More-than-Human

This text offers the first book-length introduction to more-than-human geography, exploring its key ideas, main debates, and future prospects.

An opening chapter traces the origins and emergence of this field of enquiry and positions more-than-human geography as a response to a set of intellectual and political crises in Western thought and politics. It identifies key literatures and thinkers and reflects on the varying usages and meanings of the idea of the more-than-human. Three subsequent sections explore cross-cutting themes that draw together the disparate strands of more-than-human geography: examining new materialisms developed in the field, analysing knowledge practices and methodologies, and finally reflecting on the political and ethical implications of a more-than-human approach. A final chapter examines the tensions between this approach and cognate work in environmental geography to review the strengths and the limitations of more-than-human geographies, and to speculate as to their near future development.

Introducing the key idea of more-than-human geography, this book will be an important resource for undergraduate and postgraduate students of human geography, environmental geography, cultural and social geography, and political geography.

Jamie Lorimer is Professor of Environmental Geography in the School of Geography and the Environment at the University of Oxford. He completed a PhD at the University of Bristol in 2005 and has since lectured at Kings College London, before moving to Oxford in 2012.

Timothy Hodgetts is Lecturer in Human Geography in the School of Geography and the Environment at the University of Oxford, where he is the Course Director of the MSc in Nature, Society and Environmental Governance.

Key Ideas in Geography
Series editors: Noel Castree, *University of Wollongong* and
Audrey Kobayashi, *Queen's University*

The *Key Ideas in Geography* series will provide strong, original and accessible texts on important spatial concepts for academics and students working in the fields of geography, sociology and anthropology, as well as the interdisciplinary fields of urban and rural studies, development and cultural studies. Each text will locate a key idea within its traditions of thought, provide grounds for understanding its various usages and meanings, and offer critical discussion of the contribution of relevant authors and thinkers.

Landscape
John Wylie

Scale
Andrew Herod

Rural
Michael Woods

Citizenship
Richard Yarwood

Wilderness
Phillip Vannini and April Vannini

Creativity
Harriet Hawkins

Migration, 2nd Edition
Michael Samers and Michael Collyer

Mobility, 2nd Edition
Peter Adey

City, 2nd Edition
Phil Hubbard

Resilience
Kevin Grove

Postcolonialism
Tariq Jazeel

Non-representational Theory
Paul Simpson

Climate Change
Mike Hulme

Space
Peter Merriman

Home, 2nd Edition
Alison Blunt and Robyn Dowling

Nationalism
David Kaplan and Kathryn Hannum

More-than-Human
Jamie Lorimer and Timothy Hodgetts

For more information about this series, please visit: www.routledge.com/series/KIG

More-than-Human

Jamie Lorimer and Timothy Hodgetts

Routledge
Taylor & Francis Group

LONDON AND NEW YORK

Designed cover image: © 'Micropia man' by Bianca Pilet

First published 2024
by Routledge
4 Park Square, Milton Park, Abingdon, Oxon OX14 4RN

and by Routledge
605 Third Avenue, New York, NY 10158

Routledge is an imprint of the Taylor & Francis Group, an informa business

© 2024 Jamie Lorimer and Timothy Hodgetts

British Library Cataloguing-in-Publication Data
A catalogue record for this book is available from the British Library

Library of Congress Cataloging-in-Publication Data
Names: Lorimer, Jamie, 1979- author. | Hodgetts, Timothy, 1978- author.
Title: More-than-human / Jamie Lorimer and Timothy Hodgetts.
Description: Abingdon, Oxon; New York, NY: Routledge, 2024. |
Series: Key ideas in geography | Includes bibliographical references and index.
Identifiers: LCCN 2023044546 (print) | LCCN 2023044547 (ebook) |
ISBN 9781138058309 (hardback) | ISBN 9781138058392 (paperback) |
ISBN 9781315164304 (ebook)
Subjects: LCSH: Human geography.
Classification: LCC GF41.L673 2024 (print) | LCC GF41 (ebook) |
DDC 304.2—dc23/eng/20231222
LC record available at https://lccn.loc.gov/2023044546
LC ebook record available at https://lccn.loc.gov/2023044547

ISBN: 9781138058309 (hbk)
ISBN: 9781138058392 (pbk)
ISBN: 9781315164304 (ebk)

DOI: 10.4324/9781315164304

Typeset in Optima
by codeMantra

To Donna Haraway and Bruno Latour

Contents

Figures and tables

Figures

Tables

Boxes

About the authors

Jamie Lorimer is Professor of Environmental Geography in the School of Geography and the Environment at the University of Oxford. He completed a PhD at the University of Bristol in 2005 and has since lectured at Kings College London, before moving to Oxford in 2012. His research explores public understandings of nature and how these come to shape environmental governance. Past projects have examined the histories, politics, and cultures of wildlife conservation ranging across scales from elephants to the microbiome. Jamie is the author of *Wildlife in the Anthropocene: Conservation after Nature* (Minnesota, 2015) and *The Probiotic Planet: Using Life to Manage Life* (Minnesota, 2020). His current research explores transitions in agriculture in the context of growing concerns about the relationships between farming, biodiversity loss, and global heating. He has extensive teaching experience and has taught and developed modules on more-than-human geography for both undergraduate and postgraduate students.

Timothy Hodgetts is Lecturer in Human Geography in the School of Geography and the Environment at the University of Oxford, where he is the Course Director of the *MSc in Nature, Society and Environmental Governance*. He completed a PhD in Geography & the Environment at the University of Oxford in 2015. His research focuses on the governance and lived geographies of more-than-human life, particularly animals in the UK. He has taught more-than-human geography to undergraduate and postgraduate students, and in more recent years mainly teaches postgraduates on topics of environmental governance, more-than-human, and animal geographies.

Acknowledgements

This book has been a long time in the making. We would like to thank Andrew Mould and his team at Routledge for their patience and gentle encouragement, as well as their help in bringing it to completion. The work has benefitted from comments by the series editor Noel Castree and from several anonymous referees.

The book has been developed from over a decade of lectures delivered to both undergraduate and masters students in the School of Geography and the Environment at the University of Oxford – especially those on the Nature, Society, and Environmental Governance MSc course that we direct, and on the Geographies for the Anthropocene BA course that Jamie co-teaches with Beth Greenhough and Hannah Fair. We would like to thank our students for their engagement with our lectures and for their critical feedback on our teaching materials. We would also like to think Lorraine Wild, Lucy Young, Caroline Anderson, and Alison Attwell, and the larger team of administrative staff at Oxford who run the undergraduate and Masters programmes and who do so much behind the scenes to make lecturing such a pleasure.

A book like this owes debts of academic gratitude to the wide range of scholars working under the banner of more-than-geography. It has been shaped by much published work as well as by conversations at conferences and workshops over the last 15 years. There are too many contributors to list here, but we would like to highlight some significant influences.

We have been lucky participants in the Technological Life and More-than-Human research groups at Oxford and are indebted to our PhD students, postdoctoral researchers, and academic colleagues who make these such lively, supportive, and generative fora for developing ideas. Special thanks to Beth Greenhough, along with Maan Barua, Mark Bomford, Myung-Ae Choi,

Thomas Cousins, George Cusworth, Jenny Dodsworth, Joshua Evans, Hannah Fair, Oscar Hartman-Davies, Eben Kirksey, Ian Klinke, Javier Lezaun, Derek McCormack, Jasper Montana, Kelsy Nagy, Cyrus Nayeri, Khatijah Rahmat, Gillian Rose, Adam Searle, Filipa Soares, Theo Stanley, Jonny Turnbull, Anna-Lora Wainwright, and Annie Welden.

Jamie would also like to thank the postdoctoral researchers he has worked with over the last decade, who have contributed greatly to the ideas presented in this book. These include Nathan Clay, Clemens Driessen, Marion Ernwein, Carmen McLeod, Matthew McMullen, and Alex Sexton.

We would like to thank Sarah Whatmore for her time in interview and for her wider role in helping found the field of more-than-human geography, along with Steve Hinchliffe who served as Jamie's external PhD examiner. Thanks also to Andrew Barry, Bruce Braun, Henry Buller, Nigel Clark, Gail Davies, David Demeritt, Julie Guthman, Ann Kelly, Alex Loftus, Hayden Lorimer, Mara Miele, Emma Roe, Krithika Srinivasan, and Kathryn Yusoff for influential conversations over the years.

Jamie would like to thank Magali, Amelie, and Louis for their love and support. Tim would like to thank Becca, Bethan, and Caitlin for the same. And of course Hester, whose lessons in attunement remain influential.

Funding to support the research that underpins this book has come from the Economic and Social Research Council, the British Academy, the Wellcome and Leverhulme Trusts, the John Fell Fund, and the Canadian Institute for Advanced Research.

Prologue

Limbering up

Nature. Animal. Human. Science.

Take a moment to think about what each of these terms mean to you.

What images come to mind?

There is no right answer, and we would hope to find some variation. But we might expect some readers to converge on the following:

Nature: the great green world out there, separated from Society. A valued place or thing that is often under threat, as well as an external force with the power to harm. You might imagine a park, a garden, the countryside, or the wilderness?

Animal: a mobile, living organism visible to the naked eye. Generally, not a human. Perhaps a dog or cat? Or maybe a tiger, panda, or polar bear? These might be seen as beasts of lesser moral status?

Human: a person. A special lifeform, blessed with language and a thinking (perhaps even rational) mind, superior to animals. Living in a body that is separate from the environment. Perhaps you saw yourself, a friend, a statue, or a famous person?

Science: the truth about the natural world. An objective way of producing knowledge that is not shaped by personal and social interests. Perhaps you see a person in a white coat in a laboratory, or in a suit reassuring the public? Maybe an explorer in some natural environment?

Were your answers similar to those above? Or were they different – perhaps a little, perhaps a lot? Take another moment to reflect on why there might be variations in how people respond to these prompts.

Introduction

I.1 Are humans exceptional?

Are humans exceptional beings? Are humans distinct from the rest of Nature, perhaps separated by virtue of having souls, language, or the capacity to reason enabling self-conscious actions in the world? Or are humans a part of nature, not a distinct category but an entangled part of the whole? Maybe they are both – is that possible? Or perhaps neither?

These are profound questions that have long troubled thinkers. Many different responses have been given throughout human history and across different cultures. Answers are found in poetry and philosophy, in religion and art, in agriculture and architecture, in science and technology and law (Soper, 1995; Castree, 2005). These answers sometimes assert human exceptionalism, sometimes assert versions of human-nature holism, and sometimes attempt a middle ground (Figure I.1). Similar arguments for each of these positions have been made in different times and in different places, even when the specific words and ideas differ.

This book traces a recent chapter in these conversations about the relationships between humans and worlds, this time situated within the academic discipline of human geography (and the related fields of anthropology and science studies). These 'more-than-human' geographers, and their colleagues in the wider academy, begin by rejecting a dualistic ontology (see Box I.1) that understands humans as exceptional and defined in opposition to Nature. They do so largely in a Western intellectual culture that has been dominated for several centuries by the assertion of human exceptionalism. As we shall see in Chapter 1, criticisms of exceptionalism have been building across the academy and in wider societies for some time. Indeed,

DOI: 10.4324/9781315164304-1

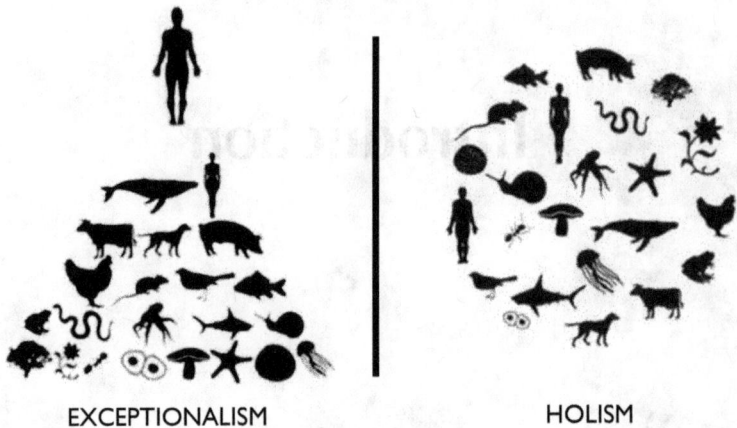

EXCEPTIONALISM   HOLISM

Figure I.1 Different visualisations of human relationships with the Earth and other lifeforms.

Box I.1 Ontology: dualism, holism, monism, hybridity, and entanglement

Ontology is the branch of philosophy concerned with the nature of being or existence. An ontology is a theory of what the world is. Many different ontologies exist, they have important consequences for how the world is understood, and on how different people act in the world. A group of people sharing the same ontology may come into conflict with another group when their different ontologies are incompatible or incommensurable.

We use the term *dualism* to describe an ontology in which humans are understood as separate from and distinct to Nature. Dualism asserts a very particular understanding of humans as exceptional beings, elevated from the rest of the world. It asserts a very loaded understanding of Nature (as indicated by the capitalisation 'N'), which is held to be a singular, timeless, and universal material world that pre-exists human action (an earlier book in this series explores the concept in detail, see Castree, 2005).

In the tradition of Western empirical philosophy, the dualist position is usually identified with the work of French philosopher Rene Descartes, who emphasised the distinction between (i) humans as thinking beings with souls, and (ii) the soul-less, unthinking material world. As such, it is commonly known as Cartesian dualism. We explore this philosophy, and its implications, in more detail in Chapter 1.

By contrast, the philosophical idea of *holism* suggests that the things of the world exist as, and can only be understood as, parts of a whole. A holist ontology thus directs analytical attention to the relations through which worlds are made and re-made. A similar, although not identical, philosophical concept is *monism* which asserts the one-ness of all existence. Rather than two kinds of existence (like thought/matter, or souls/bodies in Descartes' work for example), a monist holds that there is but a single substance. In Western thought, monism is usually associated with European continental philosophy but both monist and holist views are also widespread in systems of thought beyond the Western tradition.

As this book proceeds, we will introduce a further range of non-dualist ontologies, all of which emerge out of criticisms of Cartesian dualism. We will encounter *hybrids* composed of a mixture of Nature and Society. We will meet *cyborgs*: part human, part animal, and part machine. We will be presented with a figure of the human as a superorganism, a multispecies ecology, or a *holobiont* composed of microbial life. We will move far from the false certainties of the dualism to encounter a world of *entanglement*: a *meshwork* of beings in constant processes of becoming otherwise.

Box I.1: Different ontologies

criticism or outright rejection of dualistic ontologies have been consistently asserted by a diversity of marginalised and often colonised peoples, whose views have often been stifled, ignored, or violently repressed.

I.2 Five beginnings

But we are getting ahead of ourselves. Let's begin with five events that illustrate this shift away from human exceptionalism:

First, on 20 March 2017, the New Zealand Parliament passed the Te Awa Tupua (Whanganui River Claims Settlement) Bill to recognise the understandings of the Whanganui River held by the indigenous iwi tribe. The official parliament website explained how the Bill:

> Was widely reported in New Zealand and overseas for one particularly innovative effect: it confers a legal personality on the Whanganui River. A legal person is an entity that has the same rights and responsibilities as a person. In New Zealand law, a number of entities have legal personhood including companies, trusts, and societies. The move reflects Whanganui iwi's unique ancestral relationship with the river. Iwi who lived along the river not only relied on it as an essential food source, but held with it a deep spiritual connection. From the 1880s to 1920s, the Crown – with little or no iwi consultation – conducted works to establish a steamer service on the river and extract minerals from its bed, eroding its ecological quality, destroying eel weirs and fisheries, and degrading the river's cultural and spiritual value. Whanganui iwi first petitioned Parliament in the 1870s, continuing for decades to seek compensation and justice through several courts and the Waitangi Tribunal. The bill will provide a settlement of $80 million to redress these "actions and omissions" of the Crown. It will recognise Te Awa Tupua as an indivisible and living whole, comprising the Whanganui River from the mountains to the sea, and all its physical and metaphysical elements.
>
> (NZ Parliament, 2017)

Second, on 18 August 2012, *The Economist* magazine (for many decades a publishing stalwart of Western liberalism) pictured on its cover a re-worked version of Michelangelo's drawing of the Vitruvian Man, with the head replaced with an artist's impression of microbial life. The issue was entitled 'Microbes Maketh Man' and the accompanying leader article explained that

> Political revolutionaries turn the world upside down. Scientific ones more often turn it inside out. And that, almost literally, is happening to the idea of what, biologically speaking, a human being is. The traditional view is that a human body is a collection of 10 trillion cells which are themselves the products of 23,000 genes. If the revolutionaries are correct, these numbers radically underestimate the truth. For in the nooks and crannies of every human being, and especially in

his or her guts, dwells the microbiome: 100 trillion bacteria of several hundred species bearing 3m non-human genes.

(Anon, 2012)

Third, on 31st August 2016, the American magazine *National Geographic* (a bastion of armchair exploration) published a video on their website entitled 'Rare Video Shows Elephant's 'Mourning' Matriarch's Death'. The scare quotes around the idea of 'mourning' suggested that this was, in some sense, a controversial suggestion. The accompanying text explained that:

It has become rare for wild African elephants to live to old age, thanks to their brutal slaughter by ivory poachers. Rarer still is the chance for scientists to observe elephants as they cope with the death of their family leader. Shifra Goldenberg, a Colorado State University doctoral student, is among the lucky few. She watched the final days as Queen Victoria, one of the last surviving old matriarchs in the Samburu National Reserve in northern Kenya, died of natural causes in 2013, with her family members close by. When Goldenberg returned to the carcass a few weeks later, she encountered elephants from three separate families inspecting the bones. Were they paying respect? ... Elephants have long been regarded for their ability, along with dolphins and chimpanzees, among others, to express emotion, even empathy. But their response to death remains a mystery. Do they have the human characteristic of grief? The examples are mounting, though the science remains incomplete.

(Parker, 2016)

Fourth, on 10 December 2021, Netflix released a dark comedy with a cast list including some of Hollywood's most famous actors. Don't Look Up! is a film about irrational human behaviour; the failures of climate change policy; and the relationships between scientists, the media, and politicians. It is described in its own promotional material thus:

Kate Dibiasky (Jennifer Lawrence), an astronomy grad student, and her professor Dr Randall Mindy (Leonardo DiCaprio) make an astounding discovery of a comet orbiting within the solar system. The problem — it's on a direct collision course with Earth. The other problem? No one really seems to care. Turns out warning mankind about a planet-killer the size of Mount Everest is an inconvenient fact to navigate. ... With only six months until the comet makes impact, managing the 24-hour news cycle and gaining the attention of the social media obsessed public before it's too late proves shockingly comical — what will it take to get the world to just look up?!

(Anon, 2022)

These four events all speak in different ways to a wider fifth event: the diagnosis of the Anthropocene (Box I.2). Taken together, these five developments illustrate the themes of this book. As we shall see, grieving elephants, microbial companions, and rivers that are legal persons challenge Western ideas of human exceptionalism. Recognising human actions as capable of shaping global-scale earth systems undermines the idea of the natural world as singular, timeless, and separate to humans. In different ways, each of the events illustrates the nuanced relationships between science and politics, and they each point to the possibility of multiple understandings of material worlds. And we learn that even bingeing on films can help to reinforce the sense that all is not well with the rationalist model of Science and Politics that undergirds Western liberalism.

Box I.2   The Anthropocene and the end of nature

On 21 May 2019, a working group of the International Commission on Stratigraphy recommended that the Earth be placed in a new unit of geological time (AWG, 2019). They formally approved the concept of the Anthropocene, defined as

> The epoch of geological time during which human activity is considered to be the dominant influence on the environment, climate, and ecology of the earth, a formal chrono-stratigraphic unit with a base which has been tentatively defined as the mid-twentieth century.
>
> (OED, 2016)

This was a significant step in long process that began in 2000 when the atmospheric chemist Paul Crutzen (2002) first proposed the

---

Anthropocene as a replacement for the Holocene – suggesting that the Holocene no longer existed due to the magnitude of human impacts on the Earth System.

The Anthropocene Working Group suggest that a new division be made in the timeline of Earth history to recognise that humans (as a singular species) have become a planet changing force. They have proposed a start date of 1945, indexed to the first tests of nuclear weapons, whose fallout will leave a clear, universal, and synchronous signal in the fossil record, thus providing the evidence that future geologists will need to indicate the start of a new epoch (Lewis and Maslin, 2018).

The diagnosis of the Anthropocene has catalysed much debate in the natural sciences (Malhi, 2017), and it quickly escaped the confines of the sciences as it was picked up by a range of environmental activists and social scientists who found it useful as an umbrella term for a related collection of contemporary environmental crises (Bonneuil and Fressoz, 2017). The Anthropocene describes the contemporary environmental zeitgeist – or the spirit of the age (Lorimer, 2016).

The Anthropocene also gives general expression to the growing unease with models of human exceptionalism and the models of development it underpins. For some, it serves as a public proclamation of 'the end of Nature' – where nature is only natural when it is unmarked by human influence. For environmental activists like Bill McKibben (1989), there can be no such thing as Nature on a used planet in which human influence is ubiquitous.

Meanwhile, the naming of the Anthropocene has been contested by social scientists who suggest it is unjust to attribute responsibility to humans as a species, given the vast social inequalities in causing environmental harm, in benefitting from environmental change, and in the ability to adapt to future environments (Malm and Hornborg, 2014). They propose that we 'name the system, not the species' offering alternative titles like the Capitalocene or the Plantationocene (Moore, 2016).

1.3 More-than-human geography

In this book, we set out the challenges that have been posed to the taken-for-granted assumptions of Western social science, and specifically geography, by those rethinking nature and humans in non-dualistic ways. We trace how geographers (and related scholars) have grappled with questions about human relationships with nature during the early decades of the 21st century. We explore the understandings they have developed from the non-dualistic starting point of human-nature hybridity and entanglement. The work that we focus on emerges from a specific set of conversations, debates, empirical investigations, experiments, and conceptual developments situated within the academic discipline of geography. We write as two white, male Anglophone geographers working at the University of Oxford in the UK, with research interests in animals, nature recovery, agriculture, and the microbiome. Our positionality and our interests shape our account, but we draw widely across relevant literatures and from work coming from other authorial positions. We hope that the audience of this book will range beyond geography. Geography is a capacious field of enquiry and geographers populate a distinctly undisciplined discipline, lacking a canon of texts and figures and thus open to borrowing ideas and sharing them with others. Sometimes, in the text, we will refer to more-than-human geography, at other times to more-than-humanism and to more-than-humanists to include a broader set of scholars working in other disciplines.

The assertion that humans are a part of nature is not all that novel, unique, or even that unusual outside of this specific intellectual context. Sometimes, the geographers whose work we review have drawn on non-dualistic concepts from everyday and indigenous ontologies, either directly (like Sarah Whatmore or Bawaka Country et al.,) or more often by borrowing from anthropologists who study non-Western peoples (like Tim Ingold and Anna Tsing). Often, these geographers have also drawn on alternative philosophical traditions from within the European canon, particularly theories of monism (e.g. from Baruch Spinoza), processes (e.g. Henri Bergson), and becoming (e.g. Gilles Deleuze) that challenge the humanist ideal of the rational, separate, and elevated human. And often, these geographers are informed by their own training, background, and experiences in various environmental movements in which non-dualistic ideas of varied provenance have long circulated. In this book, we hope to show that this geographical research has developed important insights for understanding and engaging in worlds marked by environmental crisis and entrenched inequalities.

We will present more-than-human geography as marked by flourishing diversity, with a proliferation of conceptual developments and empirical foci. Yet despite the diversity, we suggest that this work is shaped by three key concerns that each derive from rejecting the separation of humans and nature. These are: (i) an interest in material agency, (ii) acknowledging situated and multiple knowledges, and (iii) a focus on relations and processes. Let's briefly introduce each in turn:

First, **material agency**. Agency is usually understood as the capacity to produce effects. In the dualistic humanist tradition, the focus is firmly on human agency. Humans are understood as the only actors with the power to shape worlds, and agency is conceptualised in terms of conscious human intentions. However, if humans are not held to be separated from nature, then agency can be re-conceptualised as distributed. Agency can be extended to many actors other than humans. In some cases, this may extend the scope of who or what is understood to perform intentional or even (rarely) moral agency. We might accept that humans are not unique animals in terms of having intentions, rational thoughts, emotions, or perhaps even forms of morality. In other cases, it may involve re-conceptualising agency in non-intentional forms and paying attention to capacities of different entities to affect the worlds around them. We would all likely agree that hurricanes, floods, and volcanoes are not intentional, but they certainly shape (more-than-human) worlds. The same is also true for some viruses, as we saw with the COVID-19 pandemic. In Chapter 2, we trace how engagements with feminist theory, science studies, and anthropology that emphasise nonhuman forms of agency have enabled geographers to appreciate various forms of nonhuman material agency and their impacts on social worlds.

Second, **situated and multiple knowledges**. As we saw in the New Zealand example above, a river can be known in many ways. More-than-human geography expands the prevailing knowledge system of Western science, and its unrelenting and often uncompromising focus on generating claims to universal truth through the knowledge practices of objective reason (see Box I.3). Instead, drawing on a range of insights from feminist theory, anthropology, and science studies, this work examines how knowledge is always made (not found) and that this making (or construction) requires specific, skilled material bodies, practices, and technologies. In Chapter 3, we show how this model of epistemic pluralism helps us to recognise multiple forms of legitimate natural knowledge, and that it also allows us to see some non-humans as experts on their own terms. Asserting that knowledge is always situated in place and time, and that diverse beings will understand worlds in diverse ways, does not lead inexorably to the 'anything goes' of relativism; instead, it offers an account of knowledge that allows truth claims to be examined alongside their claims to legitimacy. It also helps understand the type of political problems that face science and scientists in Don't Look Up! And it enables geographers to work with scientists to develop more democratic and participatory forms of environmental decision making.

Third, a focus on relations and processes. Asserting that humans are not separate from Nature (or the world) does not mean that the category of 'human' becomes meaningless. There are still distinguishable human beings, identifiable from each other and from other animate and inanimate forms; human beings that are locatable in time and place. But asserting that humans are inextricably parts of worlds turns analytical attention to the relations and processes through which humans exist. What defines humans, on these logics, is not what separates them from all others. Instead, humans are defined through their *relations with* all manner of animate and inanimate beings. Furthermore, not all relations are equally desirable since relations can be unequal, violent, homogenising, and environmentally harmful. Analytical attention shifts to understanding which relations are more or less fixed; how they change through time; and the processes through which relations (and thus humans) are made, un-made, and re-made. As we explain in Chapters 4 and 5, this allows more-than-human geographers to tackle political questions, positioning this work alongside vibrant (though not always sympathetic) strands of critical theory.

Box I.3 Epistemology, nature, and politics

Epistemology refers to the branch of philosophy that studies knowledge and understanding. An epistemology is a theory of knowledge; it establishes how knowledge ought to be produced, and what counts as truth.

Modern Western philosophy holds the scientific method in highest regard as a means for producing knowledge about the natural world.

Adherence to the scientific method is fundamental to the natural sciences, and natural scientists are widely held to be the legitimate spokespeople for Nature.

We discuss the scientific method in more detail in the following chapter, but its key principles include a commitment to transparency, objectivity, and reason. It advocates that scientists set themselves outside of society and seek to remove themselves from the world under observation – ideally achieving a 'view from nowhere' (Haraway, 1988). From this position, it becomes possible to identify universal patterns and processes and to reveal the laws of Nature. In John Law's (2015) terms, it reveals a 'one world world' whose operations everybody can agree on.

Science is done best by disciplined, rational minds that are in control of their bodies and the passions and emotions which might influence and compromise their work. Sight is the paramount sense here: visionary scientists see things that others can't. They learn to doubt bodily feelings.

But some Western publics have come to doubt and distrust science and scientists, seeing them as too removed from Nature, not connected to their emotions, or too driven by personal gain. Instead, they place trust in the alternative epistemologies of those with close lived experience of interacting with Nature. Valued lay experts include indigenous peoples, farmers, hunters, and patients, amongst others. Here it is proximity to Nature that grants expertise.

In both cases, natural scientists and lay experts will often refer to truths about a singular Nature. They will argue that something or someone is normal, natural, and right, and by extension, someone or something is abnormal, unnatural, and wrong. The critics that we encounter in this book suggest that they are therefore involved in an 'anti-politics of Nature' (Latour, 2004), in which reference to Nature is used to short cut or overrule the necessary political processes of discussion, debate, and disagreement. Instead, they suggest we need to recognise the knowledge is 'situated' (Haraway, 1988), that we must acknowledge multiple legitimate epistemologies and find ways of deliberating between them (Hinchliffe, 2007).

I.4 Multinaturalism

If 'humans' are not conceptualised as separate to 'Nature', then the concept of Nature also needs to be reimagined beyond the dualistic ideal of a separate, singular, and timeless material world. One way to do so, that is congruent with the three concerns above, is through the concept of multinaturalism. In response to the crisis in the modern figure of Nature and the failures of the modern settlement between science and politics to which it has given rise (see Chapter 1), sociologist of science Bruno Latour turns to the work of the Amazonian anthropologist Viveiros de Castro (1998).[1] De Castro first proposed multinaturalism as a way to understand the multiplicity of natural worlds. Latour (2011) develops this idea and proposes it as a new foundation for a post-Natural politics. He starts by questioning why many Western citizens are happy to accept the idea of multiculturalism (even if they might not agree with the policies to which it gives rise) but struggle with the idea of multinaturalism. We accept that there are multiple cultures, he suggests, but are uneasy with the multiple natures. Latour argues that a pluralism about natures offers a useful place to begin again. For advocates, multinaturalism has two key dimensions:

- First, it asserts that there are **multiple forms of situated knowledge**, recognising that there are different forms of expertise and authority that should have a stake in deliberating about more-than-human worlds. These include the natural sciences, but are not confined to them, and extend to a range of lay, indigenous, and other epistemologies that we will encounter in the following chapters. In some manifestations of multinaturalism, these knowledges are also possessed by nonhuman subjects, like animals, plants, and even geomorphic agents like rivers.
- Second, it attends to the contingent **relations and processes** through which worlds are made, recognising the **material agency** of humans and nonhumans alike. Multinaturalism accepts that there is no single, timeless, equilibrium Nature cut off from humanity. It acknowledges the reality of different worlds which emerge from the multiple, hybrid forms and trajectories that any ecology can take. These forms and trajectories are shaped to differing degrees by human actions and are thus the subject of political processes. So, for example, a forest is a very different entity to a forester, a zoologist, an eco-tourist, a shaman, or even a squirrel. All of whom may have legitimate ideas of what a forest is, that likely give rise to politics should any one of them be given sole charge of forest management.

This multinatural model is certainly more complicated than the model of a singular Nature revealed by Natural Science (Lorimer, 2012). It suggests that there are lots of experts and lots of natures and that there will thus be lots of disagreement between a wider range of political parties, all of whom need to be involved in decision making. But enthusiasts suggest that it provides a more convincing, useful, and just way of engaging with the political realities of the present. While these arguments have gained a significant amount of traction in the academy, and particularly amongst the more-than-humanists discussed in this book, they also have their opponents (whose arguments we review in Chapter 5). They have also yet to fully impact on popular environmental discourse, in which the modern idea of Nature as a stable and timeless source of value dies hard, seeming to be something we cannot do without (Castree, 2012).

1.5 Why 'more-than' human?

In the chapters that follow, we will encounter a diversity of approaches to theorising the more-than-human. Something we will encounter from the start is the difficulty of writing about the entanglement of humans and nature in a multinatural way that rejects their separation while holding on to some sense of what it means to be human. For example, one early suggestion came from geographer Sarah Whatmore (2002), whose work was foundational to the development of more-than-human geographies. Her notion of 'hybridity' (which she developed from the writings of Bruno Latour and Donna Haraway) sought to conceptualise non-dualistic relations between humans and worlds. Yet for some commentators (e.g. Lulka, 2009), the word 'hybrid' still seems to assert a residual dualistic distinction, of two pre-existing entities coming together to create something new (which is not what Whatmore intended, indeed far from it). Other suggestions for new terms, such as 'socio-natures' (Swyngedouw, 1996)[2] and 'nature-cultures' (Fuentes, 2010),[3] have suffered similar problems. In a way, this difficulty of proceeding (at least in English, French, Spanish, and other European languages) points to how engrained the notion of human exceptionalism is within Western cultures.

The concept of the 'more-than-human' is our favoured term to foreground how human lives are best understood as 'always already' entangled in the material worlds of which they are a part.[4] It signals a theoretical approach that pays attention to the three key concerns noted above: material agency, situated and multiple knowledges, and relations/processes. But the label 'more-than-human' is by no means accepted or used by all those whose work we encounter in the chapters that follow. For example, there are some academics in the humanities and the social sciences who favour the labels posthumanism and posthuman, using them to describe their work and the contemporary realities they aim to examine. Chronologically, the label post-human came before 'more-than-human' in the writings of figures like Katherine Hayles (1999) and Neil Badmington (2000). In their case, and in many others, it has come to be near synonymous with more-than-human (Castree and Nash, 2004). But there is one powerful version of posthumanism that takes the posthuman as a specific historical moment at which the human is seen to be either threatened (Fukuyama, 2002), or able to be overcome, by developments in the biosciences. In the latter case, advocates celebrate a coming 'transhumanism' in which fleshly humans are enhanced, or even superseded by artificial intelligence (Kurzweil, 2005; Lovelock, 2019).[5]

For Sarah Whatmore, the periodisation implicit in this idea of posthumanism is problematic because 'implicit in such terminology is a particular kind of historicity that holds onto the idea that things have not always been this way; that in times past the human was more self-evidently and reliably itself' (Whatmore, 2013, 81). Instead, she suggests that 'whether one works through the long practiced intimacies between human and plant communities or the skills configured between bodies and tools, one never arrives at a time/place when the human was not a work in progress' (ibid.). She explains how she prefers the label 'more-than-human' over posthuman because 'it is what exceeds rather than what comes after the human, however configured in particular times and places, which is the more promising and pressing project' (ibid.). For fellow more-than-geographer Bruce Braun, what matters is 'human becomings': 'the ongoing differentiation of ways of life and modes of being' (2004, 1355) over the celebration of, or nostalgia for, the 'historical fiction' of human being.

Other critics have suggested that humanism is so tainted by its associations with racism, anthropocentrism, and colonial capitalism that it must be rejected entirely, not supplemented with a 'more-than' (see discussion in Anderson, 2014). Some prefer the label antihumanism, drawing on the rich and varied vein of work in critical theory by authors like Nietzsche, Foucault, and Althusser (Soper, 1986). In place of the human, they tend to centre the subject of their enquiries in the title of their approach, leading to the fields of subaltern studies, Black studies, women's studies, etc. The geographer Kathryn Yusoff (2021) takes this critique in a different direction and advocates for the 'inhuman' and 'the inhumanities' (see Box 4.5). She acknowledges that

> Although the human is a ritual object of self-flagellation for Western thought (through the Enlightenment and then its critiques of post-colonialism, poststructuralism, and posthumanism), it nonetheless remains a dominant figure that marshals the horizons of meaning with an irrepressible recurrence.
>
> (2021, 665)

Drawing on work in antiracist and Black geographies, she proposes the inhumanities as an approach that moves away from the human altogether, in that it 'registers a commitment to dismantling the humanist subject and the white supremacy that characterized its geographic project of the differentiation of subjects' (2021, 672).

Despite these criticisms, synonyms, and alternatives, 'more-than-human' remains the term of choice for the majority of the scholars whose work we review in the chapters that follow. Their aims, we suggest, include expanding the scope of who and what the Human is, while maintaining elements of the critical ethos of the Enlightenment, harnessing the powers of science and reason to equitable and sustainable ends. To do so, they have often drawn together insights from both the sciences and the humanities to forge novel methodologies and concepts for pioneering forms of interdisciplinary research. Here, in Jonathan Murdoch's terms, more-than-humanism becomes 'the unfinished working through of humanism' (see Castree and Nash, 2004, 1357). Whether they achieve these aims is a theme that we return to throughout the chapters that follow and is ultimately a question for you to decide upon.

1.6 The structure of the book

In the following chapter (Chapter 1), we expand on the claims in this introduction. We situate the rise of more-than-humanism through a history of humanism, providing an overview of its central concepts and summarising the range of critical perspectives and real-world developments that have precipitated the current crisis in humanism. Chapters 2, 3, and 4 outline the key principles of more-than-humanism. In Chapter 2, we introduce more-than-human materialisms, focusing on the different, non-dualistic ontologies that characterise the field. In Chapter 3, we examine the more-than-human knowledge practices through which these ontologies are known and illustrate more-than-human methodologies for geographical research. In Chapter 4, we turn to the politics and ethics of more-than-humanism. In the final chapter, we identify tensions within more-than-humanism and outline the criticisms of more-than-humanism that have been offered by a range of geographers and social scientists. We evaluate these criticisms and identify current and potential areas of reconciliation that will sharpen and strengthen more-than-human geography.

Questions for reflection

1 Are humans different from the rest of 'the natural world'?
2 Who (or what) has the ability to affect things in the world?
3 Do you understand what 'the world is' in a particular way?
4 How do relationships with organisms and objects shape your life?
5 Are there things it is natural for people to do?
6 What types of knowledge are most valid for understanding environmental issues?
7 Who should decide on environmental management and why?
8 If there are many ways to understand nature, are there multiple natures?
9 In what ways are you 'more-than-human'?

Suggestions for readings

The following offer more extended academic introductions to more-than-human geography:

Greenhough B (2014) More-than-human-geographies. In: Paasi A, Castree N, Lee R, Radcliffe S, Kitchin R, Lawson V and Withers CWJ (eds) *The Sage handbook of progress in human geography*. London: SAGE, pp. 94–119.
Hinchliffe S (2007) *Geographies of nature: Societies, environments, ecologies*. London: SAGE.
Isaacs JR (2020) More-than-human geographies. In: Richardson D, Castree N and Goodchild MF, et al. (eds) *International encyclopedia of geography*. New York: John Wiley, pp. 1–5.

Lorimer J (2012) Multinatural geographies for the Anthropocene. *Progress in Human Geography* 36(5): 593–612.

Whatmore S (2006) Materialist returns: Practising cultural geography in and for a more-than-human world. *Cultural Geographies* 13(4): 600–609.

These books provide more popular introductions to more-than-human thinking:

Abram D (2012) *The spell of the sensuous: Perception and language in a more-than-human world*. New York: Knopf Doubleday Publishing Group.

Bridle J (2022) *Ways of being: Animals, plants, machines: The search for a planetary intelligence*. London: Penguin Books Limited.

Damasio A (2005) *Descartes' error: Emotion, reason, and the human brain*. London: Penguin.

de Waal F (2016) *Are we smart enough to know how smart animals are?* New York: W. W. Norton.

Kimmerer RW (2020) *Braiding sweetgrass: Indigenous wisdom, scientific knowledge and the teachings of plants*. Minneapolis: Penguin Books Limited.

Notes

1   Nigel Clark and Bronislaw Szerszynski (2020) offer another way of conceptualising worlds of multiple natures in their book *Planetary Social Thought*, in which they introduce the concepts of 'planetary multiplicity' and 'earthly multitudes'. They explain 'we want to think through the idea that ours is a planet with a propensity for reorganizing its own component parts, for lurching or leaping from one operating state to another. The term we give to this understanding of a planet that is capable both of self-transformation and of being nudged into change by outside forces is *planetary multiplicity*. This is our way of conceiving of an Earth that has the capacity – at every scale, from the microscopic to the entire Earth system – to become other to itself, to self-differentiate' (2020, 8). But they caution that 'it is not possible to ask what planet we are on without also asking about the different ways this planet is engaged with, experienced, known and imagined. The term we give to the way that different human groups or collectives respond to the multiplicity that inheres in our planet is *earthly multitudes*' (2020, 9).

2   For an introduction, see Bear (2017).

3   For an introduction, see Malone and Ovenden (2016).

4   The phrase 'always already' as an expression of nondualism is taken from Haraway (1988).

5   For a more comprehensive overview, see Lorimer (2009).

References

Anderson K (2014) Mind over matter? On decentring the human in human geography. *Cultural Geographies* 21(1): 3–18.

Anon (2012) Microbes maketh man. *The Economist*, 18 August Available at: www. economist.com/leaders/2012/08/18/microbes-maketh-man [accessed April 2023].

Anon (2022) *DON'T LOOK UP tells the story of two low-level astronomers who must go on a giant media tour to warn mankind of an approaching comet that will destroy planet Earth*. Available at: https://www.dontlookup-movie.com/synopsis/ [accessed March 2023].

AWG (2019) *Working Group on the Anthropocene: Results of binding vote by AWG*. Available at: http://quaternary.stratigraphy.org/working-groups/anthropocene/ [accessed April 2023].

Badmington N (2000) *Posthumanism*. New York: Palgrave.

Bear C (2017) Socio-nature. In: Richardson D, Castree N, Goodchild MF, Kobayashi A, Liu W and Marston RA (eds) *International Encyclopedia of Geography: People, the Earth, Environment and Technology*. pp. 1–7. https://doi. org/10.1002/9781118786352.wbieg0212

Bonneuil C and Fressoz JB (2017) *The shock of the Anthropocene: The Earth, history and us*. New York: Verso Books.

Braun B (2004) Modalities of posthumanism. *Environment and Planning A* 36(8): 1352–1355.

Castree N (2005) *Nature*. London: Routledge.

Castree N (2012) *Making Sense of Nature*. London: Taylor & Francis.

Castree N and Nash C (2004) Mapping posthumanism: An exchange. *Environment and Planning A: Economy and Space* 36(8): 1341–1363.

Clark N and Szerszynski B (2020) *Planetary social thought: The anthropocene challenge to the social sciences*. London: Wiley.

Crutzen PJ (2002) Geology of mankind. *Nature* 415(6867): 23–23.

de Castro EV (1998) Cosmological deixis and amerindian perspectivism. *The Journal of the Royal Anthropological Institute* 4(3): 469–488.

Fuentes A (2010) Naturalcultural encounters in Bali: Monkeys, temples, tourists, and ethnoprimatology. *Cultural Anthropology* 25(4): 600–624.

Fukuyama F (2002) *Our posthuman future: Consequences of the biotechnology revolution*. New York: Farrar, Straus and Giroux.

Greenhough B (2014) More-than-human geographies. In: Paasi A, Castree N, Lee R, Radcliffe S, Kitchin R, Lawson V and Withers CWJ (eds) *The SAGE handbook of progress in human geography*. London: SAGE, pp. 94–119.

Haraway D (1988) Situated knowledges: The science question in feminism and the privilege of partial perspective. *Feminist Studies* 14(3): 575–599.

Hayles NK (1999) *How we became posthuman: Virtual bodies in cybernetics, literature, and informatics*. Chicago: University of Chicago Press.

Hinchliffe S (2007) *Geographies of nature: societies, environments, ecologies*. London: Sage.

Isaacs JR (2020) More-than-human geographies. In: Richardson D, Castree N, Goodchild MF, Kobayashi A, Liu W and Marston RA (eds) *International Encyclopedia of Geography*. 1–5. https://doi.org/10.1002/9781118786352.wbieg2041

Kurzweil R (2005) *The singularity is near: When humans transcend biology*. London: Penguin.

Latour B (2004) *Politics of nature: how to bring the sciences into democracy*. Cambridge: Harvard University Press.

Latour B (2011) From multiculturalism to multinaturalism: What rules of method for the new socio-scientific experiments? *Nature + Culture* 6(1): 1–17.

Law J (2015) What's wrong with a one-world world? *Distinktion: Scandinavian Journal of Social Theory* 16(1): 126–139.

Lewis SL and Maslin MA (2018) *The human planet: How we created the anthropocene*. London: Penguin Books Limited.

Lorimer J (2009) Posthumanism/posthumanistic geographies. *International Encyclopedia of Human Geography* 8: 344–354.

Lorimer J (2012) Multinatural geographies for the Anthropocene. *Progress in Human Geography* 36(5): 593–612.

Lorimer J (2016) The Anthropo-scene: A guide for the perplexed. *Social Studies of Science* 47(1): 117–142.

Lovelock J (2019) *Novacene: The coming age of hyperintelligence*. Cambridge: MIT Press.

Lulka D (2009) The residual humanism of hybridity: retaining a sense of the earth. *Transactions of the Institute of British Geographers* 34(3): 378–393.

Malhi Y (2017) The concept of the anthropocene. *Annual Review of Environment and Resources* 42(1): 77–104.

Malm A and Hornborg A (2014) The geology of mankind? A critique of the Anthropocene narrative. *The Anthropocene Review* 1(1): 62–69.

Malone N and Ovenden K (2016) Natureculture. In: Bezanson M, MacKinnon KC, Riley E, Campbell CJ, Nekaris KAI, Estrada A, Di Fiore AF, Ross S, Jones-Engel LE, Thierry B, Sussman RW, Sanz C, Loudon J, Elton S and Fuentes A (eds) *The International Encyclopedia of Primatology*. pp. 212–217. https://doi.org/10.1002/9781119179313.wbprim0135 1–2.

McKibben B (1989) *The end of nature*. New York: Random House.

Moore JW (2016) *Anthropocene or capitalocene? Nature, history, and the crisis of capitalism*. San Francisco: PM Press.

OED (2016) *Oxford English Dictionary*. Oxford: Oxford University Press.

Parker L (2016) *Rare video shows elephants 'mourning' matriarch's death*. Available at: https://www.nationalgeographic.com/animals/article/elephants-mourning-video-animal-grief [accessed March 2023].

Parliament NZ (2017) *Innovative bill protects Whanganui River with legal personhood*. Available at: https://www.parliament.nz/en/get-involved/features/innovative-bill-protects-whanganui-river-with-legal-personhood/ [accessed March 2023].

Soper K (1986) *Humanism and anti-humanism*. Chicago: Open Court.

Soper K (1995) *What is nature? Culture, politics, and the non-human*. Oxford: Blackwell.

Swyngedouw E (1996) The city as a hybrid: On nature, society and cyborg urbanization. *Capitalism Nature Socialism* 7(2): 65–80.

Whatmore S (2002) *Hybrid geographies: natures, cultures, spaces*. London: Sage.

Whatmore S (2006) Materialist returns: Practising cultural geography in and for a more-than-human world. *Cultural Geographies* 13(4): 600–609.

Whatmore SJ (2013) Earthly powers and affective environments: An ontological politics of flood risk. *Theory, Culture & Society* 30(7–8): 33–50.

Yusoff K (2021) The inhumanities. *Annals of the American Association of Geographers* 111(3): 663–676.

Humanism and its problems

1

Situating the emergence of more-than-human geography

1.1 Humanism

In the Introduction, we explained how more-than-human geographers believe knowledges are 'situated'. They understand that all forms of knowledge are made (rather than 'found') in specific times and places, by skilled bodies with the help of technologies. And that knowledge is interpreted through specific cultural lenses. To be consistent, then, we need to understand more-than-humanism itself as a situated form of knowledge. To explain why more-than-human geographers make their conceptual claims and ethical moves, it is necessary to trace the intellectual context in which the movement emerged, and to which it was responding – the philosophical contours of which are known as 'humanism'.

Humanism has been the dominant paradigm in Western thought and culture for several hundred years. In this chapter, we introduce its key claims, which can be summarised as follows. First, we suggest that humanism begins with the claim that humans are exceptional and separate from the rest of nature (a 'dualist ontology'). Further, it asserts that timeless 'facts' are discovered through rationalist science and that they apply equally everywhere (a rationalist and universalist epistemology). Finally, it has a politics that claims that progress in securing *human* liberties (and maybe *human* equalities) will occur through the exercise of science and reason. For each of these ontological, epistemological, and political claims, we show how mounting critiques from within and outside the academy led to the development of conceptual alternatives.

To understand how and where these ideas about 'the human' and humanism emerged, we need to tell an origin story (we say more about origin

DOI: 10.4324/9781315164304-2

stories later).[1] We must travel back in time to earlier periods in Western intellectual history and explore the radical ideas of a collection of philosophers writing in Europe between the 16th and the 19th century. Together these thinkers developed the intellectual foundations of what came to be known as the Renaissance, that was followed by the Scientific Revolution, which together culminated in the Enlightenment. Key figures like Rene Descartes, Immanuel Kant, Isaac Newton, and Francis Bacon were central in establishing what came to be known as humanism, modernity, and science. They are sometimes depicted as caricature pantomime villains in the contemporary writings of more-than-human theorists, who hold them personally responsible for the harms to which their ideas gave rise. To give them a fair hearing, we will try to set their ideas in context, for these thinkers were responding to the conditions of their time.

In particular, these thinkers were writing in response to what they perceived as the 'Dark Ages'[2] that characterised Europe following the collapse of the classical civilisations of Greece and Rome at the start of the first millennium BC, and which lasted until at least the 14th century. While civilisation flourished in other parts of the world, life in Europe was judged to be inferior to the imagined past pinnacles of Athens and Rome. They were concerned that most people lived at the mercy of famine, disease, and natural disasters, which were unpredictable, yet occurred with depressing frequency. Life expectancy was low, with many living lives not much better than their domestic animals. Power was vested in Kings or Queens by the authority of God, and the land was ruled by a small, belligerent aristocracy and aligned religious authorities. War and violence were commonplace. The architects of humanism felt that culture in this period was too centred on myth, superstition, and folk wisdom, while intellectual life was dominated by organised religion. Moral guidance and any explanation of the world were to be found in the scriptures, and official authority lay with those in charge of interpreting these religious texts. Those suggesting otherwise risked being persecuted as a heretic. For centuries, there had been little in the way of material improvement or technological development, and the prospects for cultural innovation and political expression were extremely limited.

The architects of the Renaissance and the Enlightenment took issue with these conditions, sometimes putting themselves at great personal risk as they challenged the establishment and nurtured the wider changes that were taking place in European society. They sought to outline a radical new

philosophy with profound implications for how people understood themselves and their place in the world, that aimed to challenge the prevailing
social order and to improve the human condition. The history of humanism
is long and varied.[3] Here, we sketch the main intellectual developments
behind the emergence of the modern figure of the human and of modern
humanism. We organise this account thematically, focusing on questions of
ontology, epistemology, and politics to anticipate the topics that we cover in
the next three chapters of the book.

1.2 Humanism's dualist ontology: putting the human on a pedestal

Humanism is a discourse which claims that the figure of 'Man' (sic) naturally
stands at the centre of things; is entirely distinct from animals, machines,
and other nonhuman entities; is absolutely known and knowable to 'him-
self'; is the origin of meaning and history; and shares with all other human
beings a universal essence (Badmington, 2004, 1345).

Humanists seek to establish humans as *the* special category of life,
distinct from all other animals and lifeforms, set apart from the material,
natural world, and known through science. Renaissance artists like Michelangelo (1475–1564) and Leonardo Da Vinci (1452–1519) put an idealised
figure of the Human on a pedestal, placing Man at the centre of the Universe (Figure 1.1). This ontology was best expressed by two key thinkers:
Rene Descartes (1596–1650) and Immanuel Kant (1724–1804). Their claim
of human exceptionalism was not a new idea in Western culture; humanists inherited the Judeo-Christian idea that God created Man in his image
and gave him special dominion over the Earth. But humanists sought to
justify and amplify this ontology by identifying the particular set of characteristics of Man that make him distinct. Foremost among these was the
capacity to reason.

Descartes was an influential French philosopher and mathematician, who
argued that what set humans apart from all other animals was our posses-
sion of a 'soul'. He famously stated that 'I think, therefore I am' (*cogito,
ergo, sum*) (Descartes, 1998), arguing that the essence of human being lay
in our ability to be aware of ourselves and to reason. In a key intervention
for more-than-human critics, he claimed that animals and other organisms
could not think or reason, that they did not have this soul, and therefore

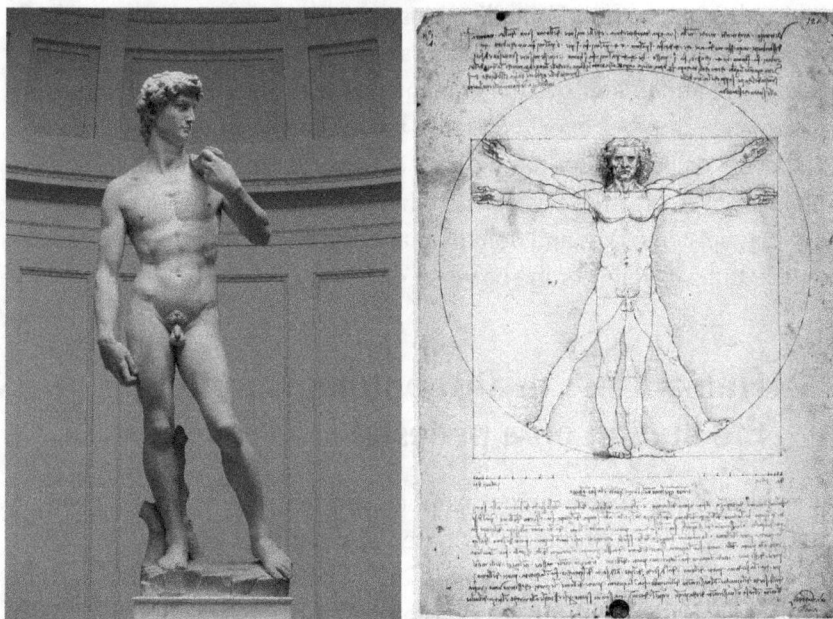

Figure 1.1 Michelangelo's five metre tall white marble statue of the biblical figure of David, the king of Israel famous for slaying Goliath (created 1501–1504), and Leonardo Da Vinci's line drawing entitled *The Proportions of the Human Figure after Vitruvius*, commonly referred to as the Vitruvian Man (c.1490). Images provided by Wikimedia Commons. The files are licensed under the Creative Commons Attribution-Share Alike 3.0 Unported licence.

should be placed alongside earth and machines and other inorganic matter as substances for human use and benefit. Descartes' conception of the human as a rational being set apart from animals and as the only subject of moral standing was developed by the German philosopher Immanuel Kant. Kant argued that humans are distinguished by our ability to think freely and to act autonomously of nature, such that we are the only source of moral value on Earth. He focused his attention on the power of thought, which he conceived of as an immaterial practice happening in a mind, which he separated from the material, natural body. Kant amplified Descartes' appeal for rational enquiry arguing in an essay entitled 'What is Enlightenment?' that it was the 'categorical imperative' of humans to 'dare to know' (*sapere aude*) (Kant, 1784/2013).

In a break with Descartes, Kant took great steps to secularise his conception of the human, as part of a wider Enlightenment project to challenge the power of organised religion. Kant was deeply marked by the impact of natural disasters, like the earthquake that destroyed the city of Lisbon in 1755. The fact that this disaster occurred on All Saints Day and disproportionately hit the religious seemed to Kant to suggest the absence of God. But Kant was more concerned that these events showed the potential of an unruly nature to threaten the future existence of human beings and thus to terminate the only source of moral value in the universe. As the geographer Nigel Clark explains:

> Kant's deepest fear was … the potential of a monstrous earth to annihilate humankind altogether: the threat of 'natural revolutions' rendering the universe's one and only moral being into just another fossil remain... For in the absence of humanity, laments Kant, 'the whole creation would be a mere waste, in vain, and without final purpose'.
>
> (Clark, 2017, 218)

In the face of these threats, Kant sought to separate human thought and moral action from nature and the material world. His aim was to establish a clear separation between the 'is' and the 'ought', to separate morality from nature (and God) and to encourage human explanation and control of the nonhuman world.

Descartes and Kant separated humans from animals and the natural world and placed an idealised figure of the Human on a pedestal. Their ontology laid the foundations for modern natural science and the later work of figures like Francis Bacon and Isaac Newton, who developed a mechanistic understanding of the natural world as a set of objects, with fixed essential properties, and adhering to universal laws that could (and should) be subject to rational, empirical enquiry, and manipulation. In the emergence of natural science, Nature was framed as a set of resources (consistent with existing cultural religious traditions), but amenable to technological improvement, laying the intellectual foundations for the industrial revolution and the rise of capitalism (Merchant, 1989).

It is important to emphasise that these philosophical ideas did not emerge in a vacuum; that they were accepted and promoted shows how they reflected and supported shifting cultural values within European societies. And there have always been counter currents to these modes of thought, both within Western thought and in the cultures to which they spread or were imposed through colonisation. Nevertheless, the influence of these humanist foundations continues to be strongly felt.

1.3 Challenges to humanism's dualist ontology: scientific revelations

Here, we flag three broad developments in the post-Enlightenment natural sciences that challenge the humanist ontology of human exceptionalism, namely theories of evolution, understandings of cognition, and the diagnosis of the Anthropocene.

1.3.1 Evolution and symbiogenesis

Ever since Charles Darwin developed and popularised the theory of evolution in the middle of the 19th century (Darwin, 1861), some natural scientists have been sceptical about claims for human exceptionalism, suggesting that it is more appropriate to see humans as part of a continuum of lifeforms with shared evolutionary histories (Dennett, 2014). This reading initially placed humans as the pinnacle of evolution, but this understanding shifted in the 20th century to understand humans as one complex lifeform alongside others. The human (as *Homo sapiens*) is one of many hominins, all of which are now extinct, is closely related to contemporary primates, and has different degrees of affinity with other organisms according to when we diverged in our evolutionary history (Figure 1.2).[4] This understanding of evolutionary kinship was powered up by the Human Genome Project (1990–2003) and similar projects to map the nuclear genome of many other organisms. This research revealed that humans commonly share 99.9% of their genes with each other, 98.8% with chimpanzees, and 60% with both fruit flies and bananas (Lee, 2018).

The scientists behind the Human Genome Project hoped that it would reveal the 'code of life' (Lee, 2013), making visible the script of human nature that would allow us to understand how each individual works, and to explain important forms of human difference like the causes of disease. Here, the data was inconclusive. It appears that humans have relatively little nuclear DNA when compared with other animals that we commonly believe we are superior to. The marbled lungfish, *Protopterus aethiopicus*, for example has more than 40 times the amount of DNA per cell than humans (Pray, 2008). It soon became clear that genetic complexity is a poor predictor of the complexity of an organism, and that the nature of being human is underdetermined by our nuclear DNA. As a result, scientific attention has turned to mapping how genes are expressed in human development

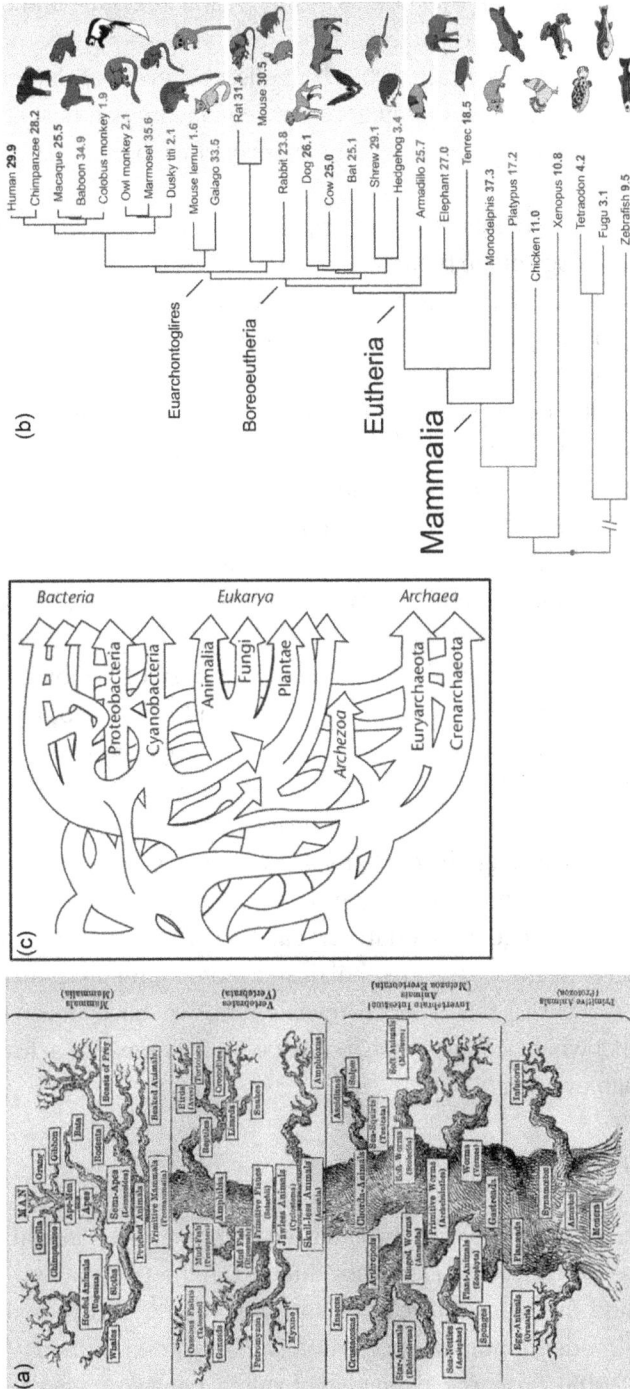

Figure 1.2 Three representations of evolution. A. Vertical model with man at the pinnacle (from Haeckel, 1879) B. Vertical model based on phylogenetic branches, with numbers showing genetic similarity to humans (from Margulies et al., 2007). C. Schematic representation of a horizontal model of evolution involving lateral gene transfer (from Doolittle et al., 1999).

and to exploring the human microbiome – the great abundance and diversity of microbial species like bacteria, fungi, and viruses that live in, on, and around us (Turnbaugh et al., 2007). Scientists believe that differences in the microbiome and in the interactions between the human host and its microbiome over the life course might help account for human difference (Yong, 2016).

The microbiome and other fields of 'post-genomic' research offer a radically different ontology of the human compared to the dualism of Descartes and Kant. Here, the human is an ecology, or what scientists describe as a 'holobiont': a host organism plus its microbes (Gilbert et al., 2012). The human is not a pure form cut off from nature and kept human by this separation. Instead, the human (and other animals) are fundamentally entangled with the world, kept alive by a diverse set of bacteria, fungi, and even viruses that digest our food, train our immune systems, and configure a wide range of bodily functions (McFall-Ngai et al., 2013). We are learning how we commonly exchange microbes with each other, our domestic animals, and the wider environment, and that most of these infections are benign or even beneficial.

Meanwhile, a new theory of evolution as a process of symbiogenesis traces the origins of humans and all other plants and animals to a distant historical moment at which one microbe ingested another to create a cell with a nucleus (Archibald, 2014). It suggests that the subsequent explosion of life happened largely because of symbiotic relations between such microbial cells. This approach flags the evolutionary importance of the continuous 'horizontal' exchange of microbial organisms and their genes between species in ways that challenge traditional 'vertical' models of evolution (image C, Figure 1.2). For science studies scholar and more-than-human theorist Donna Haraway (2016), this science reveals that 'we have never been Human', and that what we have come to think of as the human is actually a 'multispecies achievement'.

1.3.2 Human and animal cognition

A second strand of scientific work has focused on human and animal cognition. This research develops Descartes' interest in the physiology of the human mind and the nature of reason, and in so doing, has profoundly challenged his model of human exceptionalism and the mind-body dualism (Damasio, 2005). Research in the field of animal behaviour has focused on the characteristics of a small number of cognitively and behaviourally complex mammal and bird species (de Waal, 2016). Through a series of laboratory studies and periods of field observation, scientists have challenged the idea that animals are mechanistic automata that merely respond to instinctive stimuli. Instead, they demonstrate that many animals, like the mourning elephants we encountered in the previous chapter, inhabit sophisticated cognitive and emotional worlds that often involve social relations with other members of their own species, as well as other species including their human carers or antagonists (Despret, 2013). Some go so far as to suggest that some self-aware animals live in 'animal cultures': characterised by shared, learned behaviours, which differ between groups of the same species, and which are passed down over time (Safina, 2020). This research has revealed striking similarities between humans and other species, as well as profound interspecies cognitive differences, that scramble hierarchies designed to show human sophistication and superiority. More recent research has further expanded the taxonomic scope of this field to explore plant cognition and communication (Marder, 2013; Wohlleben, 2016).

Meanwhile, parallel research in the science of the mind has explored the physiology of human cognition in ways that challenge the humanist separation between the mind and the body. For example, developments in the field of neuroscience make use of new technologies for visualising the activity of the brain to map the parts responsible for particular activities, skills, and emotions (Damasio, 2005). While the research on the microbiome we introduced above has traced how microbes shape human moods along the 'gut-brain axis' (Cryan and Dinan, 2012). This builds on longer-standing research on how the consumption of foods, drugs, and other materials shapes mental health and development. This science challenges the Kantian dualisms between the mind and the body and between thought and matter, offering fields of interdisciplinary research that explore the 'embodied mind' and the 'enminded body'. Psychologists have found that a great deal of human action and thought happens well in advance of any self-conscious or deliberate reflection (i.e. before 'reasoning') (Kahneman, 2011). Just think of how much of what you do happens without conscious planning or how much your everyday actions are due to following habits and routines that you barely ever reflect upon. This work highlights the vital role of affect, feelings, and emotions (over reason) in driving individual and collective sensing and action (Simpson, 2020).

1.3.3 Environmental science and the Anthropocene

A third challenge to human exceptionalism comes from environmental scientists who have traced how humans are entangled with the environment across a range of scales. Some have explored the porosity of human and animal bodies to the artificial chemicals that are central to modern life. More than 60 years ago, Rachel Carson (1962) warned about the risks of pesticides that accumulate up the food chain and threaten species like birds. Subsequent research has traced how a promiscuous range of plastics, pesticides, fertilisers, hormones, food additives, and other waste products are incorporated into the bodies of humans and other organisms (Alaimo, 2016). It has examined how these chemicals come to configure our moods, behaviours, life chances, and evolutionary inheritance through epigenetic processes (Guthman and Mansfield, 2013). This interest in the agency of artificial materials resonates with work in the natural and the social sciences that highlights the fundamental roles of technology in making us who we are and in enabling social life to happen. Together this research offers what Donna Haraway (1991) terms a 'cyborg ontology' for a world characterised by machine-human-animal hybrids. It allows us to acknowledge the 'monsters' (Haraway, 1992) of modern life that cannot be captured by the dualisms that we identified above (Davies, 2003).

In a similar vein, the diagnosis of the Anthropocene that we introduced in the previous chapter popularises longer-standing arguments made by environmentalists like Bill McKibben (1989) that we have reached 'the end of Nature' due to the magnitude of human impacts upon the planet. For many, the Anthropocene makes manifest the impossibility of any effort to separate humans from the environment, confirming the 'entanglement' of people in nature and demonstrating that, in Latour's (1993) terms, 'we have never been modern', when being modern was premised on being separate from nature. However, for most environmental scientists, this diagnosis is not a celebration of human supremacy, in which we have fulfilled our Enlightenment destiny as the 'God Species' (Lynas, 2011) capable of the full Kantian separation from Nature. Instead, many caution that the passage into the future climate of the Anthropocene will see the return of a vengeful, 'inhuman Nature' (Clark, 2011). They exhort us to understand, in the words of the philosopher Isabelle Stengers (Stengers and Goffey, 2015), that 'Gaia is ticklish', and that our tickling might provoke the end of modern civilisations.

Taken together, this scientific research from across the life, mind, and environmental sciences, and their reception amongst activists and social theorists, have profoundly challenged the modern ontology of the human as separate from animals and from nature. It identifies the need for new, non-dualist ontologies, and they raise important questions about the nature of natural knowledge and the relationships between science and politics that we turn to below.

1.4 Humanism's rationalist epistemology: the mind in a vat

Humanism: A variety of ethical theory and practice characterised by a stress on human rationality and capacity for free thought and moral action, and a rejection of theistic religion and the supernatural in favour of secular and naturalistic views of humanity and the universe (OED, 2023).

Let's return to the key claims of humanism. In many ways, the dualistic ontology (separating humans and nature, thought and matter, etc.) was secondary to the main aim of the Enlightenment, which was to wrestle explanation and knowledge away from the power of superstition and religion. Key thinkers like Kant argued that a secular figure of the rational human, who was not influenced by the forces of nature, offered far better grounds for explaining the world and enabling social improvement. His figure of the human offered a new epistemology: a new way of producing knowledge and of checking the strength of others' claims to truth. A modern humanist epistemology is founded on the idea of objectivity – on the importance of dispassionate and distanced observation, coupled with a robust and transparent methodology for reporting, assembling, and testing the data generated by such observations.

For Descartes, such objective knowledge comes to the rational mind through vision, which he described after Aristotle as the 'most noble of the senses' (Descartes, 1998). Vision, he argued, gave the least mediated access on reality, supplying the mind with data without the corrupting influence of the body, in contrast to the more subjective information provided by touch, taste, smell, and hearing. A focus on vision and reason required downplaying the influence of affect, emotion, and the passions, centring understanding on the cold calculus of disembodied mental enquiry. This model of sense-making is thus founded on the mind-body dualism outlined in the previous section. Latour (1999) memorably parodied the humanist idea of the mind separated from the thinking body as involving a 'mind in a vat' cut off from the world around it.

The pursuit of objective knowledge became ascendent with the Scientific Revolution that culminated by the end of the 18th century in the emergence of set of norms for how knowledge should be made and evaluated. A shorthand for these norms is the scientific method that you might have been taught at school: a circular model of knowledge production based on the testing of hypotheses that is outlined in Figure 1.3. In practice, science comes in many different shapes and sizes and is done in different ways (think for example of the differences between types of human and physical geography), but for its advocates, its epistemic virtues lie in its objective and independent status: good scientists are not subject to outside interests. Science is based on empirical or observed evidence; it is factual. Scientific knowledge production is transparent and subject to critical peer review. The method for data collection is published so that the experiment can be

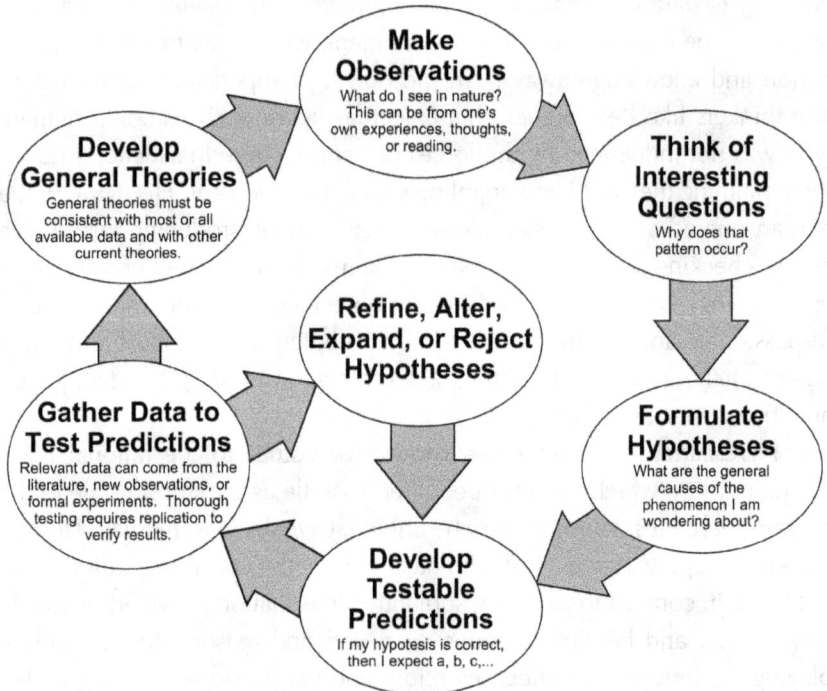

Figure 1.3 The scientific method. Image produced by ArchonMagnus, CC BY-SA 4.0, from Wikimedia Commons.

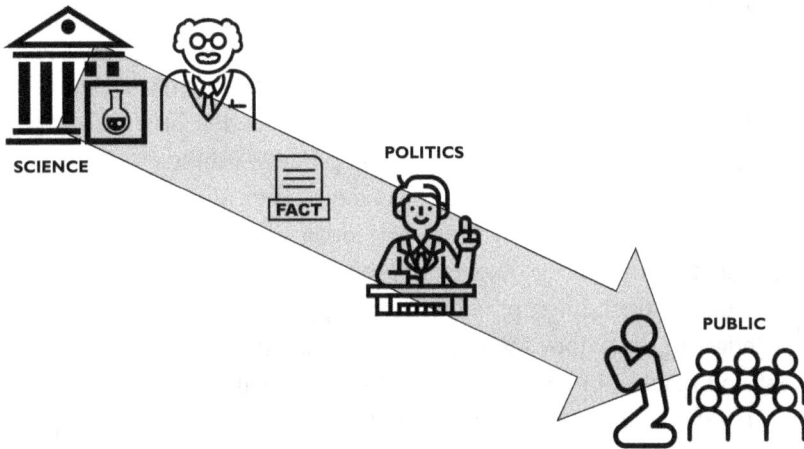

Figure 1.4 The modern settlement between science, politics, and the public (after Latour, 2004).

repeated and thus the findings should hold everywhere; science is universal. Finally, science is presented as progressive and cumulative. In the words of Isaac Newton (1675), scientists build on their predecessors by standing 'on the shoulders of giants'.

For Bruno Latour (2004) and others working in the history and the sociology of science, this model helps justify the idealised 'modern settlement' between science and politics (Figure 1.4), which we introduced in the previous chapter. This places science outside of society with scientific enquiry happening in advance of politics. Here, science is understood to generate facts in a pure domain untouched by social interests. Scientists then relay these facts to politicians and their publics, who receive them gratefully and deferentially, and then proceed to shape society and the economy in light of the information they have received.

1.5 Challenges to humanism's epistemology

This model of science and its relationships with politics has been subject to increasing criticism by social theorists, who are in turn responding to wider crises in the social legitimacy of science in Western societies over the last 60 years. Three strands of work stand out here. The first explores science in action, the second examines science in its social context, while the third emerges from Romanticism.

1.5.1 Science in action

A first challenge to the epistemology of science comes from social scientists who study 'science in action' (Latour, 1987), taking scientists as just another group of experts, and tracing the practical processes through which scientific knowledge is produced and made to travel. The critique they offer is not simply that science fails to meet its own ideals of objectivity. Instead, they suggest that the notion of objectivity promoted by scientists needs to better account for the bodies, practices, and technologies involved in creating knowledge. In short, they identify a need to take the humanist mind out of its vat and place it in back in the body situated within the wider environment. For the anthropologist Tim Ingold (2000), the humanist model of perception and knowledge production requires taking a 'building perspective' over a 'dwelling perspective' (Figure 1.5).

Ingold explains that in a building perspective, a researcher gains knowledge by abstracting themselves from the world to achieve 'a view from nowhere', gazing down onto the 'environment as globe' which is untainted

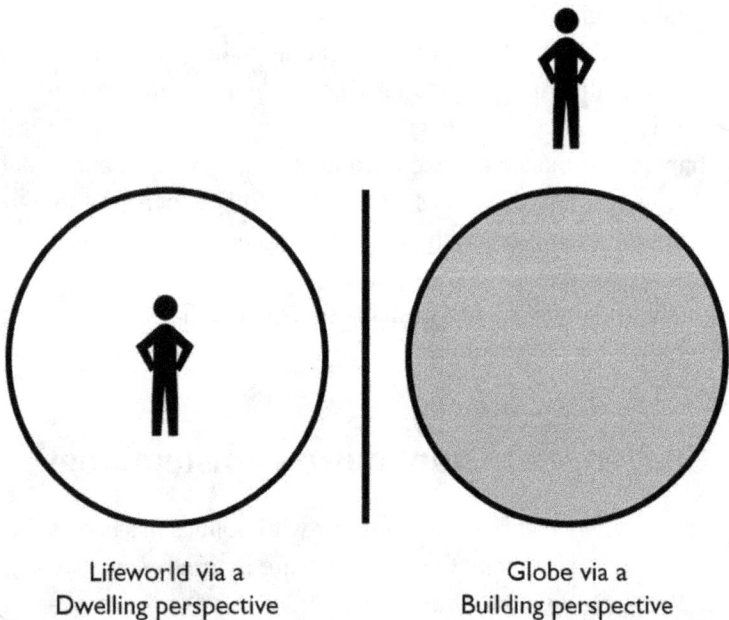

Lifeworld via a
Dwelling perspective

Globe via a
Building perspective

Figure 1.5 Two views of the environment. On the left is the lifeworld, that emerges from a dwelling perspective. On the right is the globe, which emerges from the building perspective (after Ingold, 2000).

by all the messy, material specificities of the place of observation. Here, knowledge of world is found, data is given, and there is a clear separation between thought and matter. Donna Haraway (1988) calls this 'the God trick' of scientific objectivity. In contrast, in a dwelling perspective, knowledge comes from being situated and immersed in a specific local 'lifeworld' (Ingold, 2000) that is known through the full range of bodily senses and is shaped by social context. Here, knowledge of the world is 'made' or 'constructed' through the processes of observation and data is not simply given but must be actively fabricated (for an introduction to the idea of the social construction of scientific knowledge, see Demeritt, 2002).

As we explore in the following chapter, this alternative understanding highlights that knowledge is both 'material' (it has a physical form, it is made, stored, and transmitted using various materials, tools, and techniques) and 'semiotic' (it is a system of symbols and signs that transmits knowledge). To illustrate this claim, just think of how dependent you are on your computer and phone to access and produce knowledge about the world, and how these screens require all sorts of cables, energy sources, plastics, and metals to work. Knowledge does not float in the ether but is always materialised into texts and other objects. Those tracing science in action focus on the 'assemblage' of bodies and technologies through which scientists come to speak about the world and on how different assemblages frame and order the world in particular and partial ways (Latour, 2005). This approach disputes any clear line between objective representation and reality, tracing how scientific and other forms of knowledge can be performative, shaping the world to conform with particular representations, for example of human nature, of idealised wild places, or of models of agricultural productivity (Lansing, 2012; MacKenzie et al., 2007; Robbins, 2001).

1.5.2 Science in context

A second, connected strand of work has shown that science does not happen outside of society or take place in advance of politics. A range of critics have explored how science is shaped by its social, economic, and political contexts and have examined the proliferation of controversies about the objectivity of scientific knowledge and the politics of science (Callon et al., 2009) that speaks to a widespread loss of trust in science and technology (Whatmore, 2009). Social theorists have traced how the natural sciences – including geography, geology, biology, and anthropology –

played a central role in colonialism and the categorising and ranking of different groups of people (Radcliffe, 2022; Jazeel, 2019). Postcolonial and antiracist thinkers have demonstrated how various sciences helped to naturalise the dehumanisation and subjugation of Black and indigenous groups and to ultimately provide justification for colonial projects involving regimes of slavery, exploitation and, in extreme cases, genocide (Yusoff, 2018; McKittrick, 2015).

One striking example comes from (what we would now consider to be) 'pseudoscientific' efforts to use Darwin's theory of evolution to suggest that some ethnic groups were superior to others by virtue of their evolutionary distance from other primates. As Kay Anderson (2006) has shown in her writings on *Race and the Crisis of Humanism*, this approach used anatomical criteria, like skin colour, head or face shape to rank people so as to place the White man at the pinnacle of evolution. Similarly, feminist critics of the male-centred character of humanism, identified how patriarchy was naturalised through appeals to supposedly scientific evidence that women were weaker, less rational, or otherwise inferior to men (Rose, 1993; Haraway, 1991). We explore the political consequences of these challenges to Science in Section 1.5.

1.5.3 Romanticism

Another set of critics focused on the environmental harms they associated with the humanist nature-society binary and the primacy of science, reason, and liberal capitalism in environmental management. The second half of the 20th century saw the maturation of a long tradition of green thought, whose origins (in the Western tradition at least) lie in Romanticism (Worster, 1994). Romanticism emerged in Europe and North America as a reaction to the Enlightenment, modernity, and industrial, urban capitalism. It started as an artistic movement, expressed in the poetry, paintings, and writings of figures like Thoreau, Wordsworth, Mary Shelley, Jane Austen, and John Clare (Hall, 2016).

The Romantics were concerned about the alienation caused by rationalism, science, and the disconnection from nature associated with urban life, modern technology, and capitalist industry. They celebrated immersive, subjective, and passionate encounters. They saw nature as powerful, violent, unpredictable (in contrast to the orderly and benign nature of the Enlightenment) and sought out encounters with the sublime (Oelschlaeger, 1991). They valorised those who lived close to nature, celebrating earthy, folk wisdom, often by essentialising indigenous people as 'noble savages' (Cronon, 1996). Romanticism strove for a holistic understanding of the world over the reductionism of the scientific method. It informed the holistic writings of founding figures in geography like Alexander von Humboldt whose thinking shapes contemporary approaches to Earth System Science (Wulf, 2016). It showed the way for 20th century Western environmentalism as it offered far reaching critiques of the humanist denigration of the natural environment (Warde et al., 2018), proving highly influential in the designation of National Parks (Matless, 2016).

1.5.4 The post-truth present?

As a result of these criticisms of the humanist epistemology, there is currently a strong degree of ambivalence about the place of science and technology in modern society. There is a sense that, on the one hand, science and scientists caused the environmental crisis, while also providing great improvements to the human condition. But there is also a strong awareness that scientists and their technology are central to diagnosing environmental and health problems and to providing solutions, from vaccines to renewable energy and methods for carbon sequestration. While some would like to turn their backs on science and turn to other forms of expertise, others seek to salvage a place for science in modern democratic approaches to sustainable development.

This ambivalence about the place of science has an interesting political history and it gives rise to a distinct politics that we explore in the chapters that follow. Activist and academic criticisms of science initially came largely from the political Left, with writers in the 1960s and 1970s concerned with how science naturalised racism, patriarchy, colonial capitalism, and environmental harm. They argued that science had been co-opted by capitalism and by the State (Robbins, 2019). But as social movements based on environmentalism, feminism, and antiracism became established, so the tools for critiquing science came to be deployed by those on the political Right, who were concerned that scientific arguments threatened their ideas about race, sexuality, and gender, as well as with how the scientific consensus on the causes of climate change threatened economic interests in the exploitation of fossil fuels (Conway and Oreskes, 2011).

As a result, contemporary politics is now full of pundits spread across the political spectrum, expressing scepticism about scientific experts and expertise, from the far Left to the far Right. This situation is the subject of parody in the film Don't Look Up! that we discussed in the previous chapter. It has led some to suggest that we live in a 'post-truth' age, characterised by 'circumstances in which objective facts are less influential in shaping political debate or public opinion than appeals to emotion and personal belief' (OED, 2023). Philosophers and sociologists of science have become increasingly alarmed about this 'flight from science and reason' (Gross et al., 1996), including some on the green left, like Bruno Latour (2018), who were central to inventing the concepts and the methods for revealing the social construction of scientific knowledge. As we trace in the chapters that follow, a key contribution of more-than-human theorists has been to pioneer ways of securing a political place for scientific expertise by 'bringing the sciences into democracy' (Latour, 2004), developing concepts and methods to enable what has become known as Public Engagement with Science and Technology (PEST) (Chilvers and Kearnes, 2015).

1.6 Humanism's politics: human rights, freedom, and progress

We hold these truths to be self-evident, that all men are created equal, that they are endowed by their creator with certain unalienable rights, that among these are Life, Liberty, and the Pursuit of Happiness (Jefferson, 1776/2019).

We now turn to the politics of humanism. The ultimate intellectual imperative of the Enlightenment and the Scientific Revolution was to drag Europe and European thought out of the Dark Ages and to improve the human condition. Humanism had a clear political and ethical agenda, whose influence persists to the present day. It first emphasised the potential for human freedom and liberation by establishing radical ideas about human equality that propelled diverse political movements, including those that culminated in the French revolution (1789), the American war of independence (1765–1791), and much later the communist revolution in Russia (1917). A good example of these principles is offered by the text of the United States Declaration of Independence (1776), issued by the representatives of the 13 colonies in North America who were then at war with the British. The Declaration includes the famous statement of universal humanism quoted above.

The political project of humanism radically diminished the power of organised religion,[5] it bolstered movements towards liberal democracy, which challenged the hegemony of monarchies and their aristocracies. It shaped campaigns for civil rights and served as the foundation for the UN Declaration of Human Rights (UN, 1948). While the ideal of humanism did not always live up to the reality of the political projects forged in its name – it has done a great deal to improve the political lives of some (but not all) citizens around the world, most especially in Europe and North America.

The Scientific Revolution that was forged from the Renaissance and the Enlightenment also led to profound increases in knowledge about the nonhuman world and in the power of people to anticipate and manage the risks posed by diseases and natural disasters. For some celebrants, it established humans as the 'God Species' (Lynas, 2011): the one and only species with the power, potential, and (some would say) obligation to manage the entire planet for its own ends. Science delivered Francis Bacon's dream of freeing humans from the chains of superstition by revealing the laws of Nature. The development of liberal humanism and liberal democracy were also tightly coupled with the development of liberal capitalism. Humanist philosophy informed the science of economics which forged the ideal subject of capitalism: the individual, rational economic actor that has become so central to many modes of contemporary politics and governance. Liberal capitalism was empowered by the humanist ontology that frames nature as a set of resources available for exploitation to enable human improvement.

1.7 Challenges to the politics of humanism

For now, at least for some, life expectancy has increased, food security has improved, and many people live more comfortable lives than they did in the Middle Ages. But critics suggest that the so-called triumph of human mastery is unequally distributed, and that it has come at a cost to many humans and other lifeforms. Concerns are growing that humanism has a dark side with unanticipated and dangerous consequences. Such challenges to the politics of humanism focus on two main criticisms: (i) that in practice, humanism didn't include all humans; and (ii) excluding nonhuman nature has disastrous consequences. We will take each in turn.

1.7.1 Humanism didn't include all humans

Intellectual critics of humanism in the 20th century were deeply influenced by the experience of National Socialism and the Holocaust, by the violent histories of colonialism and slavery, and by the rise of authoritarian state socialism. They suggest that all these historical movements were entangled with humanist ideals and visions of human improvement. Philosophers like Theodore Adorno (2019), Hannah Arendt (1973), and Zygmunt Bauman (1992) note how the infrastructure of the modern life – from bureaucracy, to statistics, to railways and industrial architecture – can be deployed towards the systematic killing of innocent citizens. This was given its darkest expression in the genocidal and eugenic projects of the National Socialists that claimed to deliver a superior human in the form of the 'master race'. While these social theorists agreed that this was a monstrous bastardisation of the humanist ideal, they cautioned against the power of the modern state when in pursuit of a singular ideal of the Human, at the expense of social difference. Writing during the Cold War in the 1950s, they saw the continuation of this risk of dehumanisation in the rise of state socialism in the USSR and the types of authoritarian control satirised in the writings of authors like George Orwell in *1984* and *Animal Farm* (Orwell, 1949/2013, 1943/2003).

The writings of social theorists like Michel Foucault and Jacques Derrida are extremely influential to this critique of humanism. These thinkers were inspired by political developments in Europe and North America in the 1960s, including civil unrest in France, the civil rights protests in the USA, the sexual revolution, and the counter-cultural 'hippy movement'. As 'post-structuralists', they aimed to trace the historical intellectual conditions that gave rise to the universal humanist figure of Man, to undermine the idea of a universal human nature founded in biology and to expose the Human as a powerful social construction (Murdoch, 2006). Foucault and his contemporaries hoped to give citizens the tools to 'deconstruct' the human and the human sciences so that one day, as Foucault put it in the final paragraphs of his famous book *The Order of Things*, the singular figure of 'man' 'would be erased, like a face drawn in sand at the edge of the sea' (Foucault, 1970, 387). He hoped that by enabling this deconstruction he would open political space for other modes of living.

Foucault's writing on the intellectual history of European humanism influenced a generation of postcolonial writers, like Edward Said, who traced the histories and the geographies of the application of humanist ideas to non-Western parts of the world. Said focused on who got to be considered human and where in the world they lived, demonstrating that Western Enlightenment ideals of the human were often defined in relational opposition to a racialised and exoticised figure of the non-white, non-Western other, a process he described as 'Orientalism' (Said, 1979). Said's writings connect to a parallel strand of antiracist and decolonial scholarship responding to political movements for civil rights in places as varied as North Africa, India, the Caribbean, and in cities in the USA.

Writers like Sylvia Wynter (see McKittrick, 2015), Gayatri Spivak (1998), and Franz Fanon (2017) trace how the European Man came to be framed as the epitome of the Human, and how this process was premised on the silencing and dehumanisation of Black people and other non-White 'subaltern' subjects.[6] This process involved the denigration of other ways of knowing and being in the world as Black people were exploited as slaves or made subject to universalising ideals of social and economic development. While some of these writers seek to abandon humanism altogether, others seek to develop more cosmopolitan models of humanism, which we return to in later chapters.

In a similar vein, diverse feminist, queer, and trans theorists and activists (including those mentioned above) focused critical attention on how the humanist canon gendered the universal figure of the human as a straight Man. They argued that the common tendency to use Man as a synonym for all humans is not politically neutral but is instead symptomatic of widespread 'androcentrism' and 'heteronormativity': the propensity to centre society around men and men's needs, leading to the systematic subjugation of women, and gay and transgendered people. Feminists argued that humanism risked effacing important forms of human difference that stem from both the biological constitution of women's' bodies and the social experience of being a woman in modern society. They identified the gendering of forms of knowledge in which science, objectivity, and reason are cast as male, with female knowledge framed as subjective, emotional, and embodied. Feminist analyses of the power and problems with such 'male' forms of reasoning were instrumental in the rise of more-than-human thinking.

As we shall see in the following chapters, these diverse strands of post-structural, postcolonial, antiracist, and feminist work have all been important influences in the ongoing development of more-than-human geography.

41

1.7.2 Excluding nonhuman nature has disastrous consequences

Meanwhile, a different strand of critique drew attention to the problems with the 'anthropocentrism' – or human centrism – at the core of humanism and its implications for the rest of the world. Some focused on the consequences for animals taking issue with what the philosopher Giorgio Agamben (2004) terms the humanist 'anthropological machine' through which animals are classified as lesser organisms. Philosophers like Peter Singer (1990) and Tom Regan (2004) challenged the low status afforded to animals by thinkers like Descartes and Bacon and drew attention to how the human-animal dualism serves to naturalise animal suffering and the mistreatment of animals in modern farms and laboratories.

Instead, they mobilise other figures from the canon of Western philosophy (like Jeremy Bentham) to flag the similarities between humans and other species (based on their shared ability to suffer). They aim to undermine the different criteria that humanist philosophers have used to 'draw the insuperable line' (Bentham, 1780) between humans and other animals. Other writers like Carolyn Merchant (1989), Val Plumwood (2002), and Deborah Bird Rose (2011) drew on feminist and indigenous perspectives to challenge the human-animal binary. Together this work seeks to widen the scope of humanist concern, making diverse appeals for both 'animal liberation' (Singer, 1990) – extending the logics of humanism to a select group of animals – and for other, more animal or 'zoo-centric' approaches to taking animals seriously, that we review in future chapters.

Others have focused their criticisms of the anthropocentrism of humanism on its consequences for the wider environment, developing the legacies of Romanticism we introduced above to offer a rich and diverse body of green political thought (Radkau, 2014). This comes in different forms, some of which seek to champion the political claims of nonhumans from charismatic wild species (like tigers and elephants) to habitats (like forests) and even geomorphic features like the Whanganui river we encountered in the introduction. The rise of environmentalism in the late 20th century led to a widespread scepticism about the Enlightenment vision of science as the guarantor of human freedom. Environmental scientists in the 1970s raised the alarm about the risks of nuclear weapons and the potential for a 'nuclear holocaust'. Large Western publics and many scientists supported social movements like Friends of the Earth and Greenpeace calling for nuclear disarmament. More recently, environmental scientists have identified the fundamental role played by modern science and technology in fuelling the 'Great Acceleration' (Steffen et al., 2015) in resource use that is leading us into the Anthropocene (Bonneuil and Fressoz, 2017).

Here, the Anthropocene has become a shorthand term for a collection of related crises all ultimately linked to the excesses of modern modes of managing the environment and the forms of 'blowback' (Wallace and Wallace, 2015) to which they give rise. Blowback refers to the unexpected consequences of the success of 20th-century efforts to eradicate, simplify, rationalise, and otherwise control nonhuman systems. It is shown for example in the rise of flooding and extreme weather events, in pandemics of zoonotic disease associated with intensive agriculture, and in the threat of antimicrobial resistance and the rise of pesticide-resistant pest species (Lorimer, 2020). Environmental science and environmental scientists have been powered up by this diagnosis, taking responsibility for delivering 'Earth System Governance and Stewardship' (Biermann et al., 2012), perhaps leading to various programmes for geoengineering (Buck, 2019; Morton, 2015).

The diagnosis of the Anthropocene brings debates about the politics of humanism to the fore. For some, like the authors of one popular 'ecomodernist manifesto' (Asafu-Adjaye et al., 2015) (see Box 4.1), the Anthropocene serves as a further, perhaps final, challenge to modern humans to achieve their Enlightenment destiny to deliver a 'good Anthropocene', doubling down on the promise of science and reason to stabilise the planet through acts of geoengineering. For others, like James Lovelock or Elon Musk, it should accelerate the transhumanist pursuit of artificial intelligence and extra-terrestrial colonialisation. While for a third group, including the anthropologist Anna Tsing (2015) and geographer Nigel Clark (2011), the prediction of a future hothouse planet represents the resurfacing of the figure of the volatile and unstable earth that was so feared by Immanuel Kant in his writings in the aftermath of the Lisbon earthquake. It makes visible the 'radical asymmetry' (Clark, 2011) of earth forces – we need them, but they don't need us – and the hubris of humanist dreams of the mastery and control of nature.[7] They suggest a political focus on the survival strategies of those living amidst the ruins of contemporary colonial capitalism.

1.8 Summary: humanism in binaries

Many commentators suggest that the diverse strands of humanist thinking that we have reviewed and critiqued in this section are united by their
shared commitment to binary thinking: an understanding that the world is
ultimately characterised by a set of dualisms. A dualism holds that there are
two types of things in relation to any given category, that these two types are
defined in opposition to one another, and that these identities are fixed and
essentially unchanging in time and space; they are transcendent. Furthermore, this style of dualistic thinking often ranks one side of the dualism over
another, holding one to be superior to the other. We summarise the main
dualisms that define humanism in the table below (Table 1.1). Here, the element listed in the left-hand column is held to be superior to that on the right.

Taken together, the varied body of critical scholarship we have reviewed in
this chapter, and the activism and social movements from which it emerged,

Table 1.1 The key humanist dualisms

+ Human	Animal −
Humans are different from and superior to all other animals by virtue of a specific cognitive ability. Descartes' focus on reason has been expanded/revised by others to include an ability to use language, tools, etc. Animals lack these properties and are not agents or moral subjects.	
Society	Nature
Humans are autonomous agents able to make their own destiny not influenced or hindered by nature. Nature is comprised of a background of essential forms obeying fixed laws. Humans are the only location of history and moral value and have an obligation to control and improve nature.	
Reason	Emotion
Reason is the universal and desirable human property, that needs protection and cultivation. Reason comes from the mind and is marked by the absence of emotion, which comes from the body.	
Mind	Body
The mind is separate from the body and is the locus of reason. The mind is the locus of thought. The body is the site of passions, is part of nature, and is untrustworthy. Vision is the most trustworthy of the senses and the one less mediated by the body.	
Science	Superstition
Knowledge produced through the scientific method is universal, objective, and progressive. It is grounded in empirical observation. It is superior to knowledge based on subjective feelings and unverifiable beliefs.	

raise profound questions about the ontology, knowledge practices, and politics of humanism. They challenge the possibility of placing any single figure of the Human on a pedestal and suggest we need a more capacious understanding of the human capable of accommodating myriad forms of human (and in some cases even) animal difference. Some critics want to pull the human down off its pedestal, while others want to remodel and pluralise the identity that humanism celebrates. In the chapters that follow, we explore how more-than-human geographers have sought to develop alternatives to these humanist binaries.

Questions for reflection

Here is a list of statements that capture some of the claims of Humanism, with questions that convey how they have been challenged by critics. How would you respond?

1 The human is universal. What about difference?
2 Humans are biologically discrete. But what about microbes?
3 Humans are separate from animals. On what grounds?
4 Humans are separate from nature. What about the Anthropocene? What about technology?
5 The mind is separate from the body. What about affect?
6 Humans can know the world objectively. Why the public distrust of science?
7 Science sets us free. Why the continued risks and crises?

Suggestions for reading

The following provide helpful introductions to the history of humanist thought and its influence on geography:

Castree N (2005) *Nature*. London: Routledge.
Creswell T (2013) *Geographic thought: A critical introduction*. Oxford: Wiley.
Livingstone D (1993) *The geographical tradition: Episodes in the History of a contested enterprise*. Oxford: Wiley.
The following offer key contributions to the critique of humanist thinking:
Anderson K (2006) *Race and crisis of humanism*. London: Routledge

Clark N (2011) *Inhuman nature: Sociable living on a dynamic planet.* London: SAGE.

Cronon W (1996a) The trouble with wilderness; or, getting back to the wrong nature. In: Cronon W (ed) *Uncommon ground: Rethinking the human place in nature.* New York: Norton, pp. 69–90.

Haraway DJ (2008) *When species meet.* Minneapolis: University of Minnesota Press.

Latour B (1993) *We have never been modern.* Cambridge: Harvard University Press.

Radcliffe SA (2022) *Decolonizing geography: An introduction.* Oxford: Polity Press.

Tsing AL (2015) *The mushroom at the end of the world: On the possibility of life in capitalist ruins.* Princeton: Princeton University Press.

Whatmore S (2002) *Hybrid geographies: Natures, cultures, spaces.* London: SAGE.

Notes

1   In telling the story of the flaws of Western humanism and the affirmative possibilities of more-than-human alternatives, there is a risk that this seems like a logical and necessary historical progression. That is, as a set of thoughts and actions that led inexorably from one to the next, as though the flaws of humanism were fated to be remedied through the emergence of more-than-human thought; that one would always lead to the other. This is not our intention; nor is it accurate. Not only has more-than-human thought not led to widescale shifts in (Western) societal understandings of the categories 'humans' and 'nature', but this thought itself seeks to emphasise the contingency of worlds. If worlds are made, they can be remade, and there are no guarantees about which ideas and actions will gain ascendancy.

2   The term 'dark ages' is commonly attributed to the Italian scholar Petrarch writing in 1330s about what he saw as the lack of art, culture, and progress during the post-Roman centuries in Europe, in comparison to the imagined high point of classical antiquity. The term has fallen out of favour with contemporary historians who have a more detailed understanding of the diversity and sophistication of European culture during what are now known as the Middle Ages, as well as intellectual developments in other parts of the world.

3   For wider background on humanism, the Enlightenment, and the Scientific Revolution, see Law (2011), Robertson (2015), Shapin and Schaffer (1985), and Soper (1986). For an historical account of the relationships between humanism and geography, see Livingstone (1993), Livingstone and Withers (1999), and Withers (2007).

4   Somewhat paradoxically contemporary secular Humanists use the theory of evolution to undermine the claims of Christian groups who believe in creation and a moral code derived from religious authority. Some poke fun with a car bumper sticker that adds feet to the Christian symbol of the fish to suggest that it was from fish that our ancestors evolved. Search for 'Darwin Fish'.

5   The most vocal contemporary advocates for humanism are the Humanists who claim ownership of this label through societies, writing, and campaigns that are avowedly secular and direct much of their attention to promoting atheism. See for example Humanists UK or the American Humanist Association.

6   In conversation with Sylvia Winter, James Scott suggests that this work chal-
     lenges the narrative arc of humanism, which: is often told as a kind of Euro-
     pean coming-of-age story. On this account, humanism marks a certain stage
     in Europe's consciousness of itself – that stage at which it leaves behind it the
     cramped intolerances of the damp and enclosed Middle Ages and enters, finally,
     into the rational spaciousness and secular luminosity of the Modern. As such,
     it forms a central, even defining, chapter in Europe's liberal autobiography. But
     that coming-of-age story has another aspect or dimension that is often relegated
     to a footnote, namely the connection between humanism and dehumanization
     (Scott, 2000 in Yusoff, 2021, 119).
7   For the influential Belgian philosopher Isabelle Stengers (2015), the Anthropo-
     cene represents 'the intrusion of Gaia' into the hubris of Western environmental
     thought and a politics based on the nature-society binary and dreams of human
     mastery.

References

Adorno T (2019) *The authoritarian personality.* New York: Verso Books.

Agamben G (2004) *The open: Man and animal.* Stanford: Stanford University Press.

Alaimo S (2016) *Exposed: Environmental politics and pleasures in posthuman times.*
    Minneapolis: University of Minnesota Press.

Anderson K (2006) *Race and the crisis of humanism.* London: Routledge.

Archibald J (2014) *One plus one equals one: Symbiosis and the evolution of complex
    life.* Oxford: Oxford University Press.

Arendt H (1973) *The origins of totalitarianism.* New York: HarperCollins.

Asafu-Adjaye J, Blomqvist L and Brand S, et al. (2015) *An ecomodernist manifesto.*
    Oakland: Breakthrough Institute.

Badmington N (2004) Mapping posthumanism. *Environment and Planning A* 36(8):
    1344–1351.

Bauman Z (1992) *Modernity and the holocaust.* New York: Cornell University Press.

Bentham J (1780) *An introduction to the principles of morals and legislation.* London:
    T. Payne and Son.

Biermann F, Abbott K and Andresen S, et al. (2012) Navigating the anthropocene:
    Improving earth system governance. *Science* 335(6074): 1306–1307.

Bonneuil C and Fressoz JB (2017) *The shock of the anthropocene: The earth, history
    and us.* New York: Verso Books.

Buck HJ (2019) *After geoengineering: Climate tragedy, repair, and restoration.* New
    York: Verso Books.

Callon M, Lascoumes P and Barthe Y (2009) *Acting in an uncertain world: An essay
    on technical democracy.* Cambridge, MA: MIT Press.

Carson R (1962) *Silent spring.* Fawcett Crest: New York

Chilvers J and Kearnes M (2015) *Remaking participation: Science, environment and
    emergent publics.* Abingdon: Taylor & Francis.

Clark N (2011) *Inhuman nature: Sociable living on a dynamic planet*. Thousand Oaks, CA: SAGE Publications.

Clark N (2017) Politics of strata. *Theory, Culture & Society* 34(2–3): 211–231.

Conway EM and Oreskes N (2011) *Merchants of doubt: How a handful of scientists obscured the truth on issues from tobacco smoke to global warming*. London: Bloomsbury.

Cronon W (1996) *Uncommon ground: Rethinking the human place in nature*. New York: W. W. Norton.

Cryan JF and Dinan TG (2012) Mind-altering microorganisms: The impact of the gut microbiota on brain and behaviour. *Nature Review Neuroscience* 13(10): 701–712.

Damasio AR (2005) *Descartes' error: Emotion, reason, and the human brain*. London: Penguin.

Darwin C (1861) *On the origin of species by means of natural selection; or, the preservation of favoured races in the struggle for life*. New York: D. Appleton and Company.

Davies G (2003) A geography of monsters? *Geoforum* 34(4): 409–412.

de Waal F (2016) *Are we smart enough to know how smart animals are?* New York: W. W. Norton.

Demeritt D (2002) What is the 'social construction of nature'? A typology and sympathetic critique. *Progress in Human Geography* 26(6): 767–790.

Dennett DC (2014) *Darwin's dangerous idea: Evolution and the meaning of life*. London: Simon & Schuster.

Descartes R and Cress DA (1998) *Discourse on method; and, meditations on first philosophy*. Indianapolis, IN: Hackett Pub.

Despret V (2013) Responding bodies and partial affinities in human–animal worlds. *Theory, Culture & Society* 30(7/8): 51–76.

Doolittle WF (1999) Phylogenetic classification and the universal tree. *Science* 284(5423): 2124–2128.

Fanon F, Markmann CL and Gilroy P (2017) *Black skin, white masks*. London: Pluto Press.

Foucault M (1970) *The order of things: An archaeology of the human sciences*. London: Tavistock Publications.

Gilbert S, Sapp J and Tauber A (2012) A symbiotic view of life: We have never been individuals. *Quarterly Review of Biology* 87(4): 325–341.

Gross PR, Levitt N and Lewis MW (1996) *The flight from science and reason*. New York: The New York Academy of Sciences.

Guthman J and Mansfield B (2013) The implications of environmental epigenetics: A new direction for geographic inquiry on health, space, and nature-society relations. *Progress in Human Geography* 37(4): 486–504.

Haeckel E (1879) *The evolution of man: A popular exposition of the principal points of human ontogeny and phylogeny*. New York: Appleton.

Hall DW (2016) *Romantic naturalists, early environmentalists: An ecocritical study, 1789–1912*. Abingdon: Taylor & Francis.

Haraway D (1988) Situated Knowledges: The Science Question in Feminism and the Privilege of Partial Perspective. *Feminist Studies* 14(3): 575–599.

Haraway D (1992) The promises of monsters: A regenerative politics for inappropriate/d others. In: Grossberg L, Nelson C and Treichler P (eds) *Cultural studies*. New York: Routledge, pp. 295–336.

Haraway DJ (1991) *Simians, cyborgs, and women: The reinvention of nature*. New York: Routledge.

Haraway DJ (2016) *Staying with the trouble: Making Kin in the Chthulucene*. Durham, NC: Duke University Press.

Ingold T (2000) *The perception of the environment: Essays on livelihood, dwelling and skill*. London: Routledge.

Jazeel T (2019) *Postcolonialism*. Abingdon: Taylor & Francis.

Jefferson T (1776 / 2019) *The declaration of independence*. New York: Verso Books.

Kahneman D (2011) *Thinking, fast and slow*. London: Penguin Books Limited.

Kant I (1784/2013) *An answer to the question: 'What is enlightenment?'*. London: Penguin Books Limited.

Lansing DM (2012) Performing carbon's materiality: the production of carbon offsets and the framing of exchange. *Environment and Planning A* 44(1): 204–220.

Latour B (1987) *Science in action: How to follow scientists and engineers through society*. Milton Keynes: Open University Press.

Latour B (1993) *We have never been modern*. Cambridge, MA: Harvard University Press.

Latour B (1999) *Pandora's hope: Essays on the reality of science studies*. Cambridge, MA: Harvard University Press.

Latour B (2004) *Politics of nature: How to bring the sciences into democracy*. Cambridge, MA: Harvard University Press.

Latour B (2005) *Reassembling the social: An introduction to actor-network-theory*. Oxford: Oxford University Press.

Latour B (2018) *Down to earth: Politics in the new climatic regime*. London: Wiley.

Law S (2011) *Humanism: A very short introduction*. Oxford: Oxford University Press.

Lee T (2018) *Human genome project results*. Available at: https://www.genome.gov/human-genome-project/results [accessed March 2023].

Lee TF (2013) *The human genome project: Cracking the genetic code of life*. New York: Springer US.

Livingstone D (1993) *The geographical tradition: Episodes in the history of a contested enterprise*. London: Wiley.

Livingstone DN and Withers CWJ (1999) *Geography and enlightenment*. Chicago: University of Chicago Press.

Lorimer J (2020) *The probiotic planet: Using life to manage life*. Minneapolis: University of Minnesota Press.

Lynas M (2011) *The God species: How the planet can survive the age of humans*. London: Fourth Estate.

MacKenzie DA, Muniesa F and Siu L (2007) *Do economists make markets? On the performativity of economics*. Princeton: Princeton University Press.

Marder M (2013) *Plant-thinking: A philosophy of vegetal life*. New York: Columbia University Press.

Margulies EH, Cooper GM and Asimenos G, et al. (2007) Analyses of deep mammalian sequence alignments and constraint predictions for 1% of the human genome. *Genome Res* 17(6): 760–774.

Matless D (2016) *Landscape and englishness: Second expanded edition*. London: Reaktion Books.

McFall-Ngai M, Hadfield MG and Bosch TCG, et al. (2013) Animals in a bacterial world, a new imperative for the life sciences. *Proceedings of the National Academy of Sciences* 110(9): 3229–3236.

McKibben B (1989) *The end of nature*. New York: Random House.

McKittrick K (2015) *Sylvia Wynter: On being human as praxis*. Durham: Duke University Press.

Merchant C (1989) *The death of nature: Women, ecology, and the scientific revolution*. New York: Harper & Row.

Morton O (2015) *The planet remade: How geoengineering could change the world*. Princeton: Princeton University Press.

Murdoch J (2006) *Post-structuralist geography: A guide to relational space*. London: Sage.

Nations U (1948) *The universal declaration of human rights*. New York.

Newton I (1675) *Letter from Sir Isaac Newton to Robert Hooke*. Philadelphia: Historical Society of Pennsylvania.

OED (2023) *Oxford English Dictionary*. Oxford: Oxford University Press.

Oelschlaeger M (1991) *The idea of wilderness: From prehistory to the age of ecology*. New Haven: Yale University Press.

Orwell G (1943/2003) *Animal farm*. London: Penguin Books Limited.

Orwell G (1949/2013) *Nineteen eighty four*. London: Penguin UK.

Plumwood V (2002) *Environmental culture: The ecological crisis of reason*. London: Routledge.

Pray L (2008) Eukaryotic genome complexity. *Nature Education Knowledge* 1(96): 1–7.

Radcliffe SA (2022) *Decolonizing geography: An introduction*. London: Polity Press.

Radkau J (2014) *The age of ecology*. London: Wiley.

Regan T (2004) *The case for animal rights*. Berkeley: University of California Press.

Robbins P (2001) Fixed categories in a portable landscape: The causes and consequences of land-cover categorization. *Environment and Planning A* 33(1): 161–179.

Robbins P (2019) *Political ecology: A critical introduction*. London: Wiley.

Robertson J (2015) *The enlightenment: A very short introduction*. Oxford: Oxford University Press.

Rose DB (2011) *Wild dog dreaming: Love and extinction*. Lexington: University of Virginia Press.

Rose G (1993) *Feminism and geography: The limits of geographical knowledge*. Minneapolis: University of Minnesota Press.

Safina C (2020) *Becoming wild: How animal cultures raise families, create beauty, and achieve peace.* New York: Henry Holt and Company.

Said EW (1979) *Orientalism.* New York: Vintage Books.

Shapin S and Schaffer S (1985) *Leviathan and the air-pump: Hobbes, Boyle, and the experimental life.* Princeton: Princeton University Press.

Simpson P (2020) *Non-representational theory.* Abingdon: Taylor & Francis.

Singer P (1990) *Animal liberation.* New York: New York Review of Books.

Soper K (1986) *Humanism and anti-humanism.* Chicago: Open Court.

Spivak GC (1998) *Can the subaltern speak?* London: Verso Books.

Steffen W, Broadgate W and Deutsch L, et al. (2015) The trajectory of the anthropocene: The great acceleration. *The Anthropocene Review* 2(1): 81–98.

Stengers I and Goffey A (2015) *In catastrophic times: Resisting the coming barbarism.* London: Open Humanities Press.

Tsing AL (2015) *The mushroom at the end of the world: On the possibility of life in capitalist ruins.* Princeton: Princeton University Press.

Turnbaugh P, Ley R and Hamady M, et al. (2007) The human microbiome project. *Nature* 449(7164): 804–810.

Wallace R and Wallace RG (2015) Blowback: New formal perspectives on agriculturally driven pathogen evolution and spread. *Epidemiology and Infection* 143(10): 2068–2080.

Warde P, Robin L and Sörlin S (2018) *The environment: A history of the idea.* Baltimore: Johns Hopkins University Press.

Whatmore S (2014) Nature and human geography. In: Cloke P, Crang P and Goodwin M (eds) *Introducing human geographies.* 3rd ed. London: Routledge, pp. 152–162.

Whatmore SJ (2009) Mapping knowledge controversies: Science, democracy and the redistribution of expertise. *Progress in Human Geography* 33(5): 587–598.

Withers CWJ (2007) *Placing the enlightenment: Thinking geographically about the age of reason.* Chicago: University of Chicago Press.

Wohlleben P (2016) *The hidden life of trees: What they feel, how they communicate—Discoveries from a secret world.* London: Penguin Books Limited.

Worster D (1994) *Nature's economy: A history of ecological ideas.* Cambridge: Cambridge University Press.

Wulf A (2016) *The invention of nature: Alexander von Humboldt's new world.* New York: Knopf Doubleday Publishing Group.

Yong E (2016) *I contain multitudes: The microbes within us and a grander view of life.* New York: Random House.

Yusoff K (2018) *A billion black anthropocenes or none.* Minneapolis: University of Minnesota Press.

Yusoff K (2021) The inhumanities. *Annals of the American Association of Geographers* 111(3): 663–676.

More-than-human materialisms

Writing in the early 2000s, more-than-human geographers like Nigel Thrift (2000b) and Sarah Whatmore (2006), were concerned about the 'dead' geographies that they felt characterised research during the cultural turn of the 1990s. During the cultural turn, geographers focused on the power of representations, like books, films, and other texts to shape individual and collective thought and behaviour. Thrift, Whatmore, and others argued that this was too 'idealist' an approach, too steeped in the humanist separation of the mind from the body that we encountered in the previous chapter. They suggested that it gave too much power to representations in shaping human action, that it had too narrow a model of who could act in the world, and that it neglected the roles played by a range of nonhuman actors in shaping spatial practices. In response, they called for an expansion in the focus of human geography, to encompass the wide array of nonhuman actors that make up our worlds and that come to shape how they work.

This chapter introduces the diverse and ongoing efforts of these more-than-human geographers to 'rematerialise' their discipline, focusing on the ontological problems with humanism that we discussed in the previous chapter. These geographers developed new vocabularies for thinking through how agency – the capacity to produce effects – is distributed among a wide range of material things. They argued that agency is not, as humanists would assert, solely a human achievement performed by intentional beings. Instead, they propose that human action can only be understood in terms of the wider relations through which it occurs, and that humans perform one form of agency among many others. We review the proliferation of work developing different more-than-human materialisms.

DOI: 10.4324/9781315164304-3

Before doing so, we should offer three clarifications. First, more-than-human accounts of materiality should not be confused with claims of *biological* or *environmental determinism*: the idea that human lives are determined in a mechanistic way by some element of our physical constitution or by the physical geography of the locations where we live. Determinism leads to claims that these people are like this because they live in a hot climate. Or that these people are like this because of their genes. There is a regrettable history of this type of determinist thinking in geography and anthropology associated with racism and imperialism (see discussion in Castree, 2005). Acknowledging that humans are not the only material forces shaping worlds does not lead to mechanistic assertions of determinism. In the relational, processual model that we outline below, nonhuman forces configure possibilities, rather than determining outcomes.

Second, geographers are not claiming that agency is *equally distributed*, either between people or among different kinds of entity. Different people and different material things have different capacities to produce effects. For example, the collective actions of some (but not all) humans may, through changing the climate, lead to more extreme storm events; but humans cannot stop the hurricane when it blows.

Third, more-than-humanists within Anglophone geography do not commonly assert *animism*, which is a set of beliefs common (but not identical) to many indigenous peoples that all animals, plants, objects, and landscapes are alive and share a spiritual essence. Asserting that trees have agency is not the same as recognising them as kin; recognising the material effects of rock strata or flowing waters is not the same as claiming that they have spirit (see, for example, discussions of indigenous animacy in Kimmerer, 2013). However, while more-than-human approaches always reject environmental determinism, they sometimes engage with, draw on, and think-with animistic understandings. This engagement with animist ontologies is most evident in some explicit collaborations between geographers and indigenous scholars (e.g. Bawaka Country et al., 2016), but it can also be traced in some of the lineages of thought that have inspired more-than-human conceptual developments that we trace below (e.g. Haraway's, 2016, ruminations on making kin). We discuss the flawed citational practices through which this engagement with indigenous thought has sometimes occurred in Chapter 5.

We divide our review of more-than-human materialisms into five sections, each focused on a key type of material. We start with (i) the no-longer-separated human body and then proceed out from the human focusing on:

(ii) animal bodies; (iii) biological processes; (iv) technologies and infrastructures; and finally (v) the elemental. In each case, we introduce the theorists who argued for their importance and provide examples of how their new materialist thinking shapes geographic scholarship. There are many connections between these five strands, but we will see how the various authors we encounter often have differing concerns and foci. They do not always agree on the extent to which humanity should be decentred in a rematerialised theory.

The accounts of agency that emerge from this work are diverse, but they nonetheless assert some shared characteristics to more-than-human materialities, suggesting they are

- Affectual – emphasising how materials of diverse kinds come together to shape 'intensities' that are felt in sensing bodies. The concept of *'affect'* has been developed and utilised in a variety of ways in geographic and wider social theory.
- Processual – emphasising that materialities are not fixed or static, but contingent and in the process of becoming otherwise. Often talked about in terms of the difference between *being* (stable and unitary) and *becoming* (in process).
- Relational – emphasising that material agencies are generated through sets of relations between multiple 'actors'. Drawing on the points above, these relations are not fixed but can change through time and space.
- Holistic – emphasising not only that materials come together as parts of wholes, but that they cannot be adequately understood in isolation from those wider relations.

We expand on these characteristics in the final section of the chapter.

2.1 Human bodies

We start our review with the long-standing interest amongst geographers in human bodies: in how our bodies allow us to perceive the world, and in how different bodies are shaped and spaced according to powerful ideas of what is normal, natural, and right. Geographical interest in the materiality of the human body precedes the emergence of more-than-human geography and is expressed most effectively in the work of feminist geographers and non-representational theorists.

2.1.1 Feminist geographies of the body

One strand of feminist work is critical of essentialist or determinist ideas that hold that women are closer to nature by virtue of their biology. It argues against this binary ontology, demonstrating that gender is a social construction that is laid over biological difference, that gender identities naturalise patriarchal forms of social organisation, while also shaping the bodies and behaviours of men and women as they perform their ascribed gender identities (Butler, 2006). Subsequent work has focused more on the fleshy materiality of the body and the ontology of sexual difference, tracing the specific ways in which women's bodies shape their lived experience (Butler, 2014).

The work of American feminist science studies scholar Donna Haraway was very influential (see Box 2.1) for geographers like Sarah Whatmore (2002), Bronwyn Parry (2004), and Catherine Nash (2015), who developed her analysis of biotechnology to examine a wide range of scientific practices through which women's bodies are ordered, including work on genetics, pharmaceuticals, and reproductive technologies.

Box 2.1   Donna Haraway, cyborgs, and companion species

Donna Haraway is a feminist anthropologist and science studies scholar who works at the University of California in the United States of America. Haraway has been one of the most important figures in the development of more-than-humanism and her work informs all of the materialisms we discuss, as well as the approaches to knowledge and politics we cover in later chapters.

In her early work, Haraway (1989) examined how sciences like primatology naturalised patriarchal and heteronormative ideals, by mapping ideals of the submissive female and the nuclear family onto representations of primates. For example, offering a compelling analysis of what she termed 'teddy bear patriarchy' (Haraway, 1984) in her deconstruction of how animals are displayed in the American Museum of Natural History.

She became interested in how modern innovations in biotechnology challenge conservative understanding of the relationships between technology, animals, and the human body, particularly the female body. She suggested that instead of seeing these as separate domains with fixed identities, we acknowledge their 'cyborg' ontology (Haraway, 1991). Modern women, she argued, are part organism and part machine, folded into the information bioeconomy through their use of computers or their exposure to artificial chemicals. She proposed the cyborg as a radical ontology that recognised the material realities of modern life, tracing how cyborgs are shaped by capitalist technoscience, and offered a 'cyborg manifesto' (Box 4.2) for how life might be lived otherwise.

In later work, she focused on proximal human-animal relations through a detailed autoethnographic account of dog agility racing with Cayenne, her Australian shepherd dog (Haraway, 2008). She develops her figure of the cyborg to present Cayenne as a 'companion species', tracing the co-evolutionary entanglements between people and dogs that led to Cayenne's ancestors' close relationships with humans, following long histories of domestication and the development of mutualistic relationships for herding, guarding, and companionship. She argues that dogs have shaped us as much as we have shaped them. She zooms in on the mundane and intimate practices through which she and Cayenne 'learn to be affected' by each other to become successful athletes, tracing processes of interspecies communication, affection, and understanding. She builds from this analysis to offer a 'companion species manifesto' (Haraway, 2003) (Box 4.3) for multispecies flourishing.

In her most recent writing, Haraway (2016) engages with the concept of the Anthropocene, taking issue with the use of Anthropos in the title and reflecting on the merits of alternative names like the Capitalocene, Plantationocene, and (her own preferred neologism) 'the Chthulucene'. Drawing on the mythological, tentacular figure of Chthulu, she argues that the diagnosis of a new epoch demands a recognition of the fundamental entanglements between people, the planet, and other forms of life and the need to cultivate multispecies ways of 'becoming-with' other lifeforms.

Further work by feminist geographers draws on philosophers like Elizabeth Grosz, Karen Barad, and Rosi Braidotti who are concerned with the materialities of women's bodies. For example, Rachel Colls (2007) builds from the earlier writings of Robyn Longhurst (2001) on the gendered experiences of female 'fluid' or 'leaky bodies', to explore the materiality of fat and fat female bodies. She argues that fat gets materialised through the intra-action between a fleshy, bodily substance and the lived, spatial experience of being a woman in specific cultural contexts. Comparable research by the antiracist geographer Arun Saldanha (2006) challenges both the essentialist understandings of race as a natural category determined by biology and prevalent idealist critiques of race as a social construction. Instead, and in a similar way to Colls' writings on fat, he develops a materialist account of race that focuses on how differences in human phenotype – the material expression of the human genome in skin, hair, eye colour, body shape, hair, etc. – are ordered, experienced, and resisted by different groups of people. Further research that shares these anti-essentialist approaches to materiality has explored how bodily difference shapes the lived experiences of trans-sexual (Nash, 2010), gay (Brown et al., 2012), differently aged (Hopkins, 2010), and differently abled bodies (Hall and Wilton, 2017).[1]

2.1.2 Non-representational theory

A second sustained interest in the materiality of the human body in human geography came through the development of 'non-representational theory' (for an introduction, see Simpson, 2020). Like actor-network theorists (whose work we consider below), non-representational theorists were uneasy with the focus in social science on disembodied minds and immaterial representations. Geographers like Nigel Thrift (2007) and anthropologists like Tim Ingold (2000) argued that the mind-body and reason-emotion binaries, that we introduced in the previous chapter, deny the fleshy materiality of the human body, downplay the practical nature of human knowledge, and denigrate the affective dimensions of social life. As Tim Ingold puts it: 'something … must be wrong somewhere, if the only way to understand our own creative involvement in the world is by first taking ourselves out of it' (2000, 173). In response, they suggested that geographers focus on the everyday bodily practices, habits, and the spatio-temporal rhythms through which different groups of people come to inhabit the world.

Ingold drew on the phenomenology of Martin Heidegger and Maurice Merleau-Ponty to develop his 'dwelling perspective' on human-environment-technology interactions that we introduced in the previous chapter (see Figure 1.5). For Ingold, a dwelling perspective 'treats the immersion of the organism-person in an environment or lifeworld as an inescapable condition of existence' (2000, 153). Ingold's concept of dwelling has enabled geographers to rethink a wide range of human-environment interactions (Jones, 2019). For example, the cultural geographer John Wylie (2005) used dwelling to develop new approaches to understanding landscapes while walking the South-West Coast Path in the UK. Departing from the cultural geography focus on the iconography of landscape, in which landscape is a text to be read, he develops Ingold's (2000) conception of landscape as a 'taskscape'. As a taskscape, landscape is sensed and known through movement; it is felt in the ache of the legs, the memory of diurnal and seasonal movements, and in dramatic vertiginous encounters with features like cliffs. This approach focuses on the material forms of landscape as they are encountered by moving bodies: including its topography and geomorphic features, its rivers, wind and weather, and the plants and animals encountered along the way (see also Ingold, 2011).

While Ingold's concept of dwelling has proved popular, some expressed reservations about a tendency to romanticise local, rural, bounded (and potentially exclusive) relations between human bodies and their environments and to neglect the influence of modern technology and digital media on lived experience (Massey, 2005). They sought ways of exploring dwelling in modern, urban, and networked worlds involving encounters with screens and other digital technologies. For example, Nigel Thrift (Thrift, 2007) (Box 2.2) brought Ingold and actor-network theory (see Section 2.4 below) into conversation with a wider range of non-representational theories drawn from both philosophy and the natural sciences to understand the affective, embodied dimensions of social life. Thrift's work formed part of a wider 'affective turn' in social theory, which challenged the model of the human subject as a rational and objective mind-in-a-vat to explore how thought is always embodied and is often habituated.

Non-representational geographers also examined human-animal and human-environment relations exploring a wide range of bodily materialities and human-nonhuman encounters. For example, Emma Roe (2006) has explored the affective dimensions of cooking and eating – tracing the experimental practices through which 'things' – like different sorts of carrots –

Box 2.2   Nigel Thrift and affect theory

Nigel Thrift is a cultural and economic geographer who spent his most influential years at the University of Bristol in the UK. Thrift is best known for his development of non-representational theory – a slightly nebulous set of conceptual approaches – that rose to prominence in cultural geography in the 2000s.

Non-representational theorists were responding to the cultural turn in geography and the wider humanities which placed great attention on the power of representations to shape individual and collective behaviour. Thrift and others found this account limiting, as it did not account for the role of the body, materials, and the wider environment in shaping human action. They suggest that we needed to supplement a focus on representation with an attention to the body and the affective dimensions of social life, leading Hayden Lorimer (2005) to suggest that it is more useful to understand this work as 'more-than-representational', rather than non-representational.

In turning to the body, Thrift draws attention to scientific work on the 'half second delay between action and cognition' (Thrift, 2004, 71). He reminds us that we commonly act before we think, and that a great deal of what we do happens by force of habit rather than as a result of intentional planning. This work recognises how the non-conscious shapes human behaviour and presents affect as a form of bodily intelligence.

Affect is a slippery term and has been subject to much discussion and dispute in geography (for an introduction, see Anderson, 2014). For Derek McCormack (2008), affect describes 'a pre-personal field of intensity' (414). It is different from a feeling, which he defines as 'that intensity registered in a sensing body' (414), and an emotion 'that felt intensity expressed in a socio-culturally recognizable form' (426). For Sarah Whatmore (2006), affect refers to 'the force of intensive relationality – intensities that are felt but not personal; visceral but not confined to an individuated body' (604).

Non-representational geographers have explored the character of affect and the role it plays across a wide range of cultural, political, and economic relations. They developed the concept of the 'affective atmosphere' (Anderson, 2009) to describe the collective experience of affect in situations as varied as crowds (Wall, 2019), football stadia (Edensor, 2015), airplanes (Lin, 2015), or drinking in nightclubs and domestic settings (Wilkinson, 2017). They also explored how collective affects are generated through media (Carter and McCormack, 2006). And as we explore later, they examined how affect is created and manipulated for political ends.

Non-representational accounts of affect were criticised by feminist and antiracist geographers exploring emotional geographies, like Divya Tolia-Kelly (2006) and Deborah Thien (2005), who argued that they tended to assume a universal human subject and did not take account of how bodily experience is shaped by gender, race, sexuality, disability, and other forms of social difference.[2] They also argued that the accounts of bodily experience offered by NRT were too abstract or even 'inhuman', so that they read as 'ironically disembodied' (for a summary, see Parr, 2014).

either 'become food' or are rejected as inedible. As a 'visceral geographer' (Hayes-Conroy and Hayes-Conroy, 2010), she is interested in how bodily senses of taste, disgust, and desire play the predominant role in shaping consumption decisions. Likewise, Jamie (Lorimer, 2007) has explored the 'nonhuman charisma' of different animals in their encounters with conservation scientists. He traced how the anatomical, behavioural, and ecological properties of different organisms relative to the technologically equipped scientists configured whether and how they were perceived and how their charisma shaped how scientists and publics felt towards them – ultimately with important consequences for whether they got conserved.

2.2 Animals, plants, and other organisms

A second strand of more-than-human materialist thinking emerged as part of the wider 'animal turn' in the humanities in the 1990s that gave rise to the field of animal studies (Calarco, 2020; DeMello, 2021). This challenged human exceptionalism and the modern, humanist binary ontology that ranks humans above animals as an ontologically separate and superior category of life.

A range of authors, coming from many different philosophical positions, highlighted the difficulty of drawing any line dividing all humans and all animals. Instead, they identified a multitude of cross-species affinities and connections. They highlighted both the animal nature of human life – making connections to the work on embodiment above – and they drew attention to those animals that share in the properties that have historically been used to set humans apart, like cognition, sentience, language, and tool-use. They aimed to emphasise the agencies of animals in shaping human life and to make ethical claims on their behalf. In so doing, they also sought to open up the category 'animal' to recognise the differences between animal species that this label subsumes (Derrida, 2002).

This animal turn led to a resurgence of interest in animal geographies (for overviews, see Urbanik, 2012; Lorimer and Srinivasan, 2013). In two important edited collections produced at the end of the 1990s, geographers turned their attention to both 'animal spaces' – the ways in which humans order the lives of animals – and to 'beastly places' – the lived geographies of animals themselves (Wolch and Emel, 1998; Philo and Wilbert, 2000). Work on animal spaces focused initially on representations of animals in books and film, before expanding to consider how animals' lives are ordered. As we explore in Chapter 4 (Section 4.3), this research has focused on the spaces and relations of agriculture, conservation, pest control, and laboratory research, amongst others, looking at how these relations prescribe where and when animals are in or out of place, and how animals sometimes transgress these prescriptions. Work on the 'beastly places' of animals was less prominent in the 2000s but has come to the fore more recently with the emergence of an interest in what we have elsewhere described as 'animals' geographies' or the lived experiences of animals (Hodgetts and Lorimer, 2015; Hodgetts and Lorimer, 2020; Lorimer et al., 2019) like those of the mourning elephants we encountered in the introduction.

An understanding of animals as geographical actors in their own right was partly inspired by the work of social theorists like Gilles Deleuze, Vincianne Despret, Donna Haraway, and Tim Ingold. All of whom have engaged with the science of ethology or the study of animal behaviour. These authors looked back to the writings of the 19th-century Estonian ethologist Jacob von Uexkull (1934/2010), who understood animals as inhabiting a lifeworld or 'umwelt' (for introduction, see Ginn, 2014a). This umwelt is brought into existence by the specific relations that form between an animal's bodily capacities (or what he termed 'affects') and its wider environment. For example, most humans are bipedal, favour vision over taste or smell, are active in the day, and can't breathe unassisted underwater.[3] We have a terrestrial, vision-centred, and diurnal umwelt. These affects come to shape how most humans perceive the world, even with the rise of sophisticated scientific technologies.

Through an example of the tick – those blood-sucking insects you some-times find on your body after a day in the woods – von Uexkull shows how the curious ethologist can start to understand the specific 'soap bubbles' of perception that are inhabited by other species. He explains how a tick perched on a branch tip ready for a passing mammal has three affects: an ability to register the butyric acid emitted by a mammal's skin. Once trig-gered, the tick drops and a 'tactile organ' enables it to navigate the hairy body, until a 'temperature organ' senses warmth from a bare patch of skin and the tick drills for blood (2010, 178). These three affects create for the tick a very simple soap bubble, in comparison to those of humans.

Von Uexkull's idea of animal soap bubbles fell out of fashion in ethology with the rise of mechanistic behaviourism, in which animals are treated as instinctive machines (de Waal, 2016). But his relational understand-ing of sentient animal lifeworlds has returned to prominence, partly due to the growing scientific concern with questions of animal welfare. This resurgence has also been propelled by a growing number of interdisciplin-ary collaborations between ethologists and ethnographers and the rise of an approach known as multispecies ethnography (Kirksey and Helmreich, 2010), which tunes into the soap bubbles of animals, especially 'high-order' mammals that live lives closely entangled with humans. This work presents animals as subjects and as geographic actors that are different to humans, but no less interesting as the focus of enquiry. These interdisciplinary col-laborations have given rise to a range of new methodologies that we cover in the next chapter.

Perhaps the most well-known example of multispecies ethnography is provided by Donna Haraway (2008) in her accounts of dogs as companion species (see Box 2.1).[4] But an interest in animals as geographic actors and in multispecies entanglements has also been shaped by engagements with indigenous ontologies. For example, the Australian-based ethnographer Deborah Bird Rose worked closely with Aboriginal peoples to develop a distinct approach to understanding the lifeworlds and deaths of animals like dingoes (Rose, 2011) and flying foxes (Rose, 2022). She maps their cultural importance in the context of violent colonial histories of Aboriginal mis-treatment and of growing concerns about extinction and animal suffering.

In recent years, animal geographers have expanded their focus beyond close encounters with charismatic animals that are 'big like us' (Hird, 2009) towards a more diverse set of lifeforms and relations. For example, there is an established and growing interest in 'vegetal geographies' (Barua, 2022b; Ernwein et al., 2021; Head et al., 2014) and the agencies and lifeworlds of plants, which explores how the different needs, mobilities, and temporalities of plants come to configure human practices. Moving beyond mammals, there are growing interests in the geographies of birds (Garlick, 2019; van Dooren, 2014), insects (Abrahamsson and Bertoni, 2014; Phillips, 2013; Engelmann, 2017), and fish (Bear and Eden, 2011), that comes as part of a wider challenge to a perceived 'terrestrial' bias in human geography (see Section 2.5).

This expansion in the taxonomic scope of animal geography research has also led to a focus on less affirmative or 'awkward' (Ginn et al., 2014) encounters with abject organisms, especially invertebrates. For example, Jamie (Lorimer, 2016) has written about a group of patients, suffering from a collection of inflammatory diseases, who use hookworm to try and train and exercise their overactive immune systems. They source these worms from tropical latrines, raise them at home from their own faeces, before infecting with larvae that eat their way through the skin to find an eventual home in the gut.[5] Jamie's work on hookworm forms part of a wider interest in the human microbiome that we explore below, as well as those microbes that perform vital functions in our food and in the soil (Krzywoszynska, 2019; Folkers and Opitz, 2022).

2.3 Biological processes

While plant and animal geographers are primarily concerned with the agencies and lived experience of individual organisms, a further strand of more-than-human geography focuses on the biological processes that link these organisms together and how these come to shape, and be shaped by, human activities. This strand shifts focus away from *beings*, with stable, fixed forms and identities and balanced temporal rhythms, towards a focus on *becomings*: the dynamic and nonequilibrium ecologies and processes in and through which life evolves and within which different organisms (including humans) exchange materials. The focus here is on the interactions between things and the properties of the wider 'meshwork' (Ingold, 2011) or 'assemblages' (Latour, 2005) through which relations are configured.

This work is much inspired by the vitalist philosophy of the French theorist Gilles Deleuze and his collaborations with Felix Guattari (Deleuze and Guattari, 1987). Their writings offered geographers a materialist theory of difference, understood as the open-ended process of becoming otherwise, that has proved extremely influential in the rematerialisation of discipline and social theory more generally (for introductions, see May, 2004; Doel and Clark, 2011). In more-than-human geography, this type of materialism is most commonly associated with figures like Sarah Whatmore (Box 2.3), Doreen Massey, and Steve Hinchliffe. In this section, we give a flavour of the diversity of biological processes and interspecies entanglements that have been studied by more-than-human geographers, focusing on five key themes: urban natures, resilience, indigenous ontologies, biosecurity, and post-genomics.

Box 2.3   Sarah Whatmore and *Hybrid Geographies*

Sarah Whatmore is a British cultural and environmental geographer who worked at the University of Bristol and the Open University. She is currently a colleague of ours at the University of Oxford and she kindly offered to be interviewed for this book (see Appendix 1).

Whatmore is best known for her influential book *Hybrid Geographies* (2002), in which she challenged the modern Nature-Society binary and the types of geography to which it has given rise. Informed by Bruno Latour's (1993) argument that 'we have never been modern', she demonstrates the ontological impossibility of any pure Nature, untouched by human hands, and set apart from Society. Well in advance of the contemporary discussions of the Anthropocene, her work undermined popular environmentalist enthusiasms for a binary idea of wilderness and natural purity (for a summary, see Dyer, 2008).

Instead, she suggested that we understand the world as hybrid, a mixture of elements that subsequently get classified as either social or natural. Writing with Lorraine Thorne, she proposes 'a notion of "wildlife" as a relational achievement spun between people and animals, plants and soils, documents and devices, in heterogeneous social networks that are performed in and through multiple places and fluid ecologies' (1998, 437).

In subsequent work and in her book (with Bruce Braun) *Political Matter* (Whatmore and Braun, 2010), that we explore in more detail in later chapters, she focused her attention on the politics of Nature and questions of environmental expertise. She focused on the rise of environmental knowledge controversies as generative events in which the politics of natural science are made manifest, and in which different modes of environmental expertise come into conflict and become visible (Whatmore, 2009).

Drawing on the work of the Belgian philosopher Isabelle Stengers, she developed a novel methodology for doing public engagement with science and technology in the context of controversies about flood risk mapping, flood insurance, and the design of flood defences in a town in the North of England. She also worked closely with physical geographers like Stuart Lane, developing new approaches to intra-disciplinary geographical research (Whatmore, 2013a).

Whatmore was subsequently invited to chair the social science advisory committee for the UK Government Department for Environment, Food and Rural Affairs (DEFRA), and performed a range of public service roles for the UK government.

See Appendix 1 for an interview with Sarah Whatmore in which she reflects on the emergence of more-than-human geography and her own research career.

2.3.1 Urban natures

Hinchliffe, Whatmore, and colleagues (2005) outline the character and implications of a more-than-human process ontology in their work on urban wildlife (see Box 3.1). They identify the prevalent neglect of urban ecologies in mainstream nature conservation, suggesting that: 'not pure enough to be true and not human enough to be political, urban wilds have no constituency' (2005, 645). They argue that this anti-urbanism exemplifies a wider antipathy towards hybrid natures that get dubbed as monstrous, modified, or fake. To counter this bias and neglect, they draw on ecological writings that demonstrate the importance and the novelty of urban ecologies, to make a case for a more hybrid, open-ended, and experimental approach for conceiving human-shaped ecologies. Others subsequently developed this nondualistic ontology of wildlife in further work on urban ecologies (Barua, 2022a; Gandy, 2022; Wilson, 2022) and on rewilding, a new approach to nature conservation that values ecological processes over the composition of existing species (Lorimer, 2020).

2.3.2 Resilience

Another strand of writing links process philosophy with the theory of socio-ecological resilience (Grove, 2018). Resilience thinkers examine socio-ecological systems, which are figured as nonlinear and capable of adhering to multiple stable states. Changes between such states – for example between a forest or a savannah landscape – happen when the intensities in a system change and it crosses a threshold or tipping point – for example due to the introduction of grazing animals or a dramatic event like a fire (Adger and Brown, 2016). Resilience thinking recognises the agency of humans alongside other nonhuman actors in how functional ecologies evolve and offers a nondualistic approach for explaining environmental change. Work in this vein has explored the patterns and processes of animal movement, flagging the importance of connectivity in facilitating ecological resilience and nature recovery (Hodgetts and Lorimer, 2020). For example, Tim has examined the current enthusiasm in British nature conservation with reintroducing keystone species – like beaver or the pine marten – and installing infrastructure designed to assist their passage through fragmented landscapes to explore what happens when conservationists work with animals to manipulate ecological dynamics (Hodgetts, 2018). However, the application of resilience thinking to social policy and environmental management has proved controversial, as critics argue that it has often been used to naturalise the status quo (Nelson, 2014; Chandler, 2014), a debate we explore later in this book.

2.3.3 Indigenous ontologies

A focus on multispecies entanglements and relationships of becoming has also been developed in collaborations between more-than-human geographers and indigenous scholars and environmental activists. One compelling example is given by Bawaka Country et al. (see Box 3.3) – a collective of Australian writers – who include the place from which they write as an author in their work. Bawaka Country et al articulate a relational and processual ontology through their description of the Aboriginal concept of Country, suggesting that 'Country includes humans, more-than-humans and all that is tangible and non-tangible and which become together in an active, sentient, mutually caring and multidirectional manner in, with and as place/ space' (Bawaka Country et al., 2016, 456). They present Country as a process of 'co-becoming' and as an articulation of 'a Bawaka Yolŋu ontology within which everything exists in a state of emergence and relationality'. They explain that in this ontology: 'Not only are all beings – human, animal, plant, process, thing or affect – vital and sapient with their own knowledge and law, but their very being is constituted through relationships that are constantly re-generated' (2016, 456).

2.3.4 Biosecurity

Geographers have also shown how processual thinking helps understand less affirmative relations than those involved in conservation and rewilding, focusing on situations in which biological processes cause biosecurity risks, like the spread of invasive species or the proliferation of human, plant, and animal pathogens (Dobson et al., 2013). For example, Steve Hinchliffe and his collaborators (2016) examine the emergence and proliferation of diseases in intensive agricultural systems – like avian flu, campylobacter (a bacteria that causes food poisoning) or antimicrobial resistance. They argue that these diseases emerge from the internal *configuration* of the social-ecological relations associated with intensive agricultural production, rather than due to *contamination* from the outside. They suggest that the simplified ecologies of factory farms, coupled with the concentration of stressed and immune-compromised animal bodies, animal waste, and high levels of pharmaceutical use create 'disease hotspots': centres for the emergence of new and highly virulent strains of pathogenic microbes. They propose that we understand these as the industrial diseases of just-in-time production systems: a manifestation of the 'blowback' caused by the excesses of anti-biotic models of managing life that we introduced in the previous chapter.[6] They caution that global agricultural supply chains and human air travel network provide ample vectors for such microbes and the diseases they cause to spread. Examples include COVID-19 and African Swine Fever, alongside a growing set of antimicrobial resistant (AMR) infections. In contrast to the promotion of connectivity for nature recovery, this approach highlights how the networks of economic globalisation facilitate a space-time compression that heightens the risk of pandemics or the spread of invasive species.

2.3.5 Post-genomics

This focus on biological processes also informs work in geography that maps diverse 'molecular' exchanges between human bodies, animals, microbes, and the wider environment, tracing how such exchanges fold porous bodies into ecologies in ways that pull at modern humanist understandings of bounded autonomous self (Braun, 2007). This work bridges the three types of materialism we have reviewed in this chapter so far: bodies, animals, and processes. For example, Jane Bennett (2004) examines food as 'lively matter' tracing the actual and imagined incorporation of microbes and molecules through the act of eating. Bennett is interested in omega-3 fatty acids, a kind of fat that is prevalent in certain species of fish, following the scientific claim that these fats can improve human mood and behaviour. She explores the implications of 'the idea that lipids have the power not just to increase human flesh but also to induce human moods, modes of sociality and states of mind' (2004, 137). She is not claiming that these foodstuffs are a magic bullet, as their health-giving properties only work in some people in some contexts. Instead, she is interested in how this science pulls at the mind-body dualism by making visible the metabolic foundations of being human.[7]

Comparable challenges to the human-nonhuman and mind-body dualisms are made by the geographers interested in the philosophical implications of the science of the microbiome, that we encountered in the previous chapter (Stallins et al., 2018). For Donna Haraway (2015), this post-genomic, microbial ontology supports her claim that 'we have never been human'. Comparable work by Becky Mansfield and Julie Guthman (Guthman and Mansfield, 2015) engages with developments in epigenetics, a field of science that studies the mechanisms that change the development of the human phenotype without altering our DNA. This research has shown that exposure to different environmental stimuli can change the human phenotype within a person's lifetime, and that these changes are inheritable. They argue that epigenetics challenges fixed and essentialist ideas of genetic identity and of the bounded human body and requires a more-than-human geography that simultaneously pays 'attention to ecological processes both within and around the body' (Guthman and Mansfield, 2013, 498).[8]

A final strand of post-genomic more-than-humanism engages with new scientific understandings of human evolution to challenge claims of human exceptionalism and to rethink categories of social difference. For example, the geographer Kathryn Yusoff (2013) explores developments in human origins theory which undermine the established story of *Homo sapiens* being the sole, heroic survivor from amongst 22 now extinct hominid species. Instead, this work suggests that our ancestors bred with other hominids, including Neanderthals (which make up to 4% of the modern Eurasian genome). Yusoff argues that this research has 'reconceptualised humanity as interspecies' (787) and that it offers 'new genealogical accounts that suggest the human that we have become has no "we" at the level of genus, or in terms of racial, sexual, or geographic identity' (786).

2.4 Technologies and infrastructure

At the same time as geographers were emphasising the role of bodies, animals, and ecological processes in shaping social life, there was also a growing interest in the roles played by technologies and other human-made equipment in shaping how the world works. The work of the French sociologist of science Bruno Latour (Box 2.4) was central.

Box 2.4   Bruno Latour and actor-network theory

Bruno Latour was a French anthropologist and founding figure of the field of Science and Technology Studies (STS). Latour first worked at the Ecole de Mines before moving to the Paris Institute of Political Studies (Science Po).

Latour was interested in studying 'laboratory life' (Latour and Woolgar, 1979) and 'science in action' (Latour, 1987), in tracing how scientific knowledge is produced, how it travels, and how it comes to be accepted as fact. Early in his career, he collaborated with the American primatologist Shirley Strum to reflect on what makes baboons different from humans (Strum and Latour, 1987). They focused on the two species' use of material objects. They observed that baboons do not use material things to communicate; they don't write or arrange objects to pass on information. Instead, their social worlds are oral and remembered, local to a time and a place and performed out every day. In contrast, Latour and Strum observed how humans inscribe their social order into objects: specifically, texts and images which persist through time and over space to materialise knowledge and to make it travel.

Latour developed this seemingly straightforward insight with a collection of fellow sociologists of science (including John Law and Anne-Marie Mol). They proposed that we consider people as embedded within actor-networks or assemblages. Their actor-network theory (ANT) suggests that we see the world as composed of a great diversity of material things, all of which are endowed with some degree of agency, and they encouraged social scientists to trace these actor-networks to understand how social ordering takes place (for introductions to ANT, see Bosco, 2015; Latour, 2005).

The ANT ontology of actors in networks was central to Latour's (1993) claim that 'we have never been modern' (Latour, 1993). In his fieldwork, he traced how scientists construct networks of material instruments and texts that 'translate' the messy hybridity of the material world, before 'purifying' it into the binary categories of Nature and Society (see Figure 2.1). Latour's interests in the translation work of scientists, in the roles of technology, and in the fundamental hybridity of the world are very similar to the cyborg ontology of Donna Haraway that we encountered above. Latour and Haraway were good friends.

In later work, Latour focused on the Politics of Nature (Latour, 2004), critiquing the modern political settlement between Science and Politics that places science outside of politics (see Figure 1.4). He embarked on a wide range of collaborations with artists and natural and social scientists to develop ways of 'bringing the sciences into democracy' by developing new models for 'reassembling the social' (Latour, 2005). Latour framed this as the greatest challenge facing the social sciences in the context of the diagnosis of the Anthropocene, and the rise of post-truth models of climate denial (Latour, 2018).

Latour and ANT were criticised by figures on the Left for ignoring capitalism (discussed in Chapter 5). While fellow new materialists

WORK OF PURIFICATION

Nonhumans
Nature

Humans
Culture

WORK OF
TRANSLATION

Hybrids
Networks

Figure 2.1 The 'moderns' acts of 'translation' and 'purification' that create
the nature-culture binary.

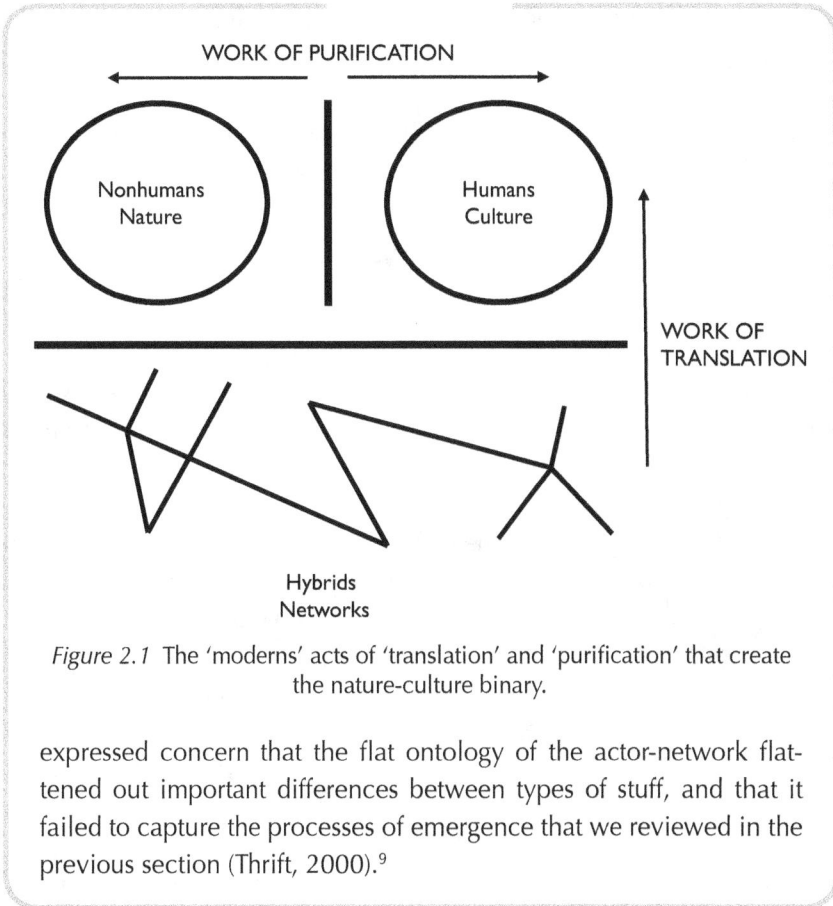

expressed concern that the flat ontology of the actor-network flattened out important differences between types of stuff, and that it
failed to capture the processes of emergence that we reviewed in the
previous section (Thrift, 2000).[9]

Early work tended to focus on the technologies of the laboratory and field
sciences and the practices of those scientists who used them to produce
representations of the world. In one famous study, Latour (1999) followed
a group of soil scientists into the Amazon, to explore how their instruments
enabled them to classify the forest boundary. He explored how the networks they used to travel and communicate enabled them to become the
recognised experts on the forest's ecology. In building their actor-network,
they translated the forest and came to speak on its behalf. Subsequent work
by sociologists and geographers like Susan Leigh Star (1991), Geoffrey
Bowker (Bowker and Star, 1999), and Paul Robbins (2001) looked at what
gets left out from these translations of forests and other nonhuman life, and
what happens when they are returned to govern the places they purport

to represent. They thus showed that specific socio-material assemblages have the power to shape the world, as the 'real' comes to converge upon its representation.

Subsequent work has developed this interest in socio-material assemblages in different directions. Some geographers have expanded the early ANT interest in scientific technologies to explore a wide array of anthropogenic assemblages through which social life is ordered. This includes work on digital and 'media ecologies': the ubiquitous and wide-reaching networks of devices, screens, cables, and data storage centres that hold the cloud and configure our information economy (Turnbull et al., 2023). This research forms part of a wider 'digital turn' (Ash et al., 2018) in geography, that examines how the specific affordances of digital media – including the ability to transform all information into binary data (0s and 1s) – radically transforms the character, reach, and power of media. It focuses on 'code': the software that runs these ecologies and ways in which code scripts social life to create 'code space' (Kitchin and Dodge, 2011). Geographers interested in technologies have also looked at the rise of surveillance networks that sense, map, model, and anticipate the movements of human and nonhuman actors, sometimes with lethal consequences. For example, Ian Shaw (2016a) has looked at the agency of killer drones that police the skies to enact US foreign policy. While Louise Amoore (2020) has examined the power of algorithmic decision-making and cloud computing.

A further strand of work has focused on the mundane infrastructure that makes modern, urban life possible. It examines pipes and sewers, roads and railways, and the architecture of buildings (Hetherington, 2019; Anand, 2017). This work has also focused on animals' interactions with infrastructure in urban environments (Barua, 2024) as well as growing efforts to use some plants and animals as infrastructure to tackle a range of environmental challenges, like flooding and climate change (Nelson and Bigger, 2022; Barua, 2021; Wakefield, 2019). Finally, a body of work in economic geography has been focused on the objects and flows that move through networks. This 'follow the thing' approach was pioneered by Ian Cook and his collaborators (Cook, 2004) and has focused on 'lifting the veil' on commodities like foodstuffs. Parallel work examines the differential movements of human bodies enabled and constrained by different transport technologies and on the uneven flow of energy and information (Graham and Marvin, 2001). There is a common interest here in questions of mobilities and logistics

(Cowen, 2014), as well as in the potential of infrastructure to go awry and cause disruption – for example, through an electricity blackout (Bennett, 2005) or a volcanic ash cloud that grounds airplanes (Adey et al., 2011).

2.5 The elements: earth, fire, air, and water

These investigations of how human lives are folded into the inorganic and technological environment is taken a step further in our final more-than-human materialism that is concerned with the agencies of 'the elemental' (Engelmann and McCormack, 2021). Here, the elemental refers to the abiotic matter from which all life is composed, which makes up a vast majority of the stuff of the world, and which has the potential for earth-quaking disasters. The drivers of this elemental focus are multiple, but three are worth mentioning here. This turn first represents the logical extension of previous waves of more-than-humanism, moving analysis ever further out beyond the human body. Second, it is driven by the growing awareness of the risks associated with the planetary transition into the Anthropocene, the return of a vengeful nature or, in Isabelle Stengers' (2017) terms, 'the intrusion of Gaia' into social thought. And finally, it emerges from increased engagement by geographers and anthropologists with indigenous ontologies that do not hold to any clear distinction between life and non-life (Povinelli, 2016), and which are held to offer promise for conceiving and living within geomorphic disruption. Here, we will flag three linked literatures, which have focused on earth and fire, air, and water.

2.5.1 Earth and fire

The diagnosis of the Anthropocene has helped propel a growing interest amongst more-than-humanists in the agency of geological and geomorphic processes, giving rise to new strands of geophilosophy, exemplified by writers like Elizabeth Grosz, who explores the 'geopower' of an unruly earth, marked by tipping points and agitated by anthropogenic climatic change (Yusoff et al., 2012). Amongst geographers, this interest is exemplified by Nigel Clark, Bron Szerszynski, and Kathryn Yusoff. In his book *Inhuman nature*, Clark (2011) focuses on powerful tectonic processes and events like earthquakes, tsunamis, and volcanic eruptions cautioning that 'what are catastrophes for soft, fleshy creatures like us are for the earth merely minor and mundane readjustments' (23). He encourages us to attend to the 'indifference' and the 'radical asymmetry' of an unruly earth: we need it more than it needs us. He focuses on human vulnerability to geopower and traces, through empirical research with those affected by these catastrophic events, how they live in the aftermath of geomorphic disasters.[10]

These elemental geographers have explored how an attention to the geo highlights the dependency of all life on the minerals and energy provided by the earth, in ways that blur the life-non-life distinction to situate the biological processes that were the focus of previous sections in their wider ontological contexts.[11] They encourage us to think with the deep time of Earth History (Clark and Szerszynski, 2020) and flag the 'debt' that modern humanity owes to the past carbon-based lifeforms that were laid down in the Carboniferous period to later become fossil fuels (Clark and Yusoff, 2014). They note the importance of fire and of combustion in mediating this relationship and highlight how 'fossil capitalism' – a term first coined by Andreas Malm (Malm, 2016) – wastefully splurges this gift from the past (Yusoff, 2016). Further work in resource geographies engages with this more-than-human agenda to explore how different forms of fossil fuel help configure different forms of political economic organisation. For example, Gavin Bridge (2009) examines coal and oil as 'geological subsidies to the present day', whose extraction constitutes 'a transfer of geological space and time that has underpinned the compression of time and space in modernity' (48). He highlights how 19th-century processes of globalisation were fuelled and accelerated by the burning of carbon.

These geographers' interests in subterranean relations and the materiality of the earth form part of a wider push across the discipline to develop more volumetric (or three-dimensional) understandings of space. Critics like Stuart Elden (2013) and Stephen Graham (2016) have argued that geography (especially urban and political geography) has for too long been wedded to studying the surfaces of a flat Earth, neglecting the spaces above, below, and around the human subject, and the agencies of the material elements of which they are composed. Geographers' engagements with Earth System Science offers a new four-dimensional spatio-temporal imaginary of 'the planetary' (Clark and Szerszynski, 2020): of an Earth configured by the historical interaction of processes in different 'spheres', including the physical spheres of the hydrosphere (water), atmosphere (air), lithosphere (land), and biosphere (life) and the human 'technosphere' (Haff, 2014). For the historian Dipesh Chakrabarty (2021), this is a radical intellectual break with past work in the humanities and social sciences in that it sees the 'entry of Earth into History', requiring analysis to acknowledge the agency of the planetary on global events.

2.5.2 Air

In our second strand of elemental research, a collection of more-than-human thinkers turned their attention to the materiality of air and to the social and spatial relations that are mediated by the atmosphere. One example of this 'aerography' is offered by Derek McCormack (2018) in his book *Atmospheric Things*. McCormack develops his earlier work on affect (see above) to think with the double meaning of atmosphere as both the gaseous substances that envelop a body, and the shared affective experience of a place, developing the common idea that places can have a friendly atmosphere, a sinister atmosphere, etc.[12] In comparable work, Tim Ingold (2007, 2010) has developed his interest in landscape and dwelling (see above) to explore the embodied experience of 'weather worlds', attending closely to the movement, humidity, sounds, smells, and tastes of air. Others have examined the human-environmental relations mediated by the lungs through the act of breathing, working with scientists and public health officials to examine how viruses, dust, and other aerosol contaminants are incorporated into the human body (Choy, 2010; Gabrys, 2022). This work is driven in part by growing public concerns with urban air quality and its effects on health, especially of children.

This attention to incorporation through breathing informs work on 'chemical geographies' (Romero et al., 2017) and the 'chemosphere' (Shapiro, 2015): the airborne chemicals to which a body is exposed, especially in domestic and institutional environments.[13] The anthropologist Nick Shapiro has examined the experience and effects of breathing formaldehyde, a common chemical in the domestic environment. He explains how formaldehyde 'seeps from the very engineered woods that give much of contemporary domestic space its comfort, security, and affordability' (2015, 372), tracing the range of toxic effects it has on human bodies, when it is inhaled at elevated concentrations over a significant period. Shapiro examines the experiences of those living in temporary accommodation provided by the US Federal Emergency Management Agency in the aftermath of Hurricane Katrina. This interest in the elemental properties of air extends to work exploring atmospheric engineering, including the use of aerosol chemicals to enact 'terror from the air' (Sloterdijk et al., 2009) upon both human and nonhuman subjects. One notorious example being the release of the herbicide 'Agent Orange' by the US military during the Vietnam War (Shaw, 2016b). It also includes research examining deliberate practices of weather modification for various political, economic, and ecological ends (Chien et al., 2017; Zee, 2022).

2.5.3 Water

A third and final strand of elemental research examines the materialities of water, developing 'wet ontologies' (Steinberg and Peters, 2015; Peters and Steinberg, 2019) to counter what was seen as a terrestrial bias in the discipline of geography. Research in this 'watery turn' (Anderson and Peters, 2014) has focused on the neglected aquatic places that are coloured blue on the map to explore the difference made by water to terrestrial understandings of space, time, and motion. This work has examined the fluid volumes and liquid materialities of oceans, rivers, and other bodies of water, as well as the human experience of being in motion on the water. For example, Jon Anderson has explored waves and the experience of surfing, suggesting that:

> 'The place of surf is the very definition of a place that is unreliable, inconsistent, wholly provisional, and unstable. It is a place that, at any moment, emerges in time and space from the web of flows and connections meeting at a particular node.'
>
> (2012, 575)

In collaborative research with anglers, Chris Bear and Sally Eden link elemental and animal geographies to develop approaches for 'thinking like a fish' (2011). Their work helps sense the liquid materialities of rivers and to begin to understand the alien lifeworlds of aquatic life. In more recent writings, Steinberg and Peters have moved away from a binary understanding of land and water, acknowledging that 'the ocean is not simply liquid; it is not simply wet. It is solid (ice) and air (mist)' (2019, 2). They explore how watery relations extend out over the land, drawing attention to scientific work that flags the evolutionary origins of life in the sea that connect to work on biological processes, suggesting that: 'we are, in a sense, soft vessels of seawater. Seventy percent of our bodies is water, the same percentage that covers Earth's surface. We are wrapped around an ocean within. You can test this simply enough: Taste your tears' (Safina, 1997, 435, in Peters and Steinberg, 2019, 6).

2.6 Key characteristics of more-than-human materialisms

This chapter has traced the gradual expansion and diversification in the types of materials that have come to interest more-than-human geographers. From a starting point that abandons the dualistic understandings of humanism, they have developed diverse accounts of materiality in which the actors are never solely human (even the humans themselves). Work in all these areas continues apace, and most more-than-human geographers span more than one of these different types of materials. On the surface, these diverse materialisations seem to be following somewhat disparate aims. Some want to talk about scientific instruments, some want to study microbes, while others worry about breathing or fear geological disasters. However, all share a common desire to move off from the nature-society, human-animal, subject-object, and thought-matter binaries that characterise humanist approaches. If we look more closely, we can identify common characteristics of the new materialisms of more-than-human geography. We flagged these at the start of the chapter and will expand on them here.

2.6.1 Affective materialities: affect over cognition

There has been a shift away from the human geography of the cultural turn that focuses on studying cognition and the textual representations and discourses through which it is shaped. The decentring of the rational mind as the locus of agency has led to a common interest in the nature and the role of affect. This redistributes agency to the body, by studying bodily movements, incorporations, and visceral processes. It offers a vocabulary for talking about feelings and emotions and how these are shared in affective atmospheres. This shift provides a very different model of the subject, as one that is first, and above all, a sensing, feeling body in the world. This figure of the affective subject comes to inform very different ideas of knowledge and of how power and politics work, that we explore in subsequent chapters. The affective turn also opens space for considering the nonhuman subjectivities of other animals, of plants, and even of ecological aggregations like forests. This idea of affective subjectivity and of life as a process of learning to be affected provides a more generous ontology of being in the world that can encompass the lifeworlds of species that don't think like us.

2.6.2 Processual materialities: becomings over beings

A second common element is the interest in the processes through which humans and nonhumans emerge, change, and are entangled together. Rather than assuming that there are fixed beings, with stable identities, that manifest essential forms, more-than-humanists take the world as fluid and caught up in constant processes of becoming. Rather than seeing the world as in balance, or progressing along predictable linear or cyclical patterns, they present a world that is nonequilibrium and sometimes marked by chaotic dynamics, tipping points and a degree of surprising unpredictability. In philosophical terms, they share an interest in immanence and the idea of difference as an ongoing process. This in turn leads to a shared commitment to what Jane Bennett (2010) terms, 'emergent causality' in which subsequent events are shaped by fine differences in the relations between elements, in ways that mitigate against the generation of universal laws of human and nonhuman behaviour. This has some profound epistemological consequences that we explore in the following chapter. It also allows more-than-human geographers to rematerialise their theories without lapsing into the forms of environmental determinism that blighted earlier work. A world of becomings and interactions provides much less solid ground for those who want to naturalise forms of social difference to legitimate political projects. This fluidity creates its own problems, that we reflect on later in the book.

2.6.3 Relational materialities: from regions to networks to intensities

In a geography premised on a world of fixed forms, it is fairly straightforward to draw lines on the map that identify what is where and to chart how things change over time. This approach gives us a world of 'regions': for example, of nation states composed of races, or wildernesses defined by human absence. It charts stable trajectories of social and ecological change. Think of your high school encounters with Rostow's model of socio-economic development or Clemens' cyclical model of ecological succession. However, a commitment to becomings and emergent causality has important implications for how more-than-human geographers conceive of space and time. It requires that we 'scrumple' (Doel, 1996) such regional maps to recognise other types of spatial-temporal relations, or what geographers describe as topologies (Murdoch, 2006; Massey, 2005). More-than-human geographers initially focused on network topologies, following things to map connections that cut across the borders of regions: from foodstuffs, to diseases, to human migrants. They traced the processes of space-time compression performed by transport and media technologies. The more recent work that we encountered above by writers like Steve Hinchliffe (Hinchliffe et al., 2013; Lorimer, 2017) uses the concepts of configuration and assemblages to trace how the intensities of the interactions between social and ecological elements at any given site can give rise to particular events: from a riot, to a disease, to a landslide.

These more-than-human approaches to space-time also unsettle familiar 'vertical' notions of scale, in which large-scale 'macro' forces determine local or 'micro' relations: the Russian doll model for explaining causation (Herod, 2010). Some have even argued for a 'geography without scale' (Marston et al., 2005) that focuses on tracing horizontal connections within assemblages without making recourse to higher explanatory categories like capitalism or colonialism. The work on biological and geological processes also stretches geographers' interests in time. It draws attention to deep time, and the ecological, epigenetic, and geological inheritances that haunt the present. It flags the 'slow violence' (Nixon, 2011) associated with chronic exposure to toxic chemicals. And it calls our attention to futures in terms of both the spectre of imminent climate catastrophe, as well as the far-off futures involved with the production of the 'future fossils' that will mark the Anthropocene.

2.6.4 Holistic materialities: holism over reductionism

Finally, recent strands of more-than-human thinking borrow extensively from holistic, systems thinking, such as Earth System Science and Ecological-Evolutionary-Developmental biology (Gilbert et al., 2015). Key thinkers like Donna Haraway, Anna Tsing, Isabelle Stengers, and Bruno Latour find in this work a liberal and ecological ontology for regrounding critical social theory (Lorimer, 2020). In their earlier writings, they took issue with the reductionism of sociobiology which sought to reduce human behaviour to genetic inheritance and to naturalise a figure of selfish human subject. In contrast, in this new alliance with science, they deploy holistic ideas of multispecies entanglement and mutualistic co-becoming. In the face of the fast unravelling of the hospitable conditions of the Holocene, they call for social theorists to work closely with natural scientists to develop democratic blueprints for bringing humans 'down to Earth' (Latour, 2018). They look for ways in which people might learn to live with the planetary boundaries identified by scientists, drawing on examples of existing practices. These alliances are premised on different epistemic relations with this new type of 'limits' thinking. They generate diverse future visions for planetary survival that we discuss in the chapters that follow.

2.7 Conclusions

Returning to the beginning of this chapter, a key common aim in all these new materialisms has been to challenge the humanist idea that the intentional human mind is the sole locus of agency in the processes that bring about social change. Decentring the human required granting some forms of agency to the nonhuman elements of the world. The concept of *'nonhuman agency'* (this specific term, not the wider idea) is commonly associated with actor-network theory whose early proponents advocated a 'generalised' symmetry in their accounts of agency. They suggested that we should not start with the presumption that it was only the human scientists doing the ordering; instead, we should be symmetrical and allow for the possibility that the nonhumans caught up in the conduct of science also have the agency to perform action. They advocated a 'flat ontology' and a 'distributed' understanding of agency that levelled out the humanist hierarchy that elevated (a small number of) humans over animals, technologies, and other things.

The merits of a flat ontology have been widely discussed, generating rich debates that we explore in Chapter 5. But as we come to the end of this chapter, it is clear that we have travelled a long way from the modern figure of the exceptional human subject. We have taken concrete steps towards understanding the first ontological dimension of the concept of multinaturalism that we outlined in the introduction. In different ways, the work considered here has recognised the impossibility of separating the world into two stable, pure, and essential categories of stuff. The various authors draw attention to the ontological impossibility of a Nature untouched by human hands, or of the human mind, let alone the human body, being somehow cut off and isolated from the world around it. They suggest that 'we have never been modern' (Latour, 1993) and that 'we have never been human' (Haraway, 2008). They propose a model of 'planetary multiplicity' (Clark and Szerszynski, 2020): 'an understanding of the Earth as characterized by diverse process of self-differentiation' (2020, 8). We are offered an Earth that can go in many different directions, partly conditional on human actions.

But has this created a new set of problems? As we discussed in the Introduction, what terms do we use to describe the world when we can't make easy recourse to Nature and Society? This chapter has traced a proliferation of terminology. Early strands of more-than-human thinking offered us 'cyborgs', 'hybrids', and 'socionatures' caught up in 'actor-networks'. Critics argue that the idea of hybridity presumes two previously pure forms that get mixed together; it suggests a point in the past at which elements were separate and a subsequent moment at which they were mixed. But most more-than-human theorists don't see the world in this way. We hear more now about entanglements and about life as a meshwork, but we are nonetheless left with something of a confusing picture. In spite of the four common characteristics outlined above, we are still surrounded by a myriad of materialisms. Is this a problem? We don't think so. Let a thousand materialisms bloom!

Questions for reflection

1 Where does your body end?
2 How much of what you do happens because you intended to do it?
3 How does your body shape what you think, feel, and do?
4 What is an animal?
5 How do plants have agency on your life?
6 Do animals have their own geographies?
7 How do technologies enable you to be student?
8 What would a day without technology be like?
9 What becomings do you desire and what do you fear?
10 How does breathing, eating, or drinking link you to the world around you?
11 How does deep time help understand where you are?
12 What will be the future fossils that last from the present day?

Suggestions for reading

The following offer more extensive discussions of the origins and character of more-than-human thinking about materialities in geography:

Anderson B, Kearnes M and McFarlane C, et al. (2012) On assemblages and geography. *Dialogues in Human Geography* 2(2): 171–189.
Clark N and Szerszynski B (2020) *Planetary social thought: The anthropocene challenge to the social sciences*. London: Wiley.
Cook I (2004) Follow the thing: Papaya. *Antipode* 36(4): 642–664.
Lorimer J and Srinivasan K (2013) Animal geographies. *The Wiley-Blackwell Companion to cultural geography*. London: John Wiley & Sons Ltd., pp. 332–342.
Simpson P (2020) *Non-representational theory*. London: Taylor & Francis.

These texts offer introductions to the 'first principles' of new materialist thinking:

Barad K (2003) Posthumanist performativity: Toward an understanding of how matter comes to matter. *Signs: Journal of Women in Culture and Society* 28(3): 801–831.
Bennett J (2004) The force of things – Steps toward an ecology of matter. *Political Theory* 32(3): 347–372.
Haraway DJ (1991) *Simians, cyborgs, and women: The reinvention of nature*. New York: Routledge.
Ingold T (2000) *The perception of the environment: Essays on livelihood, dwelling and skill*. London: Routledge.
Latour B (2005) *Reassembling the social: An introduction to actor-network-theory*. Oxford: Oxford University Press.

Notes

1   Hannah MacPherson (2009) has examined how blind people sense and experience landscapes, critiquing the 'able-ism' in much past work that assumes universal 20/20 vision. Similarly, David Bissell (2009) has explored the lives of those afflicted by chronic pain, reworking everyday, able-ist assumptions of what constitutes a comfortable body.

2   Off the record, some went so far as to suggest that non-representational theory was 'boys' theory'. This criticism forms part of a wider dissatisfaction with non-representational theory – and Nigel Thrift in particular – amongst prominent Marxist and Feminist figures on the Left of geography. See for example Smith (2005).

3   To illustrate his concept of the umwelt, von Uexkull published an article entitled *A Stroll through the Worlds of Animals and Men: A Picture Book of Invisible Worlds*. He takes us to a meadow and invites us to: 'first blow, in fancy, a soap bubble around each creature to represent its own world, filled with the perceptions which it alone knows. When we ourselves then step into one of these bubbles, the familiar meadow is transformed. Many of its colorful features

disappear, others no longer belong together but appear in new relationships. A new world comes into being. Through the bubble we see the world of the burrowing worm, of the butterfly, or of the field mouse; the world as it appears to the animals themselves, not as it appears to us' (1934, 5).

4   In comparable work, Hayden Lorimer (2006) explored the herding practices and memories of reindeer and those humans that care for them in the Highlands of Scotland. He combines an approach to landscape as taskscape with an attention to the knowledges of the animals themselves as they learn to navigate and inhabit an unfamiliar landscape. Likewise, Maan Barua (2014a, 2014b) has explored the lifeworlds and lived geographies of Asian elephants and the rural farmers with which they come into conflict in Assam in North-East India. He traces how elephants learn to navigate fragmented landscapes on the margins of national parks, how they evade detection, differentiate humans by sight and smell, and seek out gratifying encounters with illicit locally brewed alcohol. He explores how particular animals become addicted, and how they become traumatised by past violent encounters.

5   Franklin Ginn (2014b) has explored the often-lethal relationships between gardeners and slugs, while Uli Biesel and Christophe Boëte (2013) have looked at the relationships scientists and publics form with mosquitoes.

6   Anna Tsing (2017) and Julie Guthman (2019) share comparable concerns about ecological tipping points and the genesis and the proliferation of invasive pests and infectious pathogens in their work on plantation ecologies and intensive fruit production systems, respectively.

7   For further examples of work in this area, see Stassart and Whatmore (2003) and Hatch, Sternlieb and Gordon (2019).

8   In further writing, they nonetheless caution that 'epigenetics is contributing to a new biological (yet non-determinist) ontology of race' (Mansfield and Guthman 2015) that justifies a 'new science of eugenics' (2015, 5) even though models of plastic, epigenetic life might be expected to undermine categories of race premised on 'discrete kinds given in nature' (2015, 1).

9   As Thrift puts it, ANT is 'much more able to describe steely accumulation than lightning strikes' (2000a, 214).

10 Noel Castree (2012) provides a helpful summary of Inhuman Nature and its implications for geographers.

11 For Sarah Whatmore, this focus on what she terms 'earthly powers': 'conjures an ecological imagination that foregrounds the conditional openness or immanence of life such that ecology is less the interaction between prefigured life forms/material entities than their emergence and transformation in the wider field of forces, intensities and durations that give rise to them' (2013b, 36).

12 Working with McCormack, Sasha Engelman (Engelman 2015; Engelmann and McCormack 2018) has explored how artists like Dryden Goodwin and Tomas Saraceno create atmospheres through their large-scale installations. She examines how these artists work closely with solar energy, the materialities of air, and architectural and artistic technologies to shape atmospheric movement, density, and acoustic properties. Through methods we outline later in the book, they seek to witness the subsequent felt experience of the affective atmospheres engendered amongst publics in the communal settings of these art exhibitions.

13 Nick Shapiro and Eben Kirksey (2017) identify the emergence of chemo-ethnography: an interdisciplinary field of study dedicated to tracing the myriad of artificial chemicals – both life-giving and toxic – to which bodies are differentially exposed and the social relations that an awareness of these exposures brings into being.

References

Abrahamsson S and Bertoni F (2014) Compost politics: Experimenting with togetherness in vermicomposting. *Environmental Humanities* 4(1): 125–148.

Adey P, Anderson B and Guerrero LL (2011) An ash cloud, airspace and environmental threat. *Transactions of the Institute of British Geographers* 36(3): 338–343.

Adger WN and Brown K (2016) Vulnerability and resilience to environmental change: Ecological and social perspectives. In: Castree N, Demeritt D and Liverman D (eds) *A companion to environmental geography*. Oxford: Blackwell, pp. 109–122.

Amoore L (2020) *Cloud ethics: Algorithms and the attributes of ourselves and others.* Durham: Duke University Press.

Anand N (2017) *Hydraulic city: Water and the infrastructures of citizenship in Mumbai.* Durham: Duke University Press.

Anderson B (2009) Affective atmospheres. *Emotion, Space and Society* 2(2): 77–81.

Anderson B (2014) Affects. In: Cloke P, Crang P and Goodwin M (eds) *Introducing human geographies*. 3rd ed. London: Routledge, pp. 760–772.

Anderson B, Kearnes M, McFarlane C and Swanton D (2012) On assemblages and geography. *Dialogues in Human Geography* 2(2): 171–189.

Anderson J and Peters K (2014) *Water worlds: Human geographies of the ocean.* Farnham: Ashgate.

Ash J, Kitchin R and Leszczynski A (2018) Digital turn, digital geographies? *Progress in Human Geography* 42(1): 25–43.

Barua M (2014a) Bio-geo-graphy: Landscape, dwelling, and the political ecology of human-elephant relations. *Environment and Planning D: Society and Space* 32(5): 915–934.

Barua M (2014b) Volatile ecologies: Towards a material politics of human-animal relations. *Environment and Planning A* 46(6): 1462–1478.

Barua M (2021) Infrastructure and non-human life: A wider ontology. *Progress in Human Geography* 45(6): 1467–1489.

Barua M (2022) Feral ecologies: The making of postcolonial nature in London. *Journal of the Royal Anthropological Institute* 28: 896–919.

Barua M (2023) Plantationocene: A vegetal geography. *Annals of the American Association of Geographers* 113(1): 13–29. DOI: 10.1080/24694452.2022.2094326.

Barua M (2024) *Lively cities: Reconfiguring urban ecology.* Minneapolis: University of Minnesota Press.

Bawaka Country, Wright S, Suchet-Pearson S, Lloyd K, Burarrwanga L, Ganambarr R, Ganambarr-Stubbs M, Ganambarr B, Maymuru D and Sweeney J (2016) Co-becoming Bawaka: Towards a relational understanding of place/space. *Progress in Human Geography* 40(4): 455–475.

Bear C and Eden S (2011) Thinking like a fish? Engaging with nonhuman difference through recreational angling. *Environment and Planning D: Society and Space* 29(2): 336–352.

Beisel U and Boëte C (2013) The flying public health tool: Genetically modified mosquitoes and malaria control. *Science as Culture* 22(1): 38–60.

Bennett J (2004) The force of things - steps toward an ecology of matter. *Political Theory* 32(3): 347–372.

Bennett J (2005) The agency of assemblages and the North American blackout. *Public Culture* 17(3): 445–466.

Bennett J (2010) *Vibrant matter: A political ecology of things.* Durham, NC: Duke University Press.

Bissell D (2009) Obdurate pains, transient intensities: Affect and the chronically pained body. *Environment and Planning A: Economy and Space* 41(4): 911–928.

Bosco FJ (2015) Actor-network theory, networks, and relational geographies. In: Aitken SC and Valentine G (eds) *Approaches to human geography.* London: SAGE, pp. 150–162.

Bowker GC and Star S, Leigh (1999) *Sorting things out: Classification and its consequences.* Cambridge, MA: MIT Press.

Braun B (2007) Biopolitics and the molecularization of life. *Cultural Geographies* 14(1): 6–28.

Bridge G (2009) The hole world: Scales and spaces of extraction. *New Geographies* 2: 43–48.

Brown G, Lim J and Browne PK (2012) *Geographies of sexualities: Theory, practices and politics.* London: Ashgate Publishing Limited.

Butler J (2006) *Gender trouble: Feminism and the subversion of identity.* New York: Routledge.

Butler J (2014) *Bodies that matter: On the discursive limits of "sex".* Abingdon: Taylor & Francis.

Calarco MR (2020) *Animal studies: The key concepts.* Abingdon: Taylor & Francis.

Carter S and McCormack DP (2006) Film, geopolitics and the affective logics of intervention. *Political Geography* 25(2): 228–245.

Castree N (2005) *Nature.* London: Routledge.

Castree N (2012) The return of nature? *Cultural Geographies* 19(4): 547–552.

Chakrabarty D (2021) *The climate of history in a planetary age.* Chicago: University of Chicago Press.

Chandler D (2014) *Resilience: The governance of complexity.* Abingdon: Taylor & Francis.

Chien S-S, Hong D-L and Lin P-H (2017) Ideological and volume politics behind cloud water resource governance – weather modification in China. *Geoforum* 85: 225–233.

Choy T (2010) Air's substantiations. In: Rajan K (ed) *Lively capital: Biotechnologies, ethics, and governance in global markets.* Durham, NC: Duke, pp. 121–154.

Clark N (2011) *Inhuman nature: Sociable living on a dynamic planet.* Thousand Oaks, CA: SAGE.

Clark N and Szerszynski B (2020) *Planetary social thought: The Anthropocene challenge to the social sciences.* London: Wiley.

Clark N and Yusoff K (2014) Combustion and society: A fire-centred history of energy use. *Theory, Culture & Society* 31(5): 203–226.

Colls R (2007) Materialising bodily matter: Intra-action and the embodiment of 'fat'. *Geoforum* 38(2): 353–365.

Cook I (2004) Follow the thing: Papaya. *Antipode* 36(4): 642–664.

Cowen D (2014) *The deadly life of logistics: Mapping violence in global trade.* Minneapolis: University of Minnesota Press.

de Waal F (2016) *Are we smart enough to know how smart animals are?* New York: W. W. Norton.

Deleuze G and Guattari F (1987) *A thousand plateaus: Capitalism and schizophrenia.* Minneapolis: University of Minnesota Press.

DeMello M (2021) *Animals and society: An introduction to human-animal studies.* New York: Columbia University Press.

Derrida J (2002) The animal that therefore I am (more to follow). *Critical Inquiry* 28(2): 369–418.

Dobson A, Barker K and Tayor S (2013) *Biosecurity: The socio-politics of invasive species and infectious diseases.* London: Routledge.

Doel MA (1996) A hundred thousand lines of flight: A machinic introduction to the nomad thought and scrumpled geography of Gilles Deleuze and Félix Guattari. *Environment and Planning D: Society and Space* 14(4): 421–439.

Doel MA and Clark D (2011) Gilles Deleuze. In: Hubbard P and Kitchen R (eds) *Key thinkers on space and place.* London: SAGE, pp. 141–147.

Dyer S (2008) Hybrid geographies (2002): Sarah Whatmore. In: Hubbard P, Kitchen R and Valentine G (eds) *Key texts in human geography.* London: SAGE, pp. 207–214.

Edensor T (2015) Producing atmospheres at the match: Fan cultures, commercialisation and mood management in English football. *Emotion, Space and Society* 15: 82–89.

Elden S (2013) Secure the volume: Vertical geopolitics and the depth of power. *Political Geography* 34: 35–51.

Engelmann S (2015) Toward a poetics of air: Sequencing and surfacing breath. *Transactions of the Institute of British Geographers* 40(3): 430–444.

Engelmann S (2017) Social spiders and hybrid webs at studio Tomás Saraceno. *Cultural Geographies* 24(1): 161–169.

Engelmann S and McCormack D (2018) Elemental aesthetics: On artistic experiments with solar energy. *Annals of the American Association of Geographers* 108(1): 241–259.

Engelmann S and McCormack D (2021) Elemental worlds: Specificities, exposures, alchemies. *Progress in Human Geography* 0(0): 0309132520987301.

Ernwein M, Ginn F and Palmer J (2021) *The work that plants do: Life, labour and the future of vegetal economies.* London: Transcript Verlag.

Folkers A and Opitz S (2022) Low-carbon cows: From microbial metabolism to the symbiotic planet. *Social Studies of Science* 52(3): 330–352.

Gabrys J (2022) *Citizens of worlds: Open-air toolkits for environmental struggle.* Minneapolis: University of Minnesota Press.

Gandy M (2022) *Natura urbana: Ecological constellations in urban space.* Boston: MIT Press.

Garlick B (2019) Cultural geographies of extinction: Animal culture among Scottish ospreys. *Transactions of the Institute of British Geographers* 44(2): 226–241.

Gilbert SF, Bosch TCG and Ledon-Rettig C (2015) Eco-evo-devo: Developmental symbiosis and developmental plasticity as evolutionary agents. *Nature Review Genetics* 16(10): 611–622.

Ginn F (2014a) Jakob von Uexküll beyond bubbles: On umwelt and biophilosophy. *Science as Culture* 23(1): 129–134.

Ginn F (2014b) Sticky lives: Slugs, detachment and more-than-human ethics in the garden. *Transactions of the Institute of British Geographers* 39(4): 532–544.

Ginn F, Beisel U and Barua M (2014) Flourishing with awkward creatures: Togetherness, vulnerability, killing. *Environmental Humanities* 4: 113–123.

Graham S (2016) *Vertical: The city from satellites to bunkers.* New York: Verso Books.

Graham S and Marvin S (2001) *Splintering urbanism: Networked infrastructures, technological mobilities and the urban condition.* Routledge.

Grove K (2018) *Resilience.* Taylor & Francis.

Guthman J (2019) *Wilted: Pathogens, chemicals, and the fragile future of the strawberry industry.* Oakland: University of California Press.

Guthman J and Mansfield B (2013) The implications of environmental epigenetics: A new direction for geographic inquiry on health, space, and nature-society relations. *Progress in Human Geography* 37(4): 486–504.

Guthman J and Mansfield B (2015) Nature, difference, and the body. *The Routledge handbook of political ecology.* London: Routledge.

Haff P (2014) Humans and technology in the Anthropocene: Six rules. *The Anthropocene Review* 1(2): 126–136. DOI: 10.1177/2053019614530575.

Hall E and Wilton R (2017) Towards a relational geography of disability. *Progress in Human Geography* 41(6): 727–744.

Haraway D (1984) Teddy bear patriarchy: Taxidermy in the Garden of Eden, New York city, 1908–1936. *Social Text* No. 11 (Winter, 1984–1985): 20–64. DOI: 10.2307/466593.

Haraway D (2015) Anthropocene, Capitalocene, Plantationocene, Chthulucene: Making kin. *Environmental Humanities* 6: 159–165.

Haraway DJ (1989) *Primate visions: Gender, race, and nature in the world of modern science.* New York: Routledge.

Haraway DJ (1991) *Simians, cyborgs, and women: The reinvention of nature.* New York: Routledge.

Haraway DJ (2003) *The companion species manifesto: Dogs, people, and significant otherness*. Chicago, IL: Prickly Paradigm Press.

Haraway DJ (2008) *When species meet*. Minneapolis: University of Minnesota Press.

Haraway DJ (2016) *Staying with the trouble: Making kin in the Chthulucene*. Durham, NC: Duke University Press.

Hatch AR, Sternlieb S and Gordon J (2019) Sugar ecologies: Their metabolic and racial effects. *Food, Culture & Society* 22(5): 595–607.

Hayes-Conroy J and Hayes-Conroy A (2010) Visceral geographies: Mattering, relating, and defying. *Geography Compass* 4(9): 1273–1283.

Head L, Atchison J, Phillips C and Buckingham K (2014) Vegetal politics: Belonging, practices and places. *Social & Cultural Geography* 15(8): 861–870.

Herod A (2010) *Scale*. Abingdon: Taylor & Francis.

Hetherington K (2019) *Infrastructure, environment, and life in the Anthropocene*. Durham: Duke University Press.

Hinchliffe S, Allen J, Lavau S, Bingham N and Carter S (2013) Biosecurity and the topologies of infected life: From borderlines to borderlands. *Transactions of the Institute of British Geographers* 38(4): 531–543.

Hinchliffe S, Bingham N, Allen J and Carter S (2016) *Pathological lives: Disease, space and biopolitics*. London: Blackwell.

Hinchliffe S, Kearnes MB, Degen M and Whatmore S (2005) Urban wild things: A cosmopolitical experiment. *Environment and Planning D-Society & Space* 23(5): 643–658.

Hird M (2009) *The origins of sociable life: Evolution after science studies*. Basingstoke: Palgrave Macmillan.

Hodgetts T (2018) Connectivity as a multiple: In, with and as "nature". *Area* 50(1): 83–90.

Hodgetts T and Lorimer J (2015) Methodologies for animals' geographies: Cultures, communication and genomics. *Cultural Geographies* 22(2): 285–295.

Hodgetts T and Lorimer J (2020) Animals' mobilities. *Progress in Human Geography* 44(1): 4–26.

Hopkins P (2010) *Young people, place and identity*. London: Routledge.

Ingold T (2000) *The perception of the environment: Essays on livelihood, dwelling and skill*. London: Routledge.

Ingold T (2007) Earth, sky, wind, and weather. *Journal of the Royal Anthropological Institute* 13(SUPPL. 1): S19–S38.

Ingold T (2010) Footprints through the weather-world: Walking, breathing, knowing. *Journal of the Royal Anthropological Institute* 16(s1): S121–S139.

Ingold T (2011) *Being alive: Essays on movement, knowledge and description*. London: Routledge.

Jones O (2019) Dwelling. In: Kobayashi A (ed) *International encyclopaedia of human geography*. 2nd ed. Amsterdam: Elsevier. pp. 399–405. ISBN 9780081022955.

Kimmerer RW (2013) *Braiding sweetgrass: Indigenous wisdom, scientific knowledge and the teachings of plants*. Minneapolis: Milkweed Editions.

Kirksey SE and Helmreich S (2010) The emergence of multispecies ethnography. *Cultural Anthropology* 25(4): 545–576.

Kitchin R and Dodge M (2011) *Code/space: Software and everyday life.* Boston: MIT Press.

Krzywoszynska A (2019) Caring for soil life in the Anthropocene: The role of attentiveness in more-than-human ethics. *Transactions of the Institute of British Geographers.* 44: 661–675. https://doi.org/10.1111/tran.12293. DOI: 10.1111/tran.12293.

Latour B (1987) *Science in action: How to follow scientists and engineers through society.* Milton Keynes: Open University Press.

Latour B (1993) *We have never been modern.* Cambridge, MA: Harvard University Press.

Latour B (1999) *Pandora's hope: Essays on the reality of science studies.* Cambridge, MA: Harvard University Press.

Latour B (2004) *Politics of nature: How to bring the sciences into democracy.* Cambridge, MA: Harvard University Press.

Latour B (2005) *Reassembling the social: An introduction to actor-network-theory.* Oxford: Oxford University Press.

Latour B (2018) *Down to earth: Politics in the new climatic regime.* London: Wiley.

Latour B and Woolgar S (1979) *Laboratory life: The social construction of scientific facts.* Beverly Hills: Sage Publications.

Lin W (2015) 'Cabin pressure': Designing affective atmospheres in airline travel. *Transactions of the Institute of British Geographers* 40(2): 287–299.

Longhurst R (2001) *Bodies: Exploring fluid boundaries.* London: Routledge.

Lorimer H (2005) Cultural geography: The busyness of being 'more-than-representational'. *Progress in Human Geography* 29(1): 83–94.

Lorimer H (2006) Herding memories of humans and animals. *Environment and Planning D-Society & Space* 24(4): 497–518.

Lorimer J (2007) Nonhuman charisma. *Environment and Planning D-Society & Space* 25(5): 911–932.

Lorimer J (2016) Gut buddies: Multispecies studies and the microbiome. *Environmental Humanities* 8(1): 57–76.

Lorimer J (2017) Parasites, ghosts and mutualists: A relational geography of microbes for global health. *Transactions of the Institute of British Geographers* 42(4): 544–558.

Lorimer J (2020) *The probiotic planet: Using life to manage life.* Minneapolis: University of Minnesota Press.

Lorimer J, Hodgetts T and Barua M (2019) Animals' atmospheres. *Progress in Human Geography* 43(1): 26–45.

Lorimer J and Srinivasan K (2013) Animal geographies. *The Wiley Blackwell companion to cultural geography.* London: John Wiley & Sons, Ltd, pp. 332–342.

Macpherson H (2009) The inter-corporeal emergence of landscape: Negotiating sight, blindness, and ideas of landscape in the British countryside. *Environment and Planning A* 41: 1042–1054.

Malm A (2016) *Fossil capital: The rise of steam power and the roots of global warming*. New York: Verso Books.

Mansfield B and Guthman J (2015) Epigenetic life: Biological plasticity, abnormality, and new configurations of race and reproduction. *Cultural Geographies* 22(1): 3–20.

Marston SA, Jones JP and Woodward K (2005) Human geography without scale. *Transactions of the Institute of British Geographers* 30(4): 416–432.

Massey DB (2005) *For space*. London: SAGE.

May T (2004) *Gilles Deleuze: An introduction*. New York: Cambridge University Press.

McCormack DP (2008) Engineering affective atmospheres on the moving geographies of the 1897 Andree expedition. *Cultural Geographies* 15(4): 413–430.

McCormack DP (2018) *Atmospheric things: On the allure of elemental envelopment*. Durham: Duke University Press.

Murdoch J (2006) *Post-structuralist geography: A guide to relational space*. London: Sage.

Nash C (2015) *Genetic geographies: The trouble with ancestry*. Minneapolis: University of Minnesota Press.

Nash CJ (2010) Trans geographies, embodiment and experience. *Gender, Place, and Culture* 17: 579–595.

Nelson SH (2014) Resilience and the neoliberal counter-revolution: From ecologies of control to production of the common. *Resilience* 2(1): 1–17.

Nelson SH and Bigger P (2022) Infrastructural nature. *Progress in Human Geography* 46(1): 86–107.

Nixon R (2011) *Slow violence*. Cambridge: Harvard University Press.

Parr H (2014) Emotional geographies. In: Cloke P, Crang P and Goodwin M (eds) *Introducing human geographies*. London: Routledge, pp. 746–759.

Parry B (2004) *Trading the genome: Investigating the commodification of bio-information*. New York: Columbia University Press.

Peters K and Steinberg P (2019) The ocean in excess: Towards a more-than-wet ontology. *Dialogues in Human Geography* 9(3): 293–307.

Phillips C (2013) Living without fruit flies: Biosecuring horticulture and its markets. *Environment and Planning A* 45(7): 1679–1694.

Philo C and Wilbert C (2000) *Animal spaces, beastly places: New geographies of human-animal relations*. London: Routledge.

Povinelli EA (2016) *Geontologies: A requiem to late liberalism*. Durham: Duke University Press.

Robbins P (2001) Tracking invasive land covers in India, or why our landscapes have never been modern. *Annals of the Association of American Geographers* 91(4): 637–659.

Roe EJ (2006) Things becoming food and the embodied, material practices of an organic food consumer. *Sociologia Ruralis* 46(2): 104–121.

Romero AM, Guthman J, Galt RE, Huber M, Mansfield B and Sawyer S (2017) Chemical geographies. *GeoHumanities* 3(1): 158–177.

Rose DB (2011) *Wild dog dreaming: Love and extinction*. Lexington: University of Virginia Press.

Rose DB (2022) *Shimmer: Flying fox exuberance in worlds of peril*. Edinburgh: Edinburgh University Press.

Saldanha A (2006) Reontologising race: The machinic geography of phenotype. *Environment and Planning D: Society and Space* 24(1): 9–24.

Shapiro N (2015) Attuning to the chemosphere: Domestic formaldehyde, bodily reasoning, and the chemical sublime. *Cultural Anthropology* 30(3): 368–393.

Shapiro N and Kirksey E (2017) Chemo-Ethnography: An Introduction. *Cultural Anthropology* 32(4): 481–493.

Shaw IGR (2016a) *Predator empire: Drone warfare and full spectrum dominance*. Minneapolis: University of Minnesota Press.

Shaw IGR (2016b) Scorched atmospheres: The violent geographies of the Vietnam war and the rise of drone warfare. *Annals of the American Association of Geographers* 106(3): 688–704.

Simpson P (2020) *Non-representational theory*. Abingdon: Taylor & Francis.

Sloterdijk P, Patton A and Corcoran S (2009) *Terror from the air*. Cambridge: MIT Press.

Smith N (2005) Neo-critical geography, or, the flat pluralist world of business class. *Antipode* 37(5): 887–899.

Stallins JA, Law DM, Strosberg SA and Rossi JJ (2018) Geography and postgenomics: How space and place are the new DNA. *GeoJournal* 83(1): 153–168.

Star SL (1991) Power, technologies and the phenomenology of conventions: On being allergic to onions. In: Law J (ed) *A sociology of monsters?* London: Routledge, pp. 26–56.

Stassart P and Whatmore SJ (2003) Metabolising risk: Food scares and the un/remaking of belgian beef. *Environment and Planning A* 35(3): 449–462.

Steinberg P and Peters K (2015) Wet ontologies, fluid spaces: Giving depth to volume through oceanic thinking. *Environment and Planning D: Society and Space* 33(2): 247–264.

Stengers I (2017) Autonomy and the intrusion of Gaia. *South Atlantic Quarterly* 116(2): 381–400.

Strum SS and Latour B (1987) Redefining the social link - from baboons to humans. *Social Science Information Sur Les Sciences Sociales* 26(4): 783–802.

Thien D (2005) After or beyond feeling? A consideration of affect and emotion in geography. *Area* 37(4): 450–454.

Thrift N (2000a) Afterwords. *Environment and Planning D-Society & Space* 18(2): 213–255.

Thrift N (2000b) Introduction: Dead or alive? In: Cook I, Naylor S and Ryan J (ed) *Cultural turns/geographical turns: Perspectives on cultural geography*. Harlow: Longman, pp. 1–6.

Thrift N (2004) Intensities of Feeling: Towards a Spatial Politics of Affect. *Geografiska Annaler: Series B, Human Geography* 86(1): 57–78.

Thrift N (2007) *Non-representational theory: Space, politics, affect.* London: Routledge.

Tolia-Kelly DP (2006) Affect – an ethnocentric encounter? Exploring the 'universalist' imperative of emotional/affectual geographies. *Area* 38(2): 213–217.

Tsing A (2017) A threat to Holocene resurgence is a threat to livability. In: Brightman M and Lewis J (eds) *The anthropology of sustainability: Beyond development and progress.* New York: Palgrave Macmillan, pp. 51–65.

Turnbull J, Searle A, Hartman Davies O, Dodsworth J, Chasseray-Peraldi P, von Essen E and Anderson-Elliott H (2023) Digital ecologies: Materialities, encounters, governance. *Progress in Environmental Geography* onlinefirst.

Urbanik J (2012) *Placing animals: An introduction to the geography of human-animal relations.* Lanham: Rowman & Littlefield Publishers.

van Dooren T (2014) *Flight ways: Life and loss at the edge of extinction.* New York: Columbia University Press.

von Uexkull J (1934/2010) *A foray into the worlds of animals and humans: With a theory of meaning.* Minneapolis: University of Minnesota Press.

Wakefield S (2019) Making nature into infrastructure: The construction of oysters as a risk management solution in New York City. *Environment and Planning E: Nature and Space* 3(3): 761–785.

Wall Ir (2019) Policing atmospheres: Crowds, protest and 'atmotechnics'. *Theory, Culture & Society* 36(4): 143–162.

Whatmore S (2002) *Hybrid geographies: Natures, cultures, spaces.* London: Sage.

Whatmore S (2006) Materialist returns: Practising cultural geography in and for a more-than-human world. *Cultural Geographies* 13(4): 600–609.

Whatmore S (2013a) Where natural and social science meet? Reflections on an experiment in geographical practice. In: Barry A and Born G (eds) *Interdisciplinarity: Reconfigurations of the social and natural sciences.* London: Routledge, pp. 161–177.

Whatmore S and Braun B (2010) *Political matter: Technoscience, democracy and public life.* Oxford: Oxford University Press.

Whatmore S and Thorne L (1998) Wild(er)ness: Reconfiguring the geographies of wildlife. *Transactions of the Institute of British Geographers* 23(4): 435–454.

Whatmore SJ (2009) Mapping knowledge controversies: Science, democracy and the redistribution of expertise. *Progress in Human Geography* 33(5): 587–598.

Whatmore SJ (2013b) Earthly powers and affective environments: An ontological politics of flood risk. *Theory, Culture & Society* 30(7–8): 33–50.

Wilkinson S (2017) Drinking in the dark: Shedding light on young people's alcohol consumption experiences. *Social & Cultural Geography* 18(6): 739–757.

Wilson HF (2022) Seabirds in the city: Urban futures and fraught coexistence. *Transactions of the Institute of British Geographers* 47(4): 1137–1151.

Wolch J and Emel J (1998) *Animal geographies: Place, politics, and identity in the nature-culture borderlands.* London: Verso.

Wylie J (2005) A single day's walking: Narrating self and landscape on the south west coast path. *Transactions of the Institute of British Geographers* 30(2): 234–247.

Yusoff K (2013) Geologic life: Prehistory, climate, futures in the Anthropocene. *Environment and Planning D: Society and Space* 31(5): 779–795.

Yusoff K (2016) Anthropogenesis: Origins and endings in the Anthropocene. *Theory, Culture & Society* 33(2): 3–28.

Yusoff K, Grosz E, Clark N, Saldanha A, Yusoff K, Nash C and Grosz E (2012) Geopower: A panel on Elizabeth Grosz's chaos, territory, art: Deleuze and the framing of the earth. *Environment and Planning D: Society and Space* 30(6): 971–988.

Zee JC (2022) *Continent in dust: Experiments in a Chinese weather system*. Oakland: University of California Press.

3 | More-than-human knowledge practices

In the previous chapter, we outlined the common elements of a more-than-human understanding of what the world is. We presented a multinatural world in which sensing, feeling humans are entangled with diverse actors in unruly assemblages. This is a world of mixings and becomings, configured by relations rather than essential beings. It is a world of connections and disconnections, of hotspots, tipping points, and chaotic processes. This world is very different to that of the humanists we encountered in Chapter 1 in which the human observer is a rational mind-in-the-vat, blessed with a view-from-nowhere over a globe from which he is fundamentally separated.

These ontological claims by more-than-human geographers as to what the world is are premised on a set of claims about how the world might be known. They are based on an epistemology: a theory of what knowledge is and how it ought to be produced (see Box 1.2). As we outlined in Chapter 1, the world cannot be known outside of the practices through which knowledge is made. Work associated with the cultural turn convincingly demonstrates how language and other modes of representation do not hold up a mirror to the world to reflect it in a common and universal way. Instead, they serve to 'construct' the world. In the words of the American feminist theorist Karen Barad, we therefore need to explore how 'matter comes to matter' (2003) by examining the practices through which more-than-human geographers produce knowledge about the world.

More-than-human thinkers have developed original ways of understanding what knowledge is, how it is produced, and how it is legitimated and contested by different experts. This chapter provides an overview of these more-than-human knowledge practices. It looks at how more-than-human geographers have theorised knowledge and explored its practical

DOI: 10.4324/9781315164304-4

Table 3.1 Five instructions for making more-than-human knowledge

Learn to be affected!	Pay attention to the push of the world, to the capacity of more-than-human materials to generate affect.
Follow the thing!	Focus on more-than-human material actors and the relations, networks, and processes in and through which they cohere.
Experiment!	Develop novel methods of knowledge production and trace how different types of experiment produce truth claims across the arts and the sciences.
Engage publics to redistribute expertise!	Make an explicit commitment to participatory forms of research to widen what counts as expertise and to expand who/what counts as a research participant.
Make an alliance with science!	Be open to the epistemic virtues of science, take scientists as allies, and explore the potential of interdisciplinary modes of research.

production. And it also examines how this more-than-human thinking led to the development of novel methodologies for producing geographical knowledge. We focus on five interconnected developments in the emergence of more-than-human styles of knowledge production. We present these as a set of injunctions or commands (that are summarised in Table 3.1). We suggest that more-than-humanists encourage us to follow the things, learn to be affected, experiment, engage with publics to redistribute expertise, and make alliances with science.

3.1 Learn to be affected

Our first key set of more-than-human knowledge practices were developed by a range of geographers who were concerned with the materiality of the human body, and with the practical, visceral, and affective character of human experience. They shared the concern articulated by Sarah Whatmore that there was

> an urgent need to supplement the familiar repertoire of humanist methods that rely on generating talk and text with experimental practices that amplify other sensory, bodily and affective registers and extend the company and modality of what constitutes a research subject.
>
> (2006, 607)

We can identify three interwoven strands of work in more-than-human geography that responded to this appeal, coming from feminist theorists; multispecies and non-representational approaches; and research on indigenous knowledge practices.

3.1.1 Feminist knowledge practices

The first strand of work on embodiment and affect comes from feminist geographers, who have long been concerned with how the figure of the objective human and the ideal of rational, scientific knowledge is gendered as male. As we explained in Chapter 1, feminist thinkers show how a range of pseudoscientific arguments are used to both elevate forms of cognitive reasoning by gendering them 'male' and to denigrate the knowledge claims of women whose biology is said to make them irrational, too tied to bodily processes and too close to nature and its associations with superstition. While a strand of feminism embraced this idea of women being closer to nature to develop 'deep green' strands of feminist thinking (Shiva, 1988), Marxist and post-structuralist feminists deconstruct these claims, taking them as evidence of widespread patriarchy in Western science and culture (Adams and Gruen, 2021; Nightingale, 2006; Plumwood, 1993).

More-than-human feminists developed these critiques, while attending to how the materialities of women's bodies and the differential experience of being a woman come to configure knowledge about the world. For Donna Haraway (1988), this approach requires attending to the 'positionality' of those making knowledge claims and discloses the local, 'situated' character of knowledge. Her approach stands in stark contrast to the humanist ideal of knowledge as the disembodied view-from-nowhere manifest in what she terms the 'God-trick' of objective Science. Her work also challenges the privileging of vision in the Enlightenment hierarchy of the senses and encourages analysis of the other senses and of feelings and emotions.

In her book *When Species Meet*, Haraway (2008) builds from her earlier critiques of the patriarchal and heteronormative knowledge practices of primatology (see Box 2.1). She offers a more affirmative account based on the work of the primatologist Barbara Smuts. She explains how Smuts struggled with the then prevalent epistemic conventions of field primatology, which suggested that to be objective she must suppress her affections and not interact with baboons she was studying. Haraway explains how Smuts struggled with this injunction as her baboons kept trying to interact with her. Eventually she decided to enter the field as a responsive, affective subject. She began interacting with the animals, and in so doing, was drawn into their lifeworlds, and came to better understand their society and their behaviours. Haraway groups Smuts alongside a broader collection of women ethologists who are willing to 'learn to be affected' by the animals they study.

Haraway develops her understanding of knowledge as a process of 'learning to be affected' from the work of the Belgian philosopher Vincianne Despret (2004, 2013), who studies ethologists at work in their labs and in wild settings. Despret documents the frequent failure of experiments when researchers treat their animals as objects and machines that follow instinct, in contrast to the success experienced by those who enter into responsive relationships with their nonhuman research subjects. She develops her theory of learning to be affected from the work of von Uexkull, that we encountered in the previous chapter (Section 2.2), and presents animal research as a process of tuning in to the umwelten of different animals to map their affects and to gain an understanding of their lifeworlds. She explains how this often involves scientists training underused senses like hearing, smell and touch, and learning to use their bodies in unfamiliar ways.[1]

3.1.2 Multispecies and non-representational knowledge practices

Haraway and Despret are central figures in the field of 'multispecies studies' (Van Dooren et al., 2016), which bridges anthropology, ethology, geography, and science studies and combines ethnographic and ethological methods to study human-animal and human-plant relations (see example in Box 3.1).[2] This work has developed methods for researching the geographies of the animals themselves, especially those that live in close proximity to humans, or whose lifeworlds are fundamentally shaped by human-caused ecological changes (Hodgetts and Lorimer, 2015; Rubio-Ramon and Srinivasan, 2022). It recognises that affective experience is shared across species, and it enables analysis of knowledge practices that break down the humanist divide to explore the common and the different experiences of animal bodies. These methods enable forms of 'critical anthropomorphism' (Burghardt, 1990; de Waal, 1999) through which researchers feel qualified to write with authority about the lived experience of animals as individuals and as collectives.

The text boxes in this chapter give examples of more-than-human research in practice

---

Box 3.1   Learning to be affected by urban wild things

In 2002–2003, a team of geographers then based at the UK's Open University developed a form of multispecies knowledge practice to investigate the situation of small mammals living alongside humans in urban environments. The team included the geographers Steve Hinchliffe, Matthew Kearnes, Monica Degen, and Sarah What- more (2005) (see Box 2.3). The research took place in Birmingham, England, and traced the lives of urban-living water voles, a species of locally endangered semi-aquatic rodent. This species has a particular resonance in the UK, popularised in culture through the 1908 novel *The Wind in the Willows* (Grahame, 1908/2018) and its hero 'Ratty' (from 'water-rat', the species' more common name).

The research method draws on the science studies theories of Bruno Latour (see Box 2.4) in order to 'experiment with what is involved in taking these nonhuman worlds and ecologies seriously and in pro- ducing a politics for urban wilds' (2005, 643). The researchers explain how they 'learn to sense' the presence of water voles, guided by local wildlife conservationists and the tracking and tracing methodologies commonly used by field biologists:

> We start by looking for footprints, gazing about the ground with little confidence or direction. Our first problem is finding any- thing that can be described as a footprint. A few days of rain and thick summer vegetation mean that signs are difficult to locate. When a series of footprints is spotted across a mud-covered concrete support we are introduced to a second problem. Prints are far from self-evident – to the unversed this might have been any small creature, even a bird. So, out comes the field guide…
>
> (2005, 647)

Despite these problems, the team narrates how they gradually learn to trace the lives of water voles. In part, this learning comes from their teachers, the local wildlife experts from whom they learn the species' favoured habits (where the water voles wander and the signs they leave – especially their 'latrines'). But with this learning, the team further develop their own understanding through close attention to the signs of water voles around them. They explain that:

> Those previously unversed in water vole writing started to look at the landscape rather differently. As Latour might say, we had started to learn to be affected. We were bodies in process, gaining ways of looking, a new set of eyes (or newly conditioned retina), a slightly more wary nose, a different sensibility.
>
> (2005, 648)

The aim of such learning is not simply to replicate the existing knowledge practices of wildlife researchers. Instead, it is to utilise this sensibility to the presence of nonhumans to articulate for a less anthropocentric mode of urban politics. As they summarise:

> In learning new engagements we also learn new things and in particular come to see urban wilds as matters of controversy. For this reason we have borrowed and adapted Latour's language to talk of wild things. Wild things become more rather than less real as people learn to engage with them. At the same time, wild things are too disputed, sociable, and uncertain to become constant objects upon which a stable urban politics can be constructed. So a parliament of wild things might be rather different from the house of representatives that we commonly imagine. It may be closer to what Stengers (1997) has characterised as cosmopolitics, a politics that is worked out without recourse to old binaries of nature and society.
>
> (2005, 643)

In another example, the geographer Maan Barua develops the long-standing interest of animal geographers in urban animals by exploring the urban animal experience. Writing with the ethologist Anindya Sinha, he focuses on the lifeworlds of macaques living in Indian cities (Barua and

Sinha, 2017). Drawing on a methodology at the interface of ethnography, ecology, and ethology, they spent time observing animals in the city. They explain how some macaque species 'exhibit an inherent tendency to gravitate towards human habitations, thus, setting in motion an inexorable process of the urbanisation of their lifeworlds' (2017, 1162). They detail this process of urbanisation by exploring how the diets and social practices of macaques have adapted to the metabolic rhythms of the city, how macaques have developed new urban knowledges, and how they have come to reconfigure the spaces of the city, for human and nonhuman citizens alike.

For Haraway (2008), the willingness of ethologists (and other scientists) to learn to be affected by their animal subjects constitutes a distinctly feminist approach to knowledge making, that stands in contrast to the masculine norms of the objective science of animal behaviour. She describes this willingness to learn to be affected as an act of 'politeness' and of 'response-ability', suggesting that it offers grounds for a new ethics, that we discuss in the following chapter (Section 4.3).

An epistemic and methodological interest in learning to be affected is also central to the non-representational theories of geographers like Nigel Thrift (see Box 2.2). Thrift presents affect as both an ontology and a foundation for knowledge, suggesting we think of affect as 'a form of thinking, often indirect and non-reflective, it is true, but thinking all the same' (2004, 60). Thrift sees affect as a form of bodily intelligence that can be researched using methods from performance studies like dance, theatre, and yoga, in which practitioners are trained to think with and through their bodies (Cresswell, 2006; Lea, 2008; McCormack, 2002, 2005). Non-representational theorists have developed methodologies for researching 'post-phenomenological' (McCormack, 2017) approaches to affect that look beyond bounded individual bodies to consider how affect is shaped by encounters with other bodies, with technological infrastructures, and by exposure to a variety of materials. A central concern has been the role of media in shaping 'affective atmospheres' (Anderson, 2009): moods or feeling shared in common by distinct publics. Cultural geographers have developed tools for witnessing how affect is engendered and have explored how media technologies influence public sentiment and knowledges, by whipping up storms of affect to engender hate, love, violence, or even apathy (Vannini, 2015b). They have developed methods to describe diverse political 'affective logics' (Carter and McCormack, 2006) associated, for example, with specific styles of film making or advertising whose effects we explore in the next chapter (Lorimer, 2010b).

3.1.3 Indigenous knowledge practices

A final strand of work exploring knowledge as a process of learning to be affected comes from research in geography and anthropology on/with indigenous knowledge practices. This work emerges from at least two different sources. The first being a tradition of more-than-human scholars studying and borrowing from indigenous approaches. The second is work produced by indigenous academics themselves sometimes through collaborations with Western academics deploying participatory approaches, that we describe later in this chapter (see Box 3.4).

In the first strand, anthropologists seek to understand indigenous knowledge practices through ethnographic research. One approach from anthropology, that is known as 'perspectivism' (de Castro, 1998), has focused on mapping how indigenous people distinguish between humans and nonhumans in ways that are not reducible to Western distinctions between nature and culture. For example, Tim Ingold (2000) conducted ethnographic work on the knowledge practices of nomadic Sami herders in the Arctic regions of Norway, Finland, and Russia to develop his theory of dwelling that we outlined in the previous chapter. Like Haraway and a range of other anthropologists, Ingold criticises the God-trick of Western science which produced knowledge of the world as a 'globe' (Figure 1.5), seen from the outside. He is critical of the ways in which colonial scientists subjugated indigenous knowledges, dismissing them as being too situated, too local, and too close to nature. He makes an epistemic argument that Western philosophy can learn from an indigenous perspective.

Ingold suggests that we understand knowledge as emergent from the processes of dwelling in the world, which is conceived as an environment that encompasses the body. In his early work on landscape as taskscape, Ingold (2000) encouraged researchers to focus on the time-deepened rhythms through which humans – like nomadic herders – and their animals inhabit places; develop familiarity with landscapes, ecologies, and atmospheres; and get to know the world through their bodies. Ingold and his colleagues draw on phenomenology to study human sensory experience. They focus on senses other than sight, looking at the importance of touch; of movement; and of sound, taste, and smell (Pink, 2009). He presents multisensory worlds known through the body and offers a range of methodological tools for documenting these worlds, including techniques for sketching and diagramming the movements of different bodies (Ingold, 2011). This multisensory, place-based approach has been developed through the methodology of 'walking-with' (Sundberg, 2014), a particular model of participant observation in which geographers spend time with indigenous peoples and other lay experts to gain embodied as well as talk-based understandings of human-nonhuman interactions (Evans and Jones, 2011; Springgay and Truman, 2017; Wylie, 2005).

In the second strand of work, indigenous scholars and activists have articulated knowledge practices grounded in epistemic traditions that differ from Western natural science, often with the aim of showing how they might be made complementary. One high-profile example is given by the Potawatomi[3] botanist Robin Wall Kimmerer. In her book *Braiding Sweetgrass*, Kimmerer (2013) combines traditional ecological knowledge and skills in ethnobotany with her scientific training in biology and ecology. She details the relationships between indigenous peoples, plants, and the land to show how Native American traditions of foraging, burning, and otherwise caring for the land, alongside creation stories and other cultural narratives enhance scientific understandings. Kimmerer is especially interested in the epistemic potential of storytelling to develop understanding of the nonhuman world and describes her approach as a 'braid' that is woven from three strands: 'indigenous ways of knowing, scientific knowledge, and the story of an Anishinabekwe[4] scientist trying to bring them together in service to what matters most. It is an intertwining of science, spirit, and story' (2013, x). The wider potential of storytelling as a methodology for indigenous geographies research is explored in Richmond et al. (2022), in a collection that also outlines methodologies for anti-colonial and black environmental geographies (Lovell et al., 2022).

In spite of these examples, the historic and contemporary relationships between Western social science and indigenous knowledge is fraught. There are important, ongoing discussions that form part of the wider processes of decolonising geography, about the degree to which more-than-human approaches co-opt indigenous knowledges without fair attribution, as well as accusations that the application of more-than-human approaches fails to address the systemic inequalities caused by racism and colonialism (for a review, see Barker and Pickerill, 2020). We explore these criticisms in the final chapter (Section 5.2).

3.2 Follow the things

A second set of approaches to more-than-human knowledge production are influenced by the actor-network theory (ANT) and its focus on the role of technology in shaping how scientists and other powerful actors sense and represent the world. As we explained in the previous chapter, ANT presents people as actors in a network of other nonhuman actors and it grants all of these actors agency. The role of an actor-network theorist is to follow the movements of these actors, to map the network, and to describe how it operates. ANT developed out of a long tradition of work in Science and Technology Studies that examines 'science as practice' (Pickering, 1992) or 'science in action' (Latour, 1987). Rather than looking at science solely as a set of published papers, or as the stories told by scientific heroes, we are to look at science as something that gets done by scientists working in particular places (like laboratories) using specialised bits of kit: we are to 'open up the black boxes of science' (Latour, 1999) and look at how it is done. The methodological instruction we get from actor-network theorists is to *follow the things!* More-than-human geographers have taken up this instruction to explore several dimensions of how knowledge is produced (for an overview, see Whatmore, 2003).

3.2.1 Sensing devices

One important strand of work understands the scientist as Haraway's cyborg, embedded in networks of devices that extend and enhance her perceptual apparatus and enable her to detect phenomena unknown to the naked human body (Benson, 2010; Gabrys, 2016). The interest here is in how technology mediates *sensing* and enables processes of learning to be affected. For example, Vicky Mason and Paul Hope (2014) have explored how developments in ultrasound technology make it possible for amateur and professional zoologists to 'become sensitive to the experiences of bats, assisting the identification of species and the reliable study of many aspects of behaviour' (108). Ultrasound technologies allow these enthusiasts to 'become-detector'; to hear bats' 'echoes in the dark': sounds at frequencies outside of the normal range of human hearing. Comparable work by Eva Hayward (2010) has examined new camera technologies, like the 'critter-cams' that are attached to the bodies of animals to take the viewer into their alien worlds deep underwater or high in the air. Hayward argues that these provide 'fingeryeyes' that allow viewers to tune in to the beastly places of animals even at a distance.[5]

3.2.2 Technologies of translation

A second strand focuses on how the data generated by these devices is drawn together by scientists to *represent* reality. The interest here is in how scientists 'pack the world into words' (Latour, 1999) by giving words material form. Actor-network theorists follow the processes of 'translation' through which scientific texts are produced. They focus on 'circulating references' (Latour, 1999): the notes, graphs, sketches, pictures, and other inscriptions through which scientists record their observations for later analysis and for communication with others. They look at how these objects become 'immutable mobiles' (Latour, 2005): stable actors that move along networks through time and across space.[6] In one classic study, Michel Callon (1986) examines a controversy about scallop conservation in Saint-Brieuc bay in Brittany, Northwest France. He follows how a group of marine biologists 'negotiate' with their instruments, fishers, and marine life to produce a representation of the causes of the scallops' decline, and how this representation is betrayed when it transpires that the scallops and fishers they have selected as spokespeople fail to conform to the behaviours of those they are supposed to represent. Callon is interested in the challenging practicalities of representation and the persistent risk that it will fail. The key argument here is that knowledge only comes to matter when it is materialised in scientific representations.[7]

3.2.3 Networks for the circulation of knowledge

ANT informed work has also examined how these spaces of knowledge production are linked together, tracing the role of technologies in the *circulation* of knowledge. Researchers follow the things to map the networks and the connections that scientists and others make in order that their translations travel and become accepted. There has been a growing expansion and diversification in the type of technologies geographers have studied and the things they have followed. This has seen a move away from the early science studies' focus on scientific texts to incorporate a range of assemblages and nonhuman mobilities. For example, geographers interested in food began to follow commodities (Cook, 2004) – like papaya or coffee[8] – to map the 'nourishing networks' (Whatmore and Thorne, 1997) of the globalised food system. They have looked at the role of transport infrastructures and logistics in making these connections. Geographers like James Ash (Ash et al., 2018) have explored how people's knowledge about the world emerges from their practical interactions with their devices, like televisions and smart phones. This connects to work by urban geographers who are interested in how the infrastructure of the city, including signage, architecture, and the software 'code' that governs key systems, come to shape people's knowledge (Kitchin and Dodge, 2011; Thrift and French, 2002). A key focus in this work has been the digital ecologies associated with the rise of digital media (Box 3.2).

Box 3.2 Digital ecologies

One group of geographers interested in the rise of digital media and the digital turn has recently focused on 'digital ecologies'[9] noting that 'digital technologies increasingly mediate human–nonhuman relations in diverse settings including environmental governance, surveillance, and entertainment. Digitisation produces unique understandings of, and modes of access to, more-than-human worlds, and fundamentally reshapes conservation, environmentalism, and ecological politics' (Turnbull et al., 2023a, 2). They are interested in the different ways in which people are entangled with digital technologies, remaining sceptical about claims that the rise of digital media necessarily leads to either a disconnection from nature or a new technofix solution for reengaging people with the natural world.

In one empirical example, members of this group explore the rise of the 'digital peregrine' (Searle et al., 2023) in British cities, looking at how 'nestcams' with livestream broadcasts focused on these birds engage new publics with urban wildlife. They develop the range of existing qualitative methods (Rose, 2022), including interviews, oral histories, and digital ethnography (Pink et al., 2015), to explore how digital encounters with peregrines can 'create unexpected and radical opportunities for urban conviviality, signalling the positive potentials technologies host for forging meaningful more-than-human connections' (1). Geographers have developed a range of qualitative methodologies for examining human-technology-ecology interactions in these 'technonatural' spaces (Lynch and Farrokhi, 2022).

In connected work, Jonny Turnbull and his co-authors (including Jamie) (Turnbull et al., 2023b) explored the role of digital media in the Anthropause – the period of space-time decompression that accompanied the COVID-19 lockdowns (Rutz et al., 2020). Spending time on Facebook, they trace how different social groups in the UK developed new interests in mundane, domestic, and urban natures when they were confined to their homes. They explored how publics used sensing technologies – like digital cameras – to record local wildlife and how they turned to social media platforms to share their knowledge and form new virtual communities. For some participants, these digital technologies and the digital ecologies they enabled, allowed them to develop new modes of environmental citizenship and provided access to discussions from which they had previously felt excluded when they only took place face to face.

Other critical work has explored how the rise of digital technologies has enabled new forms of social and environmental governance. For example, Jennifer Gabrys traces how 'environments are increasingly becoming technologized sites of data production' (2020, 1) tracing the proliferation of digital sensing devices that lead to the rise of 'Smart Forests' that are put to work to tackle environmental problems like climate change. By following the things across digital and analogue spaces, they explore the consequences of the rise of this digital infrastructure for questions of environmental sustainability and social justice (Gabrys et al., 2022; Goldstein and Nost, 2022).

Meanwhile, other researchers have developed more quantitative methodologies for examining the social dynamics and the content of social media, gathering big data sets to explore how social media bring different publics and epistemic communities together and into conflict and exploring how platforms like Twitter and Instagram reveal public preferences towards different organisms, practices, and landscapes (Leszczynski, 2019; Rose and Willis, 2019).

3.3 Experiment

Our third common emphasis in more-than-human knowledge practices is the onus placed on experiments and experimentation. This expresses an epistemological and a political desire to actively experiment with the new worlds of the Anthropocene and its varied publics (Braun, 2015). We can trace the origins of this interest in experimentation to work exploring the geographies of scientific knowledge production.

3.3.1 Experimental sites

Geographers have examined how the locations in which science is conducted shape the character of the knowledge produced. This attention to *placing* knowledge production has focused primarily on the 'truth spots' (Gieryn, 2018) of the laboratory sciences, with secondary strands of comparative work looking at field sites (Kohler, 2002), museums, homes, offices, and online as sites for science (Naylor, 2002; Shapin, 1988). It forms part of a wider interest in geography in the 'spaces of knowledge' (Livingstone, 1995) and the 'geography of truth' (Thrift et al., 1995). Those studying laboratories argue that these are private sites securely located in universities or commercial and government institutions. They are not open to public inspection or interference. Laboratories offer highly controlled, 'made' environments in which scientists can direct their instruments at simplified models of the world without risk of the experiments overflowing to have consequences on the wider environment (Guggenheim, 2012). This control means that the findings generated from these experiments should be applicable in laboratories elsewhere in the world. Laboratories with these material properties are 'placeless places' (Kohler, 2002) that produce universal or general knowledge. In contrast, field sites like river stations or nature reserves tend to be natural or 'found' locations that are visible, public, and accessible to outsiders (Kohler, 2002). They are also highly variable and thus generate unique, site-specific knowledge through local 'practices of place'. These differences between laboratory and field sites are summarised in Table 3.2.

Geographers interested in experimental sites have also focused on the epistemic character of the experiments that are conducted in different locations. Their work maps the ambiguity of the word experiment across the lab and the field sciences. If you open the Oxford English Dictionary and search for the noun 'experiment', you get two very different meanings. One definition

Table 3.2 Comparative partial summary of the properties of ideal laboratory and field sites and sciences (from Lorimer and Driessen, 2014)

Laboratory science	Field science
Made/artificial	Found/natural
Controlled	Disordered/wild
Inconsequential	Consequential
Anywhere/placeless places	Here/practices of place
Secluded/private	Visible/public

describes an 'action or operation undertaken in order … to test a hypothesis, or establish or illustrate some known truth'. A second defines experiment as a 'tentative procedure; a method, system of things, or course of action, adopted in uncertainty' (OED, 2023). What an experiment is clearly varies. The first definition is linked to the understanding of an experiment common to positivist approaches to natural science that adhere to the scientific method. For Thomas Gieryn (2006), the ideal location for such experiments is the artificial, private, and placeless place of the laboratory, whose: 'walls enable scientists to gain exquisite control over the objects of their analysis. Wild nature gets repositioned in a technical and cultural environment that gives all power to the investigators' (5). Unfalsified (but falsifiable) hypotheses that have been tested in the lab can be taken as objective truths about a singular and stable found Nature that should inform but not be contested by politics.

Researchers have critically examined efforts to 'laboratise' other scientific locations by examining 'experiments in nature' (Kohler, 2002) conducted on islands (Greenhough, 2006) and field stations (Kelly and Lezaun, 2017). They have also contrasted laboratory experiments with the 'natural experiments' (Kohler, 2002) that are conducted in the 'found' locations of field sites. They suggest that the local 'practices of place' of field scientists are better described by the second definition of an experiment offered above – of a tentative procedure adopted in uncertainty. Gieryn argues that in the field 'a lack of control becomes its own virtue. Scientists en plein air are more likely to be open to surprises that might interrupt research expectations in promising ways' (2006, 6). Field sites are much more public and visible than laboratories, and interventions will have real-world consequences. Gaining authority within them involves very different social practices, including negotiating with and sometimes learning from diverse epistemic communities like farmers, hunters, and other amateur naturalists.

Table 3.2 offers a useful abstraction; but it should not be read as a list of binary oppositions. The philosopher-biologist Hans-Jorg Rheinberger (1997) has documented how the 'experimental systems' of laboratories are poorly described by the positivist definition of an experiment. He demonstrates that successful science is often practised without a theory or even testable hypotheses, is infused with local values, and wrestles with unpredictable and surprising materials. Ethnographers have demonstrated that, in practice, laboratories are much like field sites, in that they involve experiments that are tentative, local, and uncertain. Rheinberger presents an ideal experiment as a trial or a venture into the unknown that is designed to generate and learn from surprises. He argues that science is speculative and that a well-designed experimental system will be capable of generating and detecting difference, not confirming what is known.

3.3.2 Experimental natures

Rheinberger's understanding of an experiment has risen to prominence in more-than-human scholarship alongside the growing interest in the epistemic consequences of the Anthropocene (Braun, 2015). The new materialist thinkers like Steve Hinchliffe and Sarah Whatmore (Hinchliffe et al., 2005) who focus on biological and geophysical processes (see Section 2.3) argue that the diagnosis of the Anthropocene challenges the distinctions between the lab and the field that are illustrated in Table 3.2. They suggest that the knowledge produced by laboratory science has had such an impact on the world that it erases any boundary between the 'made' sites of the laboratory and the 'found' sites of the field. They argue that in a world marked by anthropogenic climate change, biodiversity loss, pollution, and a myriad of other impacts, there is no outside to the laboratory, there is no found Nature, nor can we think of laboratories as bounded and inconsequential sites. The whole world is fundamentally shaped by modern technology, and we are all caught up in a series of 'real-world experiments' (Krohn and Weyer, 1994) that involve ventures into the unknown. The epistemic consequences of this 'end of Nature' and the rise of new approaches to experimentation have been explored in work on wildlife conservation and rehabilitation (see Box 3.3) and have helped geographers develop a new concept of the wild experiment (Table 3.3).

Table 3.3 Key properties of two models of an environmental science experiment (from Lorimer and Driessen, 2014)

	Experiment	Wild experiments
Ontology	Transcendent order of Nature and Society	Immanent and indeterminate world of humans and nonhumans
Epistemology	Hypothetico-deductive method	Designed to generate surprises
Politics	Delegative: science creates facts, politics decides what matters	Dialogical: emergent collectives for generating and deliberating knowledge
Location	Laboratory (and occasionally the field)	The 'wild'

Box 3.3   Wild experiments at the Oostvaardersplassen

Jamie provides an example of this work in his writing with Clemens Driessen on approaches to rewilding at the Oostvaardersplassen (OVP) in the Netherlands. The OVP is a nature reserve that forms part of the Flevoland: a polder that was reclaimed from the sea in the 1970s to form the largest artificial island in the world. It lies below sea level and is kept dry through continuous pumping.

The OVP is a flagship example of rewilding – a model of nature conservation that aims to restore keystone species to deliver desired functions to an ecosystem. Dutch ecologists sought to introduce a guild of large herbivores to restore the grazing dynamics that were understood to drive vegetation succession in Europe at the end of the last ice age. They gathered herds of deer and back-bred and de-domesticated horses and cattle and introduced them to the reserve. The animals were to be left to their own devices to discover new behaviours and social dynamics and to create a 'Serengeti behind the dykes'. The animal populations grew, and they were soon dying of disease and starvation in the winter. This led to a public outcry about animal welfare, and control measures were taken in which a certain number of animals were shot by a warden acting 'with the eye of the wolf' to simulate natural predation dynamics.

As part of a wider body of work on rewilding (Lorimer and Driessen, 2013, 2014, 2016), Jamie and Clemens were interested in the knowledge practices of the Dutch ecologists who were conducting scientific experiments at the site and who were responsible for its management, as well of those contesting the project. Through a series of interviews with site managers and opponents, as well as participant observation of site management, they trace how the Dutch ecologists initially shuttled between describing the site as a found reserve for studying natural processes (the Serengeti behind the dykes), and presenting it as an artificial laboratory for testing a hypothesis about the paleoecology of Europe. Opponents argue that this was not a found site, as it was artificially created, and instead should be subject to the same rules that govern the treatment of animals in laboratory settings (like experimental farms or animal testing houses). It became clear that the different knowledge practices and the truth claims they were designed to support depended greatly on whether this was a lab or field and therefore judged by associated definitions of the experiment.

As it became clear that the OVP was fundamentally hybrid, the conservationists began to present it as a 'novel ecosystem' without historic analogue. In so doing, they shifted from using paleoecological data to generate a fixed idea of a landscape archetype to which the site should be returned, and instead, used this data to justify more open-ended visions of what the site might become. In other words, they shifted between the two models of a scientific experiment shown in Table 3.3. In comparable work on rewilding in Portugal, Caitlin DeSilvey and Nadia Bartolini (2019) describe these hybrid, open-ended visions as 'future-pasts': knowledges of the past that guide but do not determine what the site might become.

This approach generated a rich array of environmental surprises, producing new knowledge about European ecologies – for example, that sea eagles will nest below sea level. It also offered new models of environmental ethics (that we explore in Section 5.3). However, it ultimately failed to adhere to a democratic or participatory model of public engagement (see Section 4.3) to work with animal welfarists. The wild experiment at the OVP fell out of favour with the Dutch government who intervened in 2018 to compel the site managers to offer supplementary feed to the herbivores over the winter, thus changing their behaviours.

3.4 Engage publics to redistribute expertise

Arguably the paramount motivation of more-than-human geographers for thinking about experimentation is to engage with the diverse expertise of varied publics.[10] We have seen how the more-than-human turn to affect undermines the singular figure of the rational human subject as a mind in a vat and foregrounds multiple forms of subjectivity and expertise. We can now understand how the Anthropocene breaks down the walls of the laboratory to dissolve the distinction between found (natural) and made (artificial) spaces. These two developments call into question the established distinction between objective, secluded research and research done in the public eye and with public involvement. For Latour (2018) and his colleagues in science studies, the rise of the real-world experiments of the Anthropocene means that we should all be involved in deliberating as to their conduct and their consequences. In response, geographers and other practitioners of a field that has come to be known as Public Engagement with Science and Technology (or PEST) have sought to break down a third distinction shown in Table 3.3 between public and private research to initiate forms of public experimentation. The imperative here is to *engage publics and to redistribute expertise!* We will say more about the political implications of PEST and its redistribution of expertise in the following chapter. Here, we will concentrate on the knowledge practices through which it is enabled.

3.4.1 What is expertise?

We should start with the question of expertise: what is it and who has it? In an influential article, Harry Collins and Robert Evans (2002) proposed that their science studies colleagues focus on the social dimensions of expertise and experience. They argue that ethnographic work on the expertise of indigenous peoples, farmers, fishers, patients, and other 'lay experts' demonstrates that scientists are not the only people who should be empowered to make technical decisions, and that there are other experts, as well as other citizen stakeholders, who can be excluded by the modern 'political settlement' between science and politics (Figure 1.4). But they suggest that to effectively democratise science, we also need a 'normative theory of expertise' to decide on what grounds someone should be included (and others excluded) from technical decision-making. It is impractical and sometimes nonsensical, they argue, to assume that everyone can have a legitimate opinion on all technical matters. Indeed, in a later paper, they argue that in the context of the rise of post-truth politics and the distrust of experts manufactured by right-wing and other 'culture warriors', it is politically risky to assume that anyone has legitimate technical expertise (Collins et al., 2017). For if this was the case then how would we differentiate and dispute the claims of climate change deniers, or of those who downplay the health risks of smoking tobacco?

But expertise proves to be a slippery thing to nail down. Dictionaries define it as the property of experts, where an expert is someone who has 'gained skills from experience' over time (OED, 2023). In some cases, this expertise requires training and the acquisition of formal knowledge and is recognised in 'certified' experts, like professional scientists, doctors, engineers, etc. with degrees and certificates. The expertise of these certified experts is often held to apply in general, in contrast to the local, place-based, or contextual expertise of 'vernacular' experts, like some farmers, hunters, fishers, for example. Collins and Evans (2002) suggest we describe the latter as 'experience-based experts' to differentiate them from certified experts. A great deal of work has since been done to recognise the expertise of these groups, especially those of low political and economic status (Callon et al., 2009; Wynne, 1998). Collins and Evans (2002) offer 'a periodical table of expertise', with a typology too detailed to cover here. What we should take from this work are the insights that 'expertise is more widely distributed within society than many might imagine' (Lane et al., 2011, 18), that expertise is tacit, or embodied, and that it emerges out of the time-deepened processes of learning to be affected and of everyday experimentation that we encountered above.

3.4.2 Participatory research

More-than-human geographers have been part of a wider 'participatory turn' in social and political geographic research (Pain and Kindon, 2007). The move towards participation seeks to involve research participants in the design and operation of research projects – from shaping the initial research questions, to selecting methods, and to the types and uses of the research outputs thus created. These participatory approaches had been devised in the 1980s and 1990s by researchers working in community development and environmental management, as well as in diverse forms of community-based sociology, before reaching 'critical mass' in geographic research in the early 2000s (Pain and Kindon, 2007). In a review of the status of participatory geographies, the collective 'mrs kinpainsby' (2008) distinguish between 'public' and 'participatory' geographies, explaining that 'public geographies involve the promotion by academics of geography and geographical knowledge to wider publics, while participatory geographies involve academics in collaboration with wider publics to co-produce geographical knowledge' (299).[11]

More-than-human geographers have embraced this participatory model for the co-production of knowledge. For example, the human geographer Sarah Whatmore, the hydrologist Stuart Lane, and their colleagues have developed a novel approach to doing flood risk modelling. Working in Pickering, a flood-prone town in Yorkshire in the North of England, they gathered a group of local stakeholders with experience of flooding and worked with them to develop new methods for modelling rivers and for understanding flood risk (Lane et al., 2011; Landstrom et al., 2011). They developed a methodology they term 'competency groups' (Whatmore and Landstrom, 2011), which are designed to accommodate the diverse expertise of both certified and experience-based experts. They deploy an approach they term 'experimental constructivism', which adheres to the second definition of an experiment that we outlined in Table 3.3. Their experiments represent a trial or venture into the unknown which involves trying things out through experience. The scientists, modellers, farmers, and local property owners they enrolled in their project worked with models and found objects; they walked the riverbanks; and spent time together to build trust and to establish common interests and aims. This ultimately led to a new approach to flood prevention that overcame many of the political and hydrological problems that had thwarted past efforts at flood management.[12] In reflecting on this success, Whatmore and Landstrom highlight how it required

> the invention of research apparatuses that can 'slow down' expert reasoning and redistribute expertise: an inventiveness which brings the skills of social scientists to the fore in the design and conduct of research practices that stage more and different opportunities for new knowledge polities to emerge.
>
> (2011, 606)

More-than-human participatory research thus draws on wider traditions of co-production and develops these in two key ways. First, given the more-than-human commitment to multiple situated knowledges, widening expertise is about more than the democratisation of research on ethical grounds. The ethical arguments remain important, of course. Social research often has political consequences, so making room for diverse views and understandings can be important on the grounds of social justice. Indeed, deciding what is worthy of research is always a political act, hence the move to incorporate research participants in the shaping of research questions and design. Nevertheless, a commitment to multiple situated knowledges also requires widened participation because it allows greater understanding of the situation being researched – i.e. such research isn't just fairer, it's likely to be richer and more valid too. This instrumental justification for participatory research is not new, but the more-than-human approach amplifies the extent to which diverse ontologies might be incorporated, beyond the narrow logics of humanistic thought.

Second, more-than-human approaches, given their commitment to material agency, also require widening the cast of research participants beyond the human. Participatory research thus requires methodologies that can allow nonhuman participants to shape the development and operation of research projects as they unfold. This is by no means a simple task. In the example above, for example, we saw how competency groups have been developed to draw together diverse human perspectives on watershed management. On this model, the participants remain human for the most part (even if shaped and 'affected' by the turbulence of the river). Nevertheless, recent years have seen a proliferation of work that draws on a variety of interdisciplinary methods to try and extend participatory methodologies towards nonhumans more directly (Bastian et al., 2016).

Box 3.4   The Bawaka Collective 'both ways learning'

A particularly influential more-than-human and participatory approach to the co-production of knowledge has been developed and articulated since 2006 by a group of indigenous elders and human geographers known as the 'Bawaka Collective', who describe themselves as follows:

> The Bawaka Collective is an Indigenous and non-Indigenous, human-more-than-human research collective. It includes Bawaka Country, Laklak Burarrwanga, Ritjilili Ganambarr, Merrkiyawuy Ganambarr-Stubbs, Banbapuy Ganambarr, Djawundil Maymuru, Kate Lloyd, Sandie Suchet-Pearson and Sarah Wright. Bawaka Country is the diverse land, water, human, and nonhuman animals, plants, rocks, thoughts, and songs that make up the Yolŋu homeland of Bawaka in North East Arnhem Land, Australia. Laklak, Ritjilili, Merrkiyawuy, and Banbapuy are four Indigenous sisters, elders, and caretakers for Bawaka Country together with their daughter, Djawundil.

Sarah, Sandie and Kate are three non-Indigenous human geographers from the University of Newcastle and Macquarie University who have been adopted into the family as grand-daughter, sister, and daughter.

(Bawaka Collective, 2023)

The collective has developed a range of innovative collaborative methodologies for understanding human-environment interactions, drawing together the insights from different forms of expertise for what they term 'both ways learning', while remaining sensitive to where their understandings and accounts of the world differ and/or remain incommensurable. They use qualitative, narrative techniques from the humanities and the social sciences, sometimes comple-mented with approaches from the natural sciences.

In an ongoing series of live and multimedia presentations, learning resources, books, and academic papers, the Collective has articulated and shared how Yolŋu ontologies shape the way people relate to their Country. One example of their academic writings is a paper entitled 'Co-becoming Bawaka' (Bawaka Country et al., 2016), which begins

Is that gukguk calling? When we hear gukguk [a type of pigeon] calling us, here at Bawaka, we know it's time to go digging for ganguri, yams … Come, it's time to dig for gan-guri (yams) at Bawaka, our Homeland in northeast Arnhem Land. Will you join us? We'll get our wires and a bag to carry the ganguri and we will seek to trace the fine vines with their heart-shaped leaves to where they meet the sand. Then we will dig. As ever, though, when we are at Bawaka, we'll be doing more than just digging and getting food. We will be bringing ourselves and Bawaka into being, we will be living our history, our ceremonies, and our future, and we would like you to join us. We want you to experience what it might mean to under-stand space and place from an Indigenous Yolŋu perspective. We would like all geographers, all people, to learn what they can from us, about what it might mean to live in a world that is relational, that co-becomes with us and each other, that is

knowing, that is alive – even in its death. But first, as is appropriate in a Yolŋu world, we must introduce ourselves and introduce you to Bawaka, our Homeland.

(455–456)

In this work, the authors discuss the resonance between ideas of
co-becoming and relationality found in more-than-human geography and Bawaka Yolŋu ontology that we described in Section 2.3.
The collective project is more-than-human participatory research in
its fullest sense, co-producing knowledge through a process that is
co-designed, co-developed and inclusive of multiple ways of knowing, and in which the participants understood to be shaping these
practices co-become in relation with more-than-human Country.

3.5 Make an alliance with science

The previous imperatives to rematerialise social theory, to engage with publics, and to redistribute expertise have led several more-than-humanists to collaborate with scientists. The breakdown in the modern relationship between
science and politics, and growing concerns about climate denialism and
post-truth politics, have catalysed new ways of working across and between
different academic disciplines and their approaches to knowledge production. Andrew Barry, Georgina Born, and Gisa Weszkalnys (2008) provide
a useful overview of this trend towards interdisciplinarity (Table 3.4). They
first highlight three 'modes' of interdisciplinary research. In the first, which
they term 'integrative-synthesis', two pre-existing disciplines come together
symmetrically to forge new ways of working. In the second 'subordination-
service' mode, an asymmetric, or hierarchical, relationship is established
between disciplines in which the 'service discipline(s) is commonly understood to be making up for or filling in for an absence or lack in the other,
(master) discipline(s)' (29). They argue that social science often fills this service role in collaborations with natural science, for example by helping scientists address a perceived 'deficit' in public knowledge. In their third (and
preferred) 'agonistic-antagonistic' mode, interdisciplinarity springs from a
criticism of the limits of existing disciplines and a desire to forge a new 'inter-
discipline' that offers more than a synthesis of its component disciplines.[13]

Table 3.4 The modes and logics of interdisciplinarity (after Barry et al., 2008)

Three modes of interdisciplinary research	
Integrative – Synthesis	Two existing disciplines come together symmetrically to forge new ways of working
Subordination – Service	A hierarchical relationship is established between disciplines
Agonistic – Antagonistic	Interdisciplinarity springs from a criticism of the limits of existing disciplines and a desire to forge a new 'interdiscipline'
Three logics of interdisciplinarity	
Accountability	Interdisciplinarity breaks down the barriers between science and society, leading to greater interaction between scientists and various publics and stakeholders
Innovation	Social scientists and artists work with scientists and engineers in the commercial sector to better understand consumer desires
Ontology	Artists or social scientists work with scientists to interrogate the material characteristics of phenomena according to open-ended logics of experimentation

Barry et al. then identify three 'logics' of interdisciplinarity, the first being a logic of 'accountability', in which 'interdisciplinarity is guided by the idea that it helps to foster a culture of accountability, breaking down the barriers between science and society, leading to greater interaction, for instance, between scientists and various publics and stakeholders' (31). They associate this with the rise of 'mode two' science (Nowotny et al., 2001) in which interdisciplinary research is targeted at the interests of public policy, rather than the 'blue skies thinking' of mode one science. In their second 'logic of innovation', social scientists and artists work with scientists and engineers in the commercial sector to help them better understand the unsatisfied desires of their consumers and to enhance national competitiveness. Finally, Barry et al. identify a third 'logic of ontology' in which collaborating artists or social scientists work with scientists to interrogate the material characteristics of the phenomena under study according to the open-ended logics of experimentation outlined above.

Interdisciplinary research in an 'agonistic-antagonistic' mode, and guided by this 'logic of ontology', has become common amongst more-than-humanists in the last decade. For example, prominent social theorists have collaborated with scientists informed by modes of systems thinking associated with the Anthropocene and the microbiome. Like Sarah Whatmore, Bruno Latour collaborated with Earth System scientists and made frequent reference to the work of James Lovelock (Lenton and Latour, 2018; Latour, 2017). He defends Gaia as scientific framework and has developed Gaian thinking in recent books on how science and politics might be conjoined in the 'new climatic regime' (Latour, 2018) of the Anthropocene. Meanwhile, Donna Haraway has long admired the work of the biologist Lynn Margulis and has maintained close links with those involved in developing the field of ecological-evolutionary-developmental biology (Haraway, 2016).

In justifying this new alliance with science, Latour proposes a new model of 'composition' in which social and natural scientists collaborate with each other, and with publics, to develop new practices of knowledge production and new models of deliberative democracy (see Box 4.4 in the following chapter). While Haraway and Tsing have used Gaian thinking to ground interdisciplinary research programmes that foster 'arts of living on a damaged planet' (Tsing and Bubandt, 2017). Based on long histories of friendship and social interaction, trust, and mutual respect, they have worked with natural scientists to develop and refine knowledge practices that enable the types of composition envisaged by Latour. Tsing describes these as 'transdisciplinary mutualisms' (2015): experiments that cut across the spaces of knowledge production, spanning the field, the laboratory, and the artist's studio. We reflect on the political implications of these high-profile alliances with science in the next chapter, and in the final chapter, we explore some of the concerns that have been raised about a creeping 'scientism' in some strands of new materialist thinking.

These trends towards interdisciplinarity have been subject to much discussion and engagement in geography, a discipline which employs a great diversity of social and natural scientists who use a wide range of knowledge practices, spanning the 'hard' laboratory sciences and the 'soft' approaches of hermeneutic interpretation. Throughout the 20th century, geography became increasingly intellectually and institutionally divided into its human and physical strands. Geographers might teach on the same degree course and share the same building, but there are often limited degrees of integration or conversations across the divide. This division has been the subject of much hand-wringing, especially amongst environmental geographers, who feel that the subject should be especially well-placed to address the contemporary challenges of the Anthropocene (Castree et al., 2009). As Whatmore

(2013) puts it, the nature-culture binary is: 'an imaginary writ large in the disciplinary fabric of geography that, for all its talk of integrating social and natural science perspectives on the environment, practises a "human"/"physical" division of labour' (79).

However, there are some exceptions to this divide, including a body of work by environmental geographers working under Barry et al.'s logic of accountability to develop interdisciplinary approaches to tackling the problems of climate change, energy use, pollution, and biodiversity loss (Castree, 2015, 2016). One example is given by the collaboration between Sarah Whatmore, Stuart Lane, and other hydrologists that we outlined in the previous section, which shows a model of interdisciplinarity (or perhaps better *intra*-disciplinarity) that adheres to a more-than-humanist model. Whatmore claims that this project was not targeted at filling a deficit in public knowledge, in solving a problem, or in generating commercial innovation. Although it did inform the building of a new technology for flood defence, this was not its primary aim. Instead, she suggests that it followed Barry et al.'s agonistic mode of interdisciplinarity and their logic of ontology, in as much as it enabled diverse experts to learn to be affected by flooding as a material, hydrological process, and event. It also placed established knowledge of flooding 'at risk' to develop new ways of working with the unruly dynamics of a river (see Whatmore, 2009).

3.6 Conclusions

In this chapter, we have summarised more-than-human approaches to understanding what knowledge is and how it might be produced by geographers. We traced how these epistemologies follow from the more-than-human materialisms that we outlined in the previous chapter. We identified five instructions that we are given by more-than-human geographers: to learn to be affected, to follow the things, to experiment, to engage publics and redistribute expertise, and to make an alliance with science. Although there are important variations in how different more-than-human geographers have followed these instructions, it is possible to identify the following common dimensions to more-than-human knowledge practices

- In contrast to a humanist figure of knowledge as possessed by a rational mind-in-a-vat cut off from the world, they suggest that we see knowledge as a collection of material forms and processes. Feminist and science studies theorists demonstrate that knowledge is *generated*, rather than being found;

- Actor-network theorists show how knowledge is a *technological achievement*, in as much as it is made, stabilised in, and distributed by instruments and wider infrastructure. This knowledge is *contingent* upon these instruments and their assemblages;
- Non-representational theorists and indigenous studies scholars show us how knowledge is *embodied* and emerges out of habituated ways of living in a material world. They suggest that knowledge is *affective*, it is felt before it is thought, and it comes to matter when it is given emotional form. Knowledge is also *atmospheric*, as affects are shared and amplified through collective experience;
- Animal studies and indigenous scholars show us that knowledge is held by *nonhuman* subjects and that knowledges can be generated through human-animal collaboration;
- Science studies scholars show us how knowledge is *partial* and that it is *located* in particular places. They demonstrate that it is *experimental*, emerging out of open-ended experiments that are designed to learn from surprises. They suggest that knowledge leads to expertise, that expertise is based on experience, and that expertise comes in a variety of scientific and *vernacular* forms.

As a consequence, more-than-human geographers view knowledge as *multiple*, in that it comes in what Anne Marie Mol (2002) terms a 'multiplicity' of 'more than one, but less than many' legitimate forms. In so doing, they illustrate the second dimension of the concept of multinaturalism that we explained in the Introduction. If we take Chapters 2 and 3 together, we now have a solid understanding of the ontological and the epistemological dimensions of multinaturalism: we are presented with unruly and entangled worlds going in many different directions; and we can now appreciate multiple forms of expertise held by actors with legitimate claims to know about the worlds around them. With this multinatural foundation established, we can now turn to consider questions of ethics and politics and explore how more-than-human geographers understand questions of power and responsibility cast off from the modern certainties of humanism, anthropocentrism, and the primacy of scientific objectivity.

Questions for reflection

1 What counts as expertise?
2 What counts as an 'experiment'?
3 Does it matter where experiments happen?
4 How do you decide between competing knowledge claims based on different knowledge practices?
5 How might you learn to be affected like a tree, or a fish, or a seashell?
6 How might you learn from/with indigenous or lay knowledge in a non-extractive way?
7 How could you 'follow the things' that end up in your lunchtime meal?
8 How far can you include participants in setting research questions? What if the participants aren't human?
9 How does it matter if knowledge is not 'objective'?

Suggestions for reading

The following provide more information on the epistemic principles of more-than-human knowledge practices:

Braun B (2015) From critique to experiment? Rethinking political ecology for the Anthropocene. In: Perreault T, Bridge G and McCarthy J (eds) *The Routledge handbook of political ecology*. London: Taylor and Francis, pp. 102–114.

Callon M, Lascoumes P and Barthe Y (2009) *Acting in an uncertain world: An essay on technical democracy*. Cambridge, MA: MIT Press.

Despret V (2004) The body we care for: Figures of anthropo-zoo-genesis. *Body & Society* 10(2–3): 111–134.

Kirksey SE and Helmreich S (2010) The emergence of multispecies ethnography. *Cultural Anthropology* 25(4): 545–576.

Lorimer J and Driessen C (2014) Wild experiments at the Oostvaardersplassen: Rethinking environmentalism in the Anthropocene. *Transactions of the Institute of British Geographers* 39(2): 169–181.

Yandaarra with Gumbaynggirr Country including, Smith AS, Marshall UB, Smith N, Wright S, Daley L and Hodge P (2022) Ethics and consent in more-than-human research: Some considerations from/with/as Gumbaynggirr Country, Australia. *Transactions of the Institute of British Geographers* 47(3): 709–724.

These references explore more-than-human methodologies for geographical research:

Bastian M, Jones O, Moore N and Roe E (eds) (2016) *Participatory research in more-than-human worlds*. London: Routledge.

Dowling Robyn, Kate Lloyd and Sandra Suchet-Pearson (2017) Qualitative methods II: 'More-than-human' methodologies and/in praxis. *Progress in Human Geography* 41(6): 823–831.

Gorman R and Andrews G (2022) What role for more-than-representational, more-than-human inquiry? In: Lovell SA, Coen SE and Rosenberg MW (eds) *The Routledge Handbook of methodologies in human geography.* London: Routledge, pp. 381–394.

Pryke M, Rose G and Whatmore S (2003) *Using social theory: Thinking through research.* London: SAGE.

Vannini P (2015a) Non-representational ethnography: new ways of animating life-worlds. *Cultural Geographies* 22(2): 317–327.

These papers offer exemplary case studies of more-than-human approaches to knowledge production:

Barua M and Sinha A (2017) Animating the urban: An ethological and geographical conversation. *Social & Cultural Geography* 20(8): 1160–1180. DOI: 10.1080/14649365.2017.1409908.

Bawaka Country, Wright S, Suchet-Pearson S, Lloyd K, Burarrwanga L, Ganambarr R, Ganambarr-Stubbs M, Ganambarr B, Maymuru D and Sweeney J (2016) Co-becoming Bawaka:Towards a relational understanding of place/space. *Progress in Human Geography* 40(4): 455–475.

Cook I (2004) Follow the thing: Papaya. *Antipode* 36(4): 642–664.

Hinchliffe S, Kearnes MB, Degen M and Whatmore S (2005) Urban wild things: A cosmopolitical experiment. *Environment and Planning D-Society & Space* 23(5): 643–658.

Lane SN, Odoni N, Landstrom C, Whatmore SJ, Ward N and Bradley S (2011) Doing flood risk science differently: An experiment in radical scientific method. *Transactions of the Institute of British Geographers* 36(1): 15–36.

Notes

1   Despret gives the example of Farley Mowat, a biologist who spent his summers living amidst wolves in a remote part of the Arctic. Mowat wanted to understand where wolves sourced the fat in their diet. He began eating the mice that the wolves ate, to demonstrate that they could survive on a diet of rodents rather than moose. He ate them whole: skin and all, though he did cook them with a little garlic. Despret argues that in aligning his body with the wolves in this way he was able to 'incorporate what the animals may feel' (2013: 58). Charles Foster (2016) carried out similar experiments for his book Being a Beast, living as a badger in a human-sized 'earth' and eating earthworms to learn to taste and appreciate their place-based terroir. For a review of this approach and its implications for geography, see Lorimer H (2010a).

2   For reviews of multispecies studies and comparable work in animal geographies, see Buller H (2014, 2015a, 2015b), Nading A (2013), and Ogden, Hall and Tanita (2013).

3   The Potawatomi are a Native American people living in the Great Plains, upper Mississippi River, and western Great Lakes regions of the USA.

4   The Anishinabekwe are a group of culturally related Indigenous peoples living in the Great Lakes region of Canada and the United States that include the Potawatomi.

5   For a wider discussion of moving image methodologies for more-than-human geographies, see Lorimer J (2010b), and for example of using wildlife cameras in geography, see Fry (2023).

6   These approaches seek a passage beyond the impasse created by the 'science wars' in the 1990s, in which idealist social constructionists pitted themselves against staunch scientific realists (for an introduction, see Demeritt, 2002).

7   Jamie has drawn on this work in his research on corncrake conservation in the Scottish Hebrides Lorimer J (2008). He follows a group of ornithologists whose instruments enable them to detect this elusive bird, to count and map its declining population, to link its fate to the farming practices of the local crofters. He provides an account of a successful translation of people and wildlife that culminates in a set of scientific papers that legitimate a plan for managing corncrakes and crofters.

8   Ian Cook and his collaborators have spent more than a decade following a great diversity of commodities and documenting their findings on this website http://www.followthethings.com/

9   For more information on the Digital Ecologies Research Network, see http://www.digicologies.com/

10 As Sarah Whatmore puts it: 'the experimental demands of 'more-than-human' styles of working place an onus on actively redistributing expertise beyond engaging with other disciplines or research fields to engaging knowledge practices and vernaculars beyond the academy in experimental research/politics' Whatmore S (2006, 607).

11 Mrs Kinpainsby is a collective comprising social/political geographers Sara Kindon, Rachael Pain, and Mike Kesby, along with the insights of their many participant collaborators over the years.

12 Further examples of participatory research linking scientists with publics can be found in our Good Germs, Bad Germs project which developed a participatory methodology for engaging an interested public in the science of microbiology in the context of contemporary anxieties about domestic hygiene and its effects on the microbiome (Lorimer et al., 2019). Other examples are offered by Jennifer Gabrys (2022) who has worked with hackers and DIY fabricators of scientific equipment to develop affordable tools for monitoring atmospheric pollution in the home and in the urban environment.

13 Barry et al. differentiate interdisciplinarity, multidisciplinarity, and transdisciplinarity. They suggest that 'commonly, a distinction is made between multidisciplinarity in which several disciplines cooperate but remain unchanged, working with standard disciplinary framings and interdisciplinarity in which there is an attempt to integrate or synthesize perspectives from several disciplines … Transdisciplinarity, in contrast, is taken to involve a transgression against or transcendence of disciplinary norms, whether in the pursuit of a fusion of disciplines, an approach oriented to complexity or real-world problem-solving, or one aimed at overcoming the distance between specialized and lay knowledges or between research and policy' (2008, 28).

References

Adams CJ and Gruen L (2021) *Ecofeminism: Feminist intersections with other animals and the earth.* New York: Bloomsbury Publishing.

Anderson B (2009) Affective atmospheres. *Emotion, Space and Society* 2(2): 77–81.

Ash J, Kitchin R and Leszczynski A (2018) *Digital geographies.* London: SAGE Publications.

Barad K (2003) Posthumanist performativity: Toward an understanding of how matter comes to matter. *Signs: Journal of Women in Culture and Society* 28(3): 801–831.

Barker AJ and Pickerill J (2020) Doings with the land and sea: Decolonising geographies, indigeneity, and enacting place-agency. *Progress in Human Geography* 44(4): 640–662.

Barry A, Born G and Weszkalnys G (2008) Logics of interdisciplinarity. *Economy and Society* 37(1): 20–49.

Barua M and Sinha A (2017) Animating the urban: An ethological and geographical conversation. *Social & Cultural Geography* 20(8): 1160–1180. DOI: 10.1080/14649365.2017.1409908.

Bastian M, Jones O, Moore N and Roe E (2016) *Participatory research in more-than-human worlds.* Abingdon: Taylor & Francis.

Bawaka Collective (2023) *About us.* Available at: https://bawakacollective.com/about-us/ [accessed March 2023].

Bawaka Country, Wright S, Suchet-Pearson S, Lloyd K, Burarrwanga L, Ganambarr R, Ganambarr-Stubbs M, Ganambarr B, Maymuru D and Sweeney J (2016) Co-becoming Bawaka:Towards a relational understanding of place/space. *Progress in Human Geography* 40(4): 455–475.

Benson E (2010) *Wired wilderness: Technologies of tracking and the making of modern wildlife.* Baltimore: Johns Hopkins University Press.

Braun B (2015) From critique to experiment? Rethinking political ecology for the Anthropocene. In: Perreault T, Bridge G and McCarthy J (eds) *The Routledge handbook of political ecology.* London: Taylor and Francis, pp. 102–114.

Buller H (2014) Animal geographies I. *Progress in Human Geography* 38(2): 308–318.

Buller H (2015a) Animal geographies II: Methods. *Progress in Human Geography* 39(3): 374–384.

Buller H (2015b) Animal geographies III: Ethics. *Progress in Human Geography* 40(3): 422–430.

Burghardt GM (1990) Animal suffering, critical anthropomorphism, and reproductive rights. *Behavioral and Brain Sciences* 13(1): 14.

Callon M (1986) Some elements of a sociology of translation - domestication of the scallops and the fishermen of St Brieuc Bay. *Sociological Review Monograph* 32(1): 196–233.

Callon M, Lascoumes P and Barthe Y (2009) *Acting in an uncertain world: An essay on technical democracy.* Cambridge, MA: MIT Press.

Carter S and McCormack DP (2006) Film, geopolitics and the affective logics of intervention. *Political Geography* 25(2): 228–245.

Castree N (2015) Changing the anthropo(s)cene: Geographers, global environmental change and the politics of knowledge. *Dialogues in Human Geography* 5(3): 301–316.

Castree N (2016) Geography and the new social contract for global change research. *Transactions of the Institute of British Geographers* 41(3): 328–347.

Castree N, Demeritt D and Liverman D (2009) Introduction: Making sense of environmental geography. In: Castree et al (eds) *A Companion to Environmental Geography* London: Wiley, pp. 1–15.

Collins H, Evans R and Weinel M (2017) STS as science or politics? *Social Studies of Science* 47(4): 580–586.

Collins HM and Evans R (2002) The third wave of science studies: Studies of expertise and experience. *Social Studies of Science* 32(2): 235–296.

Cook I (2004) Follow the thing: Papaya. *Antipode* 36(4): 642–664.

Cresswell T (2006) 'You cannot shake that shimmie here': Producing mobility on the dance floor. *Cultural Geographies* 13(1): 55–77.

de Castro EV (1998) Cosmological deixis and Amerindian perspectivism. *The Journal of the Royal Anthropological Institute* 4(3): 469–488.

de Waal FBM (1999) Anthropomorphism and anthropodenial: Consistency in our thinking about humans and other animals. *Philosophical Topics* 27(1): 255–280.

Demeritt D (2002) What is the 'social construction of nature'? A typology and sympathetic critique. *Progress in Human Geography* 26(6): 767–790.

DeSilvey C and Bartolini N (2019) Where horses run free? Autonomy, temporality and rewilding in the Côa valley, Portugal. *Transactions of the Institute of British Geographers* 44(1): 94–109.

Despret V (2004) The body we care for: Figures of anthropo-zoo-genesis. *Body & Society* 10(2–3): 111–134.

Despret V (2013) Responding bodies and partial affinities in human–animal worlds. *Theory, Culture & Society* 30(7/8): 51–76.

Dowling R, Lloyd K and Suchet-Pearson S (2017) Qualitative methods II: 'More-than-human' methodologies and/in praxis. *Progress in Human Geography* 41(6): 823–831.

Evans J and Jones P (2011) The walking interview: Methodology, mobility and place. *Applied Geography* 31(2): 849–858.

Foster C (2016) *Being a beast: Adventures across the species divide*. New York: Henry Holt and Company.

Fry T (2023) Tracking Sonny: Localised digital knowledge of an urban fox. *Cultural Geographies:* 14744740231167601. DOI: 10.1177/14744740231167601.

Gabrys J (2016) *Program earth: Environmental sensing technology and the making of a computational planet*. Minneapolis: University of Minnesota Press.

Gabrys J (2020) Smart forests and data practices: From the internet of trees to planetary governance. *Big Data & Society* 7(1): 2053951720904871.

Gabrys J (2022) *Citizens of worlds: Open-air toolkits for environmental struggle.* Minneapolis: University of Minnesota Press.

Gabrys J, Westerlaken M, Urzedo D, Ritts M and Simlai T (2022) Reworking the political in digital forests: The cosmopolitics of socio-technical worlds. *Progress in Environmental Geography* 1(1–4): 58–83.

Gieryn TF (2006) City as truth-spot. *Social Studies of Science* 36(1): 5–38.

Gieryn TF (2018) *Truth-spots: How places make people believe.* Chicago: University of Chicago Press.

Goldstein J and Nost E (2022) *The nature of data: Infrastructures, environments, politics.* Nebraska: University of Nebraska Press, Lincoln.

Gorman R and Andrews G (2022) What role for more-than-representational, more-than-human inquiry? In: Lovell SA, Coen SE and Rosenberg MW (eds) *The Routledge handbook of methodologies in human geography.* London: Routledge, pp. 381–394.

Grahame K (1908/2018) *The wind in the willows.* London: Penguin.

Greenhough B (2006) Tales of an island-laboratory: Defining the field in geography and science studies. *Transactions of the Institute of British Geographers* 31(2): 224–237.

Guggenheim M (2012) Laboratizing and de-laboratizing the world. *History of the Human Sciences* 25(1): 99–118.

Haraway D (1988) Situated knowledges: The science question in feminism and the privilege of partial perspective. *Feminist Studies* 14(3): 575–599.

Haraway DJ (2008) *When species meet.* Minneapolis: University of Minnesota Press.

Haraway DJ (2016) *Staying with the trouble: Making kin in the Chthulucene.* Durham, NC: Duke University Press.

Hayward E (2010) Fingeryeyes: Impressions of cup corals. *Cultural Anthropology* 25(4): 577–599.

Hinchliffe S, Kearnes MB, Degen M and Whatmore S (2005) Urban wild things: A cosmopolitical experiment. *Environment and Planning D-Society & Space* 23(5): 643–658.

Hodgetts T and Lorimer J (2015) Methodologies for animals' geographies: Cultures, communication and genomics. *Cultural Geographies* 22(2): 285–295.

Ingold T (2000) *The perception of the environment: Essays on livelihood, dwelling and skill.* London: Routledge.

Ingold T (2011) *Being alive: Essays on movement, knowledge and description.* London: Routledge.

Kelly AH and Lezaun J (2017) The wild indoors: Room-spaces of scientific inquiry. *Cultural Anthropology* 32(3): 367–398.

Kimmerer RW (2013) *Braiding sweetgrass: Indigenous wisdom, scientific knowledge and the teachings of plants.* Minneapolis: Milkweed Editions.

Kitchin R and Dodge M (2011) *Code/space: Software and everyday life.* Cambridge: MIT Press.

Kohler RE (2002) *Landscapes & labscapes: Exploring the lab-field border in biology.* Chicago, IL: University of Chicago Press.

Krohn W and Weyer J (1994) Society as a laboratory: The social risks of experimental research. *Science and Public Policy* 21(3): 173–183.

Landstrom C, Whatmore SJ, Lane SN, Odoni NA, Ward N and Bradley S (2011) Coproducing flood risk knowledge: Redistributing expertise in critical 'participatory modelling'. *Environment and Planning A* 43(7): 1617–1633.

Lane SN, Odoni N, Landstrom C, Whatmore SJ, Ward N and Bradley S (2011) Doing flood risk science differently: An experiment in radical scientific method. *Transactions of the Institute of British Geographers* 36(1): 15–36.

Latour B (1987) *Science in action: How to follow scientists and engineers through society*. Milton Keynes: Open University Press.

Latour B (1999) *Pandora's hope: Essays on the reality of science studies*. Cambridge, MA: Harvard University Press.

Latour B (2005) *Reassembling the social: An introduction to actor-network-theory*. Oxford: Oxford University Press.

Latour B (2017) *Facing Gaia: Eight lectures on the new climatic regime*. London: Wiley.

Latour B (2018) *Down to earth: Politics in the new climatic regime*. Wiley.

Lea J (2008) Retreating to nature: Rethinking 'therapeutic landscapes'. *Area* 40(1): 90–98.

Lenton TM and Latour B (2018) Gaia 2.0. *Science* 361(6407): 1066–1068.

Leszczynski A (2019) Digital methods II: Digital-visual methods. *Progress in Human Geography* 43(6): 1143–1152.

Livingstone DN (1995) The spaces of knowledge - contributions towards a historical geography of science. *Environment and Planning D-Society & Space* 13(1): 5–34.

Lorimer H (2010a) Forces of nature, forms of life: Calibrating ethology and phenomenology. In: Anderson B and Harrison P (eds) *Taking-place: Non-representational theories and geography*. London: Ashgate, pp. 55–78.

Lorimer J (2008) Counting corncrakes: The affective science of the UK corncrake census. *Social Studies of Science* 38(3): 377–405.

Lorimer J (2010b) Moving image methodologies for more-than-human geographies. *Cultural Geographies* 17(2): 237–258.

Lorimer J and Driessen C (2013) Bovine biopolitics and the promise of monsters in the rewilding of Heck cattle. *Geoforum* 48: 249–259.

Lorimer J and Driessen C (2014) Wild experiments at the Oostvaardersplassen: Rethinking environmentalism in the Anthropocene. *Transactions of the Institute of British Geographers* 39(2): 169–181. DOI: 10.1111/tran.12030.

Lorimer J and Driessen C (2016) From "Nazi cows" to cosmopolitan "ecological engineers": Specifying rewilding through a history of Heck cattle. *Annals of the American Association of Geographers* 106(3): 631–652.

Lorimer J, Hodgetts T, Grenyer R, Greenhough B, McLeod C and Dwyer A (2019) Making the microbiome public: Participatory experiments with DNA sequencing in domestic kitchens. *Transactions of the Institute of British Geographers* 44(3): 524–541.

Lovell SA, Coen SE and Rosenberg MW (2022) *The Routledge handbook of methodologies in human geography*. Abingdon: Taylor & Francis.

Lynch CR and Farrokhi B (2022) Digital geographies and everyday life: Space, materiality, agency. In: Lovell SA, Coen SE and Rosenberg MW (eds) *The Routledge handbook of methodologies in human geography*. London: Routledge, pp. 196–206.

Mason V and Hope PR (2014) Echoes in the dark: Technological encounters with bats. *Journal of Rural Studies* 33: 107–118.

McCormack DP (2002) A paper with an interest in rhythm. *Geoforum* 33(4): 469–485.

McCormack DP (2005) Diagramming practice and performance. *Environment and Planning D-Society & Space* 23(1): 119–147.

McCormack DP (2017) The circumstances of post-phenomenological life worlds. *Transactions of the Institute of British Geographers* 42(1): 2–13.

Mol A (2002) *The body multiple: Ontology in medical practice.* Durham, NC: Duke University Press.

Mrs K (2008) Taking stock of participatory geographies: Envisioning the communiversity. *Transactions of the Institute of British Geographers* 33(3): 292–299.

Nading A (2013) Humans, animals, and health: From ecology to entanglement. *Environment and Society: Advances in Research* 4(1): 60–78.

Naylor S (2002) The field, the museum and the lecture hall: The spaces of natural history in Victorian Cornwall. *Transactions of the Institute of British Geographers* 27(4): 494–513.

Nightingale A (2006) The nature of gender: Work, gender, and environment. *Environment and Planning D-Society & Space* 24(2): 165–185.

Nowotny H, Scott P and Gibbons M (2001) *Re-thinking science: Knowledge and the public in an age of uncertainty.* London: Wiley.

OED (2023) *Oxford English Dictionary.* Oxford: Oxford University Press.

Ogden L, Hall B and Tanita K (2013) Animals, plants, people, and things: A review of multispecies ethnography. *Environment and Society: Advances in Research* 4: 5–24.

Pain R and Kindon S (2007) Participatory geographies. *Environment and Planning A: Economy and Space* 39(12): 2807–2812.

Pickering A (1992) *Science as practice and culture.* Chicago, IL: University of Chicago Press.

Pink S (2009) *Doing sensory ethnography.* Thousand Oaks, CA: SAGE.

Pink S, Horst H, Postill J, Hjorth L, Lewis T and Tacchi J (2015) *Digital ethnography: Principles and practice.* London: SAGE.

Plumwood V (1993) *Feminism and the mastery of nature.* London: Routledge.

Pryke M, Rose G and Whatmore S (2003) *Using social theory: Thinking through research.* London: SAGE.

Rheinberger H-J (1997) *Toward a history of epistemic things: Synthesizing proteins in the test tube.* Stanford, CA: Stanford University Press.

Richmond C, Coombes B and Louis RP (2022) Making space for indigenous intelligence, sovereignty and relevance in geographic research. In: Lovell SA, Coen SE and Rosenberg MW (eds) *The Routledge handbook of methodologies in human geography*. London: Routledge, pp. 230–248.

Rose G (2022) *Visual methodologies: An introduction to researching with visual materials.* London: SAGE.

Rose G and Willis A (2019) Seeing the smart city on Twitter: Colour and the affective territories of becoming smart. *Environment and Planning D: Society and Space* 37(3): 411–427.

Rubio-Ramon G and Srinivasan K (2022) Methodologies for animal geographies: Approaches within and beyond the human. In: Lovell SA, Coen SE and Rosenberg MW (eds) *The Routledge handbook of methodologies in human geography*. London: Routledge, pp. 110–123.

Rutz C, Loretto M-C, Bates AE, Davidson SC, Duarte CM, Jetz W, Johnson M, Kato A, Kays R, Mueller T, Primack RB, Ropert-Coudert Y, Tucker MA, Wikelski M and Cagnacci F (2020) Covid-19 lockdown allows researchers to quantify the effects of human activity on wildlife. *Nature Ecology & Evolution* 4(9): 1156–1159.

Searle A, Turnbull J and Adams WM (2023) The digital peregrine: A technonatural history of a cosmopolitan raptor. *Transactions of the Institute of British Geographers* 48(1): 195–212.

Shapin S (1988) The house of experiment in 17th-century England. *Isis* 79(298): 373–404.

Shiva V (1988) *Staying alive: Women, ecology, and development*. London: Zed Books.

Springgay S and Truman SE (2017) *Walking methodologies in a more-than-human world: Walkinglab*. Abingdon: Taylor & Francis.

Sundberg J (2014) Decolonizing posthumanist geographies. *Cultural Geographies* 21(1): 33–47.

Thrift N (2004) Intensities of feeling: Towards a spatial politics of affect. *Geografiska Annaler: Series B, Human Geography* 86(1): 57–78.

Thrift N, Driver F and Livingstone D (1995) The geography of truth. *Environment and Planning D-Society & Space* 13(1): 1–3.

Thrift N and French S (2002) The automatic production of space. *Transactions of the Institute of British Geographers* 27(3): 309–335.

Tsing A (2015) In the midst of disturbance: Symbiosis, coordination, history, landscape Lecture given at the *ASA Annual Conference 2015* Exeter.

Tsing AL and Bubandt N (2017) *Arts of living on a damaged planet: Ghosts and monsters of the anthropocene*. Minneapolis: University of Minnesota Press.

Turnbull J, Searle A, Hartman Davies O, Dodsworth J, Chasseray-Peraldi P, von Essen E and Anderson-Elliott H (2023a) Digital ecologies: Materialities, encounters, governance. *Progress in Environmental Geography* onlinefirst.

Turnbull J, Searle A and Lorimer J (2023b) Anthropause environmentalisms: Noticing natures with the self-isolating bird club. *Transactions of the Institute of British Geographers* 48: 232–248. Available from: https://doi.org/10.1111/tran.12569. DOI: 10.1111/tran.12569.

Van Dooren T, Münster U, Kirksey E, Rose DB, Chrulew M and Tsing AL (2016) *Multispecies studies*. Durham: Duke University Press.

Vannini P (2015a) Non-representational ethnography: New ways of animating lifeworlds. *Cultural Geographies* 22(2): 317–327.

Vannini P (2015b) *Non-representational methodologies: Re-envisioning research*. London: Taylor & Francis.

Whatmore S (2003) Generating materials. In: Pryke M, Rose G and Whatmore S (eds) *Using social theory: Thinking through research*. London: SAGE, pp. 89–104.

Whatmore S (2006) Materialist returns: Practising cultural geography in and for a more-than-human world. *Cultural Geographies* 13(4): 600–609.

Whatmore S (2013) Where natural and social science meet? Reflections on an experiment in geographical practice. In: Barry A and Born G (eds) *Interdisciplinarity: Reconfigurations of the social and natural sciences*. London: Routledge, pp. 161–177.

Whatmore S and Thorne L (1997) Nourishing networks: Alternative geographies of food. In: Goodman D and Watts M (eds) *Globalising food: Agrarian questions and global restructuring*. London: Routledge, pp. 287–304.

Whatmore SJ (2009) Mapping knowledge controversies: Science, democracy and the redistribution of expertise. *Progress in Human Geography* 33(5): 587–598.

Whatmore SJ and Landstrom C (2011) Flood apprentices: An exercise in making things public. *Economy and Society* 40(4): 582–610.

Wylie J (2005) A single day's walking: Narrating self and landscape on the south west coast path. *Transactions of the Institute of British Geographers* 30(2): 234–247.

Wynne B (1998) May the sheep safely graze? A reflexive view of the expert–lay knowledge divide. In: Lash S, Szerszynski B and Wynne B (eds) *Risk, Environment and Modernity: Towards a New Ecology*. London: SAGE Publications Ltd, pp. 44–83.

Yandaarra with Gumbaynggirr Country including, Smith AS, Marshall UB, Smith N, Wright S, Daley L and Hodge P (2022) Ethics and consent in more-than-human research: Some considerations from/with/as Gumbaynggirr Country, Australia. *Transactions of the Institute of British Geographers* 47(3): 709–724.

4 | More-than-human politics and ethics

We began this book by noting three important common dimensions to more-than-human geographies. The first is a commitment to taking seriously the agency of materials, be they living beings or immovable rocks. In the *Materialisms* chapter, we described how the human has been grounded in affective bodies, that are entangled in environments, and we looked at how material agency shapes the patterns and intensities of relations between diverse forms of matter, including living organisms.

Second, we suggested that more-than-human work shares a commitment to multiple forms of knowledge. In the *Knowledge practices* chapter, we showed how more-than-human geographers have engaged with diverse ways of knowing, including Western science, lay expertise, indigenous cosmologies, and even nonhuman knowledges. By listening to, learning from, and collaborating with diverse voices, more-than-human knowledge practices seek to diversify and democratise the politics of expertise.

The third commonality is the attention given to relations and processes. Politics is all about relations; it is about how humans and other-than-humans are linked together, drawn apart, arranged, moved, distributed, allowed to live, and made or left to die. It concerns how existing relations may contribute to, or prevent, just outcomes in multispecies societies. And the patterns of these relations are configured by social, ecological, and geological processes that operate through space and time. Some of these patterns are more consistent, predictable, and 'sticky'; others are much more ephemeral.

Taken together, these three more-than-human commitments establish the foundations for a multinatural approach to geography. In this chapter, we examine what this approach implies for politics and ethics;[1] exploring what happens to politics and ethics when actors and knowledges become

DOI: 10.4324/9781315164304-5

multiple. As we noted in the *Humanism* chapter, in Western, liberal, capitalist democracies politics has traditionally been conceived as a solely human affair, concerned with the competition between ideas, and with claims about how to distribute resources within and between societies. Political actors, according to humanists, are humans who (at least in theory) make political decisions based on rational objective arguments, often supported by reductive scientific analyses. Sometimes, the dominant logics are concerned with efficiency, sometimes with a concern for fairness, but there is usually agreement that the actors who count (politically) are the humans, with other forms of matter being categorised as 'goods' and 'resources' (like cows or oil) or 'bads' and 'risks' (like CO_2, viruses, or floods).

However, if we acknowledge that there are multiple political actors, and not all of them are human, as well as multiple ways in which to know worlds, then politics becomes something different. We will show how allowing for a multiplicity of actors leads to new forms of politics, with questions being raised about who and what counts as political. Allowing for a multiplicity of knowledges raises ethical and political questions about whose voices are heard in existing political systems, and whose are marginalised. It draws attention to how certain knowledge practices are silenced; for instance, cultural understandings that conceive of ecologies in different terms to the dominant discourse of a separated 'Nature'. Politics, then, might be re-thought, using Karen Barad's (2003) phrase that we encountered in Chapter 2, as the ways in which *'matter comes to matter'* within societies. As such, more-than-humanism does not simply provide a more coherent account of material worlds, but it also asserts a political and ethical project.

We structure the chapter into three parts. We start with a foundational case study, examining work on the 'politics of Nature' to illustrate how more-than-human geographers have approached questions of politics and ethics. This example demonstrates how attention to material agencies, multiple knowledges, and ecological processes and relations fundamentally unsettles a widespread approach to environmental politics based on protecting and preserving a 'pristine Nature'. We develop this analysis in more detail in the second section, which is split into three parts that review the political and ethical consequences of commitments to: (i) material agency; (ii) multiple knowledges; and (iii) relations and processes. In the third section, we look across the approaches reviewed to identify three shared normative commitments that characterise the politics and ethics of more-than-human geographies. These normative commitments are to a politics and ethics of *care, conversing, and connecting*.

The attention to *care* describes an ethics of recognition and 'response-ability' (Haraway, 2016) that flows from the understanding of humans as beings always already entangled in more-than-human worlds. The attention to *conversing* involves making room for a diversity of voices and listening carefully to what they say or otherwise suggest. The third commitment to *connecting* stems from the broad support for forms of 'affirmative critique', which flows from asserting that the relations through which beings (including humans) are positioned and governed are neither fixed, universal, nor necessary. It permits us to imagine that other futures are possible. These three commitments are grounded in an understanding that politics is a universal, necessary, and generative dimension of contemporary life, not something that can be foreclosed or avoided by deference to powerful forms of expertise (Mouffe, 2011). In the following and final chapter, we discuss the critiques that have been levelled at the politics and ethics of more-than-humanism. But for now, we begin by turning to the politics of Nature.

4.1 The (anti-)politics of nature: a case study

As we explained in Chapter 1, more-than-human approaches share a widespread dissatisfaction with the modern, dualistic idea of Nature and the forms of politics to which it has given rise. Here, Nature (in the singular, with a capital N) describes a world set apart from humans that should either be managed as a set of resources for economic growth or set aside as wilderness for conservation (Whatmore, 2002; Hinchliffe, 2007). In both cases, management decisions are to be made by objective natural scientists and economists. In this regime of understanding, 'Nature' as a category is not political: Nature is understood as a pre-existing taken-for-granted thing in the world. How to govern 'Nature' is a political question, but how to think about or understand Nature is not (Latour, 2004a).

This idea of Nature and the role it affords natural science was challenged by a range of social and environmental crises in the second half of the 20th century, including the threat of a nuclear apocalypse and of climate change. These crises led to a widespread questioning of both the purity of Nature (making 'Nature' as a category a focus of politics) and the objectivity of natural science (questioning who should make decisions about the politics of Nature). In analysing the politics of Nature, more-than-humanists have focused on three key questions:

- What is political?
- Who decides?
- How is this politics enacted in practice?

As we explained in Chapter 3, early efforts to answer these questions explored the social construction of scientific ideas of Nature (Demeritt, 2002). Ethnographers followed the things to trace how natural scientists come to speak with legitimacy about Nature: a domain that is understood to be materially separate from the social world. For Latour and others, this construction of Nature was not about revealing an underlying objective reality. Instead, it involves elaborate acts of 'purification', through which the messy hybridity of the material world is reduced to two types of stuff, and then of 'translation' through which this construction is communicated and legitimated as a powerful representation (Figure 2.1). Latour (1993) was especially concerned that these processes of purification and translation were 'black-boxed' by scientists. By this, he means they were rendered invisible in orthodox ways of reporting scientific knowledge practices that do not divulge the hard work and extensive material infrastructure required to both produce knowledge and to shut down the knowledge claims of others. In his book, *The Politics of Nature* (Latour, 2004a), he maps the modern settlement between science and politics (Figure 1.4), arguing that appeals to Nature are 'anti-political', or perform 'politics by other means', in that they shut down discussion. Here, invoking a singular Nature becomes a powerful way of foreclosing on wider dialogue and deliberation. Just think of how claims about what is normal, natural, and right are folded together in popular rhetoric about issues as diverse as food, biotechnology, gender, sexuality, or parenting.

Sarah Whatmore (Box 2.3) provides compelling illustrations of this politics of Nature in her influential book, *Hybrid Geographies* (2002). She offers a critique of the idea of wilderness, developing existing work in environmental history and cultural geography (Cronon, 1996), to trace how the landscapes that contemporary conservationists frame as wilderness can only be seen this way through power laden and colonial acts of purification. In examples drawn from Australia, North America, and Southern and Eastern Africa, these acts include effacing the long histories of indigenous land use, like hunting, burning, and low-intensity agriculture that have shaped the landscape.

They involve neglecting the often violent and colonial practices through which indigenous peoples were cleared from the land so that it could be seen as 'terra nullis': blank, unowned, and open to settler colonialism and conservation. She shows how narrating these landscapes as 'pure', 'virgin', or 'untouched' naturalises human absence and makes their current management apolitical. In so doing, it perpetuates colonial practices of conservation, including the exclusion (and sometimes genocide) of indigenous peoples (for wider discussion, see Adams and Mulligan, 2003; Brockington, 2002).

Subsequent work critically examined the political power of this singular idea of Nature across a wide array of policy domains, including biotechnology, food and agriculture, and human and environmental health (reviewed in Castree, 2005; Hinchliffe, 2007). As a consequence, environmental geographers Nick Bingham and Steve Hinchliffe (2008) argue that by the early 2000s, there was a growing sense that:

> Nature... seems to have stopped working so well. It no longer offers a stable category to which objects can be intuitively allocated. It is neither a source of smooth facts which seem to speak for themselves, nor an unchanging ground on which one might rely. Nature does not form a rallying site where an agreeable collective might be formed, or serve as an external arbiter which could speed matters along past due process. Instead, all of the time now, in all sorts of ways and in all sorts of places, these moves are being actively problematized, their costs becoming all too apparent. Refigured, in other words, from something to get in touch with or to be sure about towards a means of performing premature and hence anti-political unifications. Nature in this sense begins to look less like a good deal that can help to make a social world or cement a collective by informing 'us' of what is to be done, and emerges as more like a Faustian pact.
>
> (83)

Returning to the three questions above, what this literature argues is that when it comes to governing 'Nature':

- *What is political?* The modern ontology of 'what Nature is' has not been sufficiently political or open to contestation. Politics has been restricted to how Nature – understood in a very particular way – and should be managed by human actors;

- *Who decides?* Decisions about whose knowledge counts have also often been apolitical, with debate shut down through appeals to Science (in the singular, with a capital S) without considering the politics of how, where, and for what purposes science is done; and
- *How is the politics enacted in practice?* The politics of Nature has been enacted in undemocratic ways that perpetuate unjust, colonial, and even genocidal outcomes.

This critical work on the politics of Nature sets the agenda for a multinatural approach to politics. Nature, the singular capitalised concept, is found to be both ontologically suspect *and* implicated in depoliticising governance regimes. Through tracing how certain taken-for-granted assumptions – like that of a pristine, separate Natural world – have shaped and continue to shape environmental politics, a multinatural critique illuminates the practices that have facilitated environmental degradation and societal injustices. This analysis of the politics of Nature becomes the starting point for doing politics otherwise. One provocative example is the ecomodernist manifesto (Box 4.1). In the following section, we take up this challenge and trace some key examples of more-than-human approaches to politics and ethics that do not make recourse to a singular Nature.

The text boxes in this chapter introduce a sample of manifestoes associated with the politics of Nature and more-than-humanism

---

Box 4.1 The ecomodernist manifesto (2015)

The ecomodernist manifesto (Asafu-Adjaye et al., 2015) was published by a self-described group of ecomodernists associated with The Breakthrough Institute, a centre right think tank based in San Francisco, USA. The ecomodernists are resolutely pro-science and pro-technology. They see the diagnosis of the Anthropocene and the End of Nature as an opportunity for humans to achieve their Enlightenment destiny as the 'God Species' (Lynas, 2011), to harness the powers of science and reason to realise the modern project. In their manifesto, they promise a transition into a 'Good Anthropocene'.

The ecomodernists exemplify a rich tradition of reformist social theory that aims to decouple economic growth from the use of resources to ensure continued planetary prosperity (measured in terms of gross domestic product) while lowering environmental harm (Breewood and Garnett, 2022). This decoupling will be delivered by deploying green science and technologies (like renewable energy and nuclear power, sustainable agricultural intensification, and a shift to alternative proteins). For exemplary reports, see Stein et al. (2022) and Smith et al. (2021a).

They anticipate that the intensification of land use in some places and efficiencies in production will enable land sparing, releasing large areas for managed species introductions and wilding. Ecomodernists are antagonistic towards political projects that aim to reconcile humans and nature, being allergic to appeals to tradition or nature-based solutions (Blomqvist et al., 2015).

Their manifesto and wider writings have surprisingly little to say about power and politics, but the ecomodernists are neither neoliberal nor socialist. They advocate both government intervention and private sector innovation and leadership. They have been critiqued on political grounds in that they tend to slip into the 'species-talk' of the Anthropocene that masks differences between human social groups (Collard et al., 2016). They have also been accused of hubris, given the relative paucity of data that supports their claims of decoupling and sustainable green growth (Crist, 2016; Hamilton, 2016).

In the following sections, we review examples of more-than-human work that develop political analyses. We focus in particular on research and writing analysing the politics of materials, knowledges, and relations. In each part, we summarise a selection of key research that has influenced wider developments in the field. Our review is illustrative rather than exhaustive of all relevant work, and reference to further examples can be found in the footnotes.

4.2 A politics of materials: technologies, elements, and organisms

Having brought the human down off its pedestal, situated the mind in the body and placed bodies in their environments, some more-than-humanists have focused on the important roles played by material objects in configuring the distribution and relations of power between different human social groups and between humans and other organisms. They have become especially interested in the 'stuff of politics' or 'political matter' (Whatmore and Braun, 2010). This work is aware of the history of biological racism and environmental determinism that used appeals to nature to naturalise violence, exploitation, and inequality (see discussion at the start of Chapter 2). Instead, their approach is grounded in an ontology of becoming that allows these authors to tell nondeterministic or possibilist accounts that still do justice to the material agencies of nonhumans.

4.2.1 Infrastructure

Early work in science and technology studies was especially concerned with how scientific knowledge shapes society with often unequal social consequences. The focus was on social 'ordering' (Law, 1994) or 'scripting' (Akrich, 1992), taking a close interest in 'classification and its consequences' (Bowker and Star, 1999). Early work in this vein developed a Foucauldian concern with subjectification and governmentality to trace how scientific knowledge becomes 'performative', shaping the world in the image of the representations it presents.[2]

Jamie provides an example in his analysis of biodiversity conservation in the UK (Lorimer, 2015). Biodiversity emerged in the 1990s as a new way of understanding Nature and of doing conservation. The term sought to capture the full range of genetic, species, and habitat diversity. But as it was put into practice in conservation planning, it was scripted by the existing infrastructure for science and land management. It tended to focus on species, and for a species to be conserved, it needs to have been named, studied, and counted. It needs to feature in databases and have volunteers willing to look for it. The UK is a country of bird lovers: over 65% of all the biological records that were available to those designing biodiversity conservation in the UK in the early 2000s were about birds. The Royal Society for the Protection of Birds (RSPB) is one of the UK's largest environmental charities. They are rich, own lots of land, can mobilise thousands of volunteers and have political clout. Birds are charismatic, or at least more charismatic than most UK flora and fauna. As a result, birds feature disproportionately in UK conservation. There are good ecological reasons why saving birds helps other species. But in reality, birds do better in UK conservation because they are favoured by the historic infrastructure for wildlife science and management. Here, we see how an infrastructure becomes performative (Bowker, 2000), shaping UK nature in light of its preferences and partialities (see also Braverman, 2014; Youatt, 2008).

Subsequent work by more-than-human geographers interested in the political agency of infrastructure shifted focus to the material things involved in the everyday functioning of modern life. This interest was given early political expression in Donna Haraway's cyborg manifesto (Box 4.2).

Box 4.2   The cyborg manifesto (1985)

Donna Haraway wrote her cyborg manifesto (Haraway, 1991)[3] as a radical feminist critique of traditional feminist theory, which tended to accept an essential idea of gender identity tied to biology. She seeks to challenge forms of biological essentialism in conversation with Marxist critique of neoliberal capitalism and the then-nascent field of science studies. Her work was instrumental in unpacking the politics of Nature that we reviewed above.

Haraway starts from a cyborg ontology (Box 2.1), which is presented as a critique of modern humanism and its divides between nature and culture, mind and body, body and technology, etc. She offers the cyborg ontology as a means of blurring the boundaries between humans, animals, machines, and non-living matter. She engages with developments in the biological sciences at the time, including evolutionary theory, biotechnology, and the rise of microelectronics and computing.

Haraway offers an anti-essentialist ontology that celebrates mixtures and monsters. She does so to undermine political appeals to nature – both in terms of normative ideals of human nature that supports patriarchy (as well as nationalism, militarism, racism, and the ideal of the Capitalist subject). She also challenges the political appeals to an idealised myth of Nature as a pure Eden that underpin strands of Western Romanticism and environmentalism. She offers a figure of the cybernetic human to challenge gendered ideals of bodily purity. In the concluding words of the manifesto, Haraway quips: 'I would rather be a cyborg than a goddess' (1991, 68).

The cyborg manifesto celebrates 'the promises of monsters', making political alliance with forms and identifies that transgress simple binary divisions. She engages with the power of science fiction, or what she later terms speculative fabulation (Section 4.4 below), to imagine and prefigure other worlds and ways of living.

Although it is written as a polemic, the manifesto adopts a playful and ironic style, which makes it hard to follow in places.

As we explained in Section 2.4, urban geographers have looked at the power of infrastructure associated with energy provision, mobility, water and waste treatment, and communications (amongst others) in enabling and constraining everyday acts of citizenship. This work has revealed that where roads, paths, pipes, and cables go profoundly affects who is included and excluded from active participation in urban economic and political life. Political geographers have focused on the power of planning, architecture, and borders to shape political life, when abstract spatial visions are materialised through the construction of buildings, walls, fences, tunnels, and flyovers. This work has examined surveillance technologies – like CCTV cameras, facial recognition software, and drones – that enable powerful actors to shape the actions of others at a distance (Klauser, 2016). It explores how such technologies enable governments to control the movements of people and animals across territories and through the volume of space that sits above and below the terrestrial surface (Elden, 2013). This work attends to the power of classification, focusing on the centrality of algorithms and machine learning software to domains spanning social media to transport planning (Amoore, 2020; Adams, 2019). It explores how such software/hardware enables the 'automatic production of space' (Thrift and French, 2002), performing a material politics with limited human oversight.

Politically, this research primarily aims to educate citizens about the exclusive, scripting power of technologies. But some more activist examples, linked to the politics of multiple knowledges (see Section 4.3 below), also aim to 'hack' infrastructure to develop technologies for public engagement and empowerment (da Costa and Philip, 2008; Kirksey, 2014). For example, the sociologist Jennifer Gabrys has collaborated with designers, engineers, and urban justice activists to develop sensors that enable citizens to monitor air quality, to develop data platforms to map and analyse their data, and to 'propose action points, and circulate data stories to influence policy makers and industry' (2022, vii).

4.2.2 Geosocial formations

A second strand of work on the politics of materials explores how material resources configure the political patterns and processes that shape social life. As we explained in Section 2.5, geographers interested in the elemental have focused on the agencies of fossil fuels like coal and oil suggesting that modern life is founded on a 'gift from the Carboniferous' (Yusoff, 2013), fuelled by the combustion of fossilised plant remains. Clark and Yusoff trace the violent 'geosocial formations' (2017) of the Anthropocene through which fossil fuels were extracted, linking mining with long and violent histories of slavery, racism, and the exploitation of black bodies (Yusoff, 2018). In his book *Carbon Democracy*, the political theorist Timothy Mitchell (2011) examines how the different material properties of coal and oil gave rise to different modes of extraction and thus different concentrations of political power. He argues that because coal mining was labour intensive and required a large workforce, it gave unionised miners relative power in negotiations over employment and pay. They could down tools to disrupt supply and the circulation of capital. He suggests that the solid material properties of coal helped establish the labour movements that were so influential in 20th-century politics in Europe and North America.

In contrast, Mitchell suggests that as oil flows from the ground under pressure, it can be channelled along pipelines that are much easier to mechanise and to automate. As a consequence, fewer workers are required and their ability to disrupt production and circulation is more limited. Power and thus economic value concentrates in the hands of the sovereign or corporate owners of the resource, who are less susceptible to unionised demands. Mitchell is not suggesting that the character and distribution of fossil fuels determines global geopolitics, but he makes a compelling case for why we need to acknowledge their agency. Subsequent work has explored how forms of renewable energy – like solar and wind – which require more modest and less expensive infrastructure – might enable decentralised models of energy provision, enabling people and communities to live off-grid in potentially more egalitarian and democratic modes of social organisation (Bawaka Collective et al., 2022). Resource geographers have focused on how the material properties of different resources shape their political and economic geographies (Bakker and Bridge, 2006; Barua, 2020; Collard and Dempsey, 2013). Here, water emerges as an especially 'uncooperative commodity' (Bakker, 2003) as it is harder to bring to market, than discrete, solid materials like diamonds, for example.

Recently, geographers and environmental historians have become interested in what the historian Dipesh Chakrabarty (2009) terms 'the climate of history'. Chakrabarty criticises historians for taking the environment as a backdrop for human action and argues that a new mode of history is required for figuring elements of the environment as political actors with the power to shape diverse human futures. He is especially concerned with anticipating the disastrous futures that are anticipated to accompany the end of the Holocene and the advent of the Anthropocene. Arguably, Chakrabarty's approach is anticipated in a rich vein of work in environmental history that has examined the differential effects of past climatic and viral upheavals on society. For example, in his book *Late Victorian Holocausts*, Mike Davis (2001) traces how the conjunction of the El Nino Southern Oscillation with the instigation of colonial capitalism created famines in India, China, Brazil, and other parts of the Global South that lead to the deaths of 30–60 million people. He argues that these deaths stemmed from political and environmental causes such that they could not be explained away as 'natural' disasters.

4.2.3 Plants as agents of history

A further literature focuses on the political agencies of plants, offering revisionist accounts of the multispecies politics and ethics of domestication. Domestication narratives tend to centre human control, celebrating or bemoaning how our ancestors tamed wild species and subsumed them to human interests (Clutton-Brock, 1999). New accounts offer more reciprocal and mutualistic understandings which focus on how plants (and other organisms) domesticated us (Cassidy and Mullin, 2007; Swanson et al., 2018). For example, Michael Pollan (2001) has mapped a 'botany of desire', tracing how the tasty and/or narcotic agencies of plants like apples, chilis, and tobacco drew our hominid and human ancestors into becoming mobile vectors for their dispersal, and efficient economic actors for their careful propagation and cultivation.[4]

Such stories of planty agency are taken in a different direction by anthropologists like James Scott (2017) and Anna Tsing (2015), who argue that the biological properties of different plants help support different models of civilisation. Scott identifies a small number of what he terms 'state crops', like wheat and rice, that were central to the agricultural revolution and the rise of urban civilisation, the state, and plantation capitalism. He compares these with what he terms 'escape crops', like casava, that flourish with limited cultivation in marginal lands and thus provide succour to mobile social formations living outside of, and sometimes in opposition to, the modern state. He is not arguing that plants determine politics but offers a way of acknowledging their formative role in the histories of different civilisations. He suggests that plants become complicit in different modes of domination and liberation.[5] In a comparable analysis of the rise of palm oil plantations in West Papua, Sophie Chao (2022) suggests that 'violence reveals itself as a multispecies act' (5). A different account of planty agency is provided by work exploring the 'feral ecologies' (Barua, 2022) of weeds: plants that proliferate through the networks of globalisation and flourish in the disturbed landscapes of modern agriculture (Tsing, 2017; Tsing et al., 2019). These plants disrupt the logics of property, agricultural control, and productivity, as well as bringing harm to local ecologies (Atchison and Head, 2013; Barker, 2010).

4.3 A politics of multiple knowledges

A second more-than-human approach to politics and ethics works to identify where marginalised subjects and their knowledges have been excluded, and to actively promote their inclusion through participatory models of research and activism. This approach centres subjects and knowledges marginalised by the narrow modern figure of the human as a white, male, straight, able-bodied, and rational subject. It builds from the knowledge practices of the more-than-human researchers who engaged with publics to redistribute expertise that we encountered in the previous chapter (Section 3.4). We focus initially on work with marginal human subjects and then turn to work that has centred animals as political actors.

4.3.1 Public Engagement with Science and Technology (PEST)

In Chapter 1, we identified how a range of health and environmental crises in the second half of the 20th century engendered distrust amongst Western citizens in the objectivity of science and raised doubts about the unconditional benefits of science and technology. This led some citizens and their advocacy organisations to propose alternative visions of human development and human-environmental relations founded on different knowledge practices, causing the proliferation of knowledge controversies. While some scientists and politicians resisted these shifts, fearing a 'flight from science and reason', other social scientists have welcomed knowledge controversies as generative political events, due to their potential to both 'slow down' and 'open up' decision-making processes (Whatmore, 2009). They explore how events like a flood, an epidemic, or local pollution 'bring a public into being' (Marres, 2005).[6]

These interests in emergent publics and knowledge politics underpin the vibrant field of applied academic research for Public Engagement in Science and Technology (PEST) (Chilvers and Kearnes, 2015) that designs and applies methodologies to 'bring the sciences into democracy' (Latour, 2004a). The sociologist of science Michel Callon and his colleagues (2009) have traced the emergence and development of PEST (see summary of models and methods in Table 4.1). They suggest that early versions were premised on a 'public education model', or what is more disparagingly termed the 'deficit model'. Here, scientists work to educate a singular and ill-informed public through a one-way exchange of knowledge, in the hope that more science and reason would bring consensus. Science and scientists remain unchanged in this process. The limitations of this approach led to the emergence of the 'public debate model'. This accepts that scientific knowledge should remain provisional until all stakeholders and experience-based experts have had a chance to contribute and debate. A third, and more radical alternative, is the 'co-production of knowledge model'. Here, publics become participants in the design and conduct of the research. They are involved 'upstream', early in the research process, rather than being the 'downstream' recipients of the knowledge generated. In this model, scientists help nascent publics come into being around an issue, enable dialogue to slow down the processes of scientific reasoning and decision-making, and continually put scientific and other expert knowledges at risk. The flood risk mapping project that we introduced in the previous chapter (Section 3.4) offers a compelling example of this final model of coproduction.

More-than-humanists have been at the forefront of developing PEST methodologies, working in collaboration with scientists and their technologies to explore urban pollution (Gabrys, 2022), domestic hygiene (Greenhough

Table 4.1 Models and methods for Public Engagement in Science and Technology

Model		Public involvement	Expert involvement	Example methods
Public education (deficit model)		Learning from watching, listening, and viewing lectures, media, exhibits, etc.	Experts serve as advisers and provide expertise	Public lecture or newspaper article
		Asking questions of experts and interactive inquiry learning	Experts actively present their expertise to the public	Public consultations Focus groups
	Upstream	Consultation and sharing views and knowledge	Experts work to become skilled and informed communicators	Citizen juries Citizen science
Public debate		Deliberation with other participants and group problem solving	Experts welcome and value participant inputs and direction	Competency groups
	Downstream	Participants produce recommendations or reports	Experts act on participant input and direction	Participatory Action Research
Coproduction		Participants frame the research agenda	Experts defer to the research priorities of participants	

et al., 2018; Lorimer et al., 2019), and the soil microbiome (Granjou and Phillips, 2019), to give a few examples. They have also collaborated with artists to develop art-science methodologies for engaging publics using methods ranging from taxidermy, to bioart, to knitting to explore topics ranging from climate change, to animal testing, to resource extraction (for reviews, see Hawkins, 2017; Hawkins, 2015; Price and Hawkins, 2018). For example, the cultural geographer Sasha Engelmann (2020) has collaborated with the artist Tomas Saraceno and his studio to experiment with new means of sensing atmospheric forces through public performance artworks with a weather balloon.[7] In other examples, more-than-humanists have worked alongside lay experts likes chefs, nurses, farmers, and vets to amplify public concerns around a range of health and environmental issues (Davies et al., 2020; Greenhough and Roe, 2019; Sariola, 2021; Smith et al., 2021b). Finally, as we explored in Box 3.2, more-than-humanists have harnessed the potential of social media and digital technologies to bring new publics into being around issues, including urban conservation (Kirksey et al., 2018; Turnbull et al., 2023) and rural social exclusion (Dodsworth, 2024).

In general terms, Public Engagement with Science and Technology offers a very different imagination of the relationships between science and politics to the modern settlement that we outlined in Figure 1.4. We illustrate this in Figure 4.1. Here, (i) science is taken off its pedestal; (ii) publics are differentiated and recognised as having expertise; (iii) the flow of information between publics and scientists becomes two-way; and (iv) discussion

Figure 4.1 A new imagination of the relationships between science, politics, and publics.

centres on 'matters of concern', rather than closed down 'matters of fact' (after Latour, 2004a).

4.3.2 Indigenous and neurodiverse knowledges

In most of these examples of PEST, the collaborating academics share social and epistemic characteristics with their participating publics. For example, in the flood risk mapping case, the participating lay experts spoke the same language, were well-educated, and shared a basic ontology of rivers drawn from hydrology. This science served as a common epistemology for political action. Academics were working with marginalised subjects, but they were not all that marginal. A more radical politics is offered by a second strand of work by geographers engaging with publics marked by more profound social and epistemic difference to the humanist norm.

One example is offered by the collaborations between more-than-human geographers and indigenous peoples, like the Bawaka Collective that we encountered in the previous chapter (Box 3.4). This project, and others like it, involve collaborations that seek to provide better knowledge (in this case richer descriptions of place), while also engaging with and empowering citizens who have long been denigrated and marginalised in settler colonial societies like Australia. They also seek to find ways of including and empowering nonhumans as research participants.[8] And finally, they aim to 'decolonise the academy' by addressing the politics of knowledge production within geography and other disciplines. For Bruno Latour (2018), such engagements with indigenous knowledge practices are imperative as Western societies find ways of coming 'down to Earth' and facing up to the challenges of climate change. Latour argues that in the Anthropocene we are all experiencing the 'condition of dispossession' of which indigenous people are the experts by virtue of 400 years of colonisation, and we should learn from them by 'becoming indigenous' ourselves. We reflect on the challenges to this provocative assertion in the following chapter, in light of wider discussions about decolonising academic research (Section 5.2).

A different set of examples are offered by more-than-human geographers documenting the knowledges and experiences of disabled people (Hall and Wilton, 2017). For example, research on neurodiversity and autism spectrum disorder, some of which is autobiographical, has mapped and contested the marginal place of autistic people within geography and society more generally (Judge, 2018). It shows how neurodiverse knowledges and experiences offer unique and valuable more-than-human perspectives on social and environmental relations – focusing in particular on connections with nonhuman subjects (Davidson and Smith, 2009). One example is the writing and advocacy of the autistic animal behaviour researcher Temple Grandin. In her book *Animals in Translation*, Grandin (Grandin and Johnson, 2006) explains how her neurological difference enables her to achieve relational sensory proximity with cattle – she claims to be able to 'think like a cow'.[9] So effective is her method that she has been employed to redesign US slaughterhouses to reduce animal fear and thus improve animal welfare.[10]

4.3.3 Political animals

This interest in engaging with marginalised people and their knowledges takes a different form in strands of animal geography, which seek to include animals as political subjects. Early work emerged from the concerns of social and cultural geographers in the 1980s with the socio-spatial processes through which groups of people became 'in' or 'out of place' (Philo and Wilbert, 2000). Animal geographers took animals as 'another other', subject to the same sort of disciplinary practices that map who belongs where. For example, they examined the place of urban animals, noting how cities are commonly understood as archetypal human spaces, centres of civilisation in contrast to rural or wild spaces where animals are seen to belong (Philo, 1995). They found that urban animals – of which there are many – are out of place in the city – and they imagined alternative visions of the city as a 'zoopolis' (Wolch, 1998) to recognise the place of animals and to work with urban animal activists, planners, and architects to make cities more hospitable to animal life (Barua and Sinha, 2022).

The interest in animal spaces developed through the 2000s into a concern with (i) animal governmentality and (ii) animal biopolitics, amidst the wider interest in geography in Foucault's theorisations of how human bodies, subjects, and populations are shaped in modern societies (Chrulew and Wadiwel, 2016). Animal governmentality describes the processes through which humans train individual animals into desired animal subjects. Geographers focused on the ethics of training pets and working animals, especially dogs after the publication of Donna Haraway's companion species manifesto (Box 4.3) (Smith et al., 2021b), and the disciplining of livestock like dairy cattle, exploring their interactions with technology like milking robots (Holloway, 2007). Others explored how so-called wild animals are disciplined to perform

> **Box 4.3   Companion species manifesto (2003)**
>
> Donna Haraway wrote this manifesto as a precursor to her book length appeal for new models of 'multispecies flourishing' in *When Species Meet* (Haraway, 2008). She draws on her life experience of living with dogs, and in particular of dog agility racing with Roland (an Aussie-mix) and Cayenne Pepper (a pure-bred Aussie). She describes the close, affective, and skilful relationships and forms of interspecies communication this involves. The companion species manifesto builds on the cyborg manifesto in that it seeks to further challenge the modern human-animal binary, taking dogs as 'subjects' and as 'significant forms of otherness' – not 'furry children', different to humans – but nonetheless deserving of ethical and political status.
>
> Haraway traces the modes of governmentality and forms of biopolitics associated with canine domestication, breeding, and pet-keeping. She presents companion species as a non-innocent relationship and notes how humans and dogs are deeply entangled in historical relations that are often marked with violence – including colonial violence. She encourages researchers and activists to 'stay with the trouble', following the political and ethical tensions involved in securing multispecies flourishing, aware that the flourishing of some is always conditional on the suffering or deaths of others.
>
> Critics of the manifesto question Haraway's own positionality as a wealthy, White woman and her relative neglect of questions of race and social class (Nast, 2005), though they do feature prominently in the manifesto! Others take issue with the focus on affirmative, proximal encounters with charismatic species that are big like us and encourage a focus on awkward relations with species further from an anthropomorphic norm (Ginn et al., 2014), as well as making space for species best served by not relating with humans (Giraud, 2019). They take issue with Haraway for not taking a strong line against animal agriculture (Weisberg, 2009).

in zoos (Braverman, 2012; Rice et al., 2021) or to avoid conflict with farmers in free-ranging settings (Morizot, 2022). Taken together, this approach traces how the bodies, behaviours, and affective atmospheres of animals are shaped, often with negative consequences for animal health and welfare.

Work on animal biopolitics shifts the political focus from the individual to a collective of animals – normally a herd, breed, or species – to critically examine the scientific and management processes that govern reproductive dynamics to determine which animals are 'made to live' and which are killed or 'let die' (Foucault, 2010; Lemke, 2011; Srinivasan et al., 2020). Geographers have compared common modes of animal biopolitics, including different forms of agriculture, biosecurity, conservation, laboratory research, and pet-keeping (Biermann and Mansfield, 2014; Hetherington, 2020; Hinchliffe et al., 2016; Holloway et al., 2009; Srinivasan, 2013). They have explored the 'necropolitics' of killing animals in agriculture and conservation (Margulies, 2019; Sneegas, 2022). Their work reveals the 'ontological politics' (Mol, 1999) that is generated by conflicts between different human understandings of what animals are and how they ought to be treated. For example, those concerned with animal welfare look at a cow and see a subjective individual, while those interested in food production might see meat, and those interested in conservation might see either a representative of a rare breed or a tool for grazing (Lorimer and Driessen, 2013).

Meanwhile, a strand of work on the 'beastly places' of animals aims to witness animals' experiences and to centre the political claims of animals, especially those caught up in modern modes of captivity and agriculture. Geographers working as part of the wider field of *critical* animal studies draw on a range of moral philosophy to argue for both the rights and the welfare of animals (McCance, 2013; Gillespie and Collard, 2015). This work has documented, often in graphic and harrowing detail, the terrifying and painful experience of animals subject to the most egregious examples of careless human management. For example, in her book *Animal Traffic*, Rosemary Collard (2020) recounts the experience of animals caught and trafficked for the exotic pet trade, attending to how these animals are first severed from their ecological and familial bonds to become a commodity and then, once rescued, subjected to human aversion therapy to prepare them for their return to the wild. Likewise, Katie Gillespie (2018) offers an empathetic biography of one US dairy cow tracing its life as it moves through farms, the auction yard, the slaughterhouse, and the rendering plant. This work is careful not to simply blame agricultural workers for this mistreatment. Instead, it attends to conjoined exploitation and 'shared suffering' (Haraway, 2008) of human and animal bodies.[11]

Other work has focused on how some animals 'transgress' human efforts to discipline their behaviours, centring 'feral' animals living in collectives and in situations in which they have some autonomy. One example was given by the research we introduced in Chapter 3 on the urban animals' geographies of macaques in Delhi (Barua and Sinha, 2017), which affirms efforts by some urban residents to make the city more hospitable to these simian interlopers by nurturing the abilities of monkeys to adapt to urban life. This work exemplifies Haraway's politics and ethics of multispecies flourishing, where the normative commitment is towards enabling happy futures for 'significant forms of difference', without closing down the possibility that life will become otherwise.[12]

Work in this area has responded to criticisms of the companion species manifesto to expand the political scope of animal geography beyond a focus on charismatic beings that are big like us. It pushes down Aristotle's 'great chain of being', turning to insects, plants, and microbes to think through the challenges of flourishing. This has required a closer attention to what Franklin Ginn et al. (2014) describe as 'awkward' relations and encounters based on feeling of unease and disgust. Ginn provides a compelling illustration in an analysis of how gardeners relate to, and learn to live with, the slugs that threaten to eat their vegetables (Ginn, 2014), while Jamie has explored the challenges of flourishing alongside parasitic worms in the example mentioned in Chapter 3 (Lorimer, 2016).

4.4 A politics of relations and processes

The final strand of work on more-than-human politics and ethics focuses on relations and processes. It is concerned with the trajectories of becoming that configure subjective and collective experience, and with finding ways of living well and living justly with often unruly biological and geological processes. We describe three strands of this work that focus on human becoming, ecological relations, and geomorphic processes.

4.4.1 Human becoming and the politics of affect

As we explained in Chapter 2, non-representational, feminist, and health geographers all draw attention to how the affective dimensions of human life are configured through relations with technologies, materials, and environments. They explore how collective affects bubble up through the churning processes of political life, in response to events as diverse as earthquakes, financial crises, or sporting events. They examine how affect is governed to create political subjects, tracing how collective affects are engineered and managed in contemporary politics under various forms of government and market intervention.[13] They are interested in the political role of 'affective atmospheres', where an atmosphere describes a collective affective experience in place that is produced by an arrangement of bodies and materials, often requiring control over ephemeral and ethereal elements like the air and the weather, as well as the use of sound, light, taste, and smell.

For example, in her book *National Affects*, the political geographer Angharad Stephens (2022) examines the affective dimensions of national identify. In one compelling chapter, she traces the 'happy' affective atmosphere that bubbled up in the UK around the events of the 2012 London Olympic Games and explores how these events were carefully curated to contribute to a cosmopolitan sense of everyday nationalism in the UK. Similarly, Sean Carter and Derek McCormack (2006) have examined the 'affective logics' that shape popular representations of geopolitics on film, offering a close reading of *Black Hawk Down*, a film about US military involvement in Somalia in 1993. They explore how the film produces and amplifies collective affects that justify US military intervention and a wider politics of imperialism.[14]

Others have explored the politics of affect in relation to human-environment relations. Here, more-than-human geographers were influenced by the writings of the political theorist Jane Bennett (2001) and her book *The Enchantment of Modern Life*. Bennett disputes the popular idea that modern, urban life and scientific research necessarily lead to alienation and argues for the vital place of affects like wonder, hope, joy, and curiosity in catalysing an ethical sensibility for human and nonhuman others. This proposal, alongside Haraway's concept of response-ability that we encountered in the last chapter, has inspired a range of more-than-human scholarship developing affirmative, relational frameworks for human-nonhuman ethics.

Jamie provides an example in his work on 'nonhuman charisma' (Lorimer, 2007) that we introduced in Chapter 2. He focused on what makes environmentalists and animal enthusiasts concerned about the nonhuman world and argues that it is generally not the rational calculation of species loss or extinction that propels many people to get involved in nature conservation but formative affective experiences with certain wildlife that are amplified by the affective atmospheres of popular media. Here, the positive charisma of some 'flagship species' like pandas, tigers, and elephants has helped build public powerful political and economic support for wildlife, as well as motivating people to participate in citizen science initiatives. At the same time, the negative charisma of snakes, spiders, and many insects has made it harder to build public support for their plight.

Bruce Braun (2015) links this interest in a politics of becoming to the ethos of experimentation that we introduced in Section 3.3. He traces how a range of more-than-human scholars have turned to experimentation in response to a shared dissatisfaction with the predominant relationship between the knowledge practices of the critical social sciences and the worlds that they critique. He picks up on Bruno Latour's argument that social science critique has 'run out of steam' (Latour, 2004b) (Box 4.4): that it is limited by a

---

Box 4.4   The compositionist manifesto (2010)

This manifesto was written by Bruno Latour (Latour, 2010) to outline the principles of an approach to politics grounded in actor-network-theory (see Sections 2.4 and 3.2).

Latour is responding to a concern that the methods that he and his fellow science studies scholars developed to trace the construction of scientific knowledge are being used by climate sceptics and other conspiracy theorists to cast doubt on the truth of science. He is also developing his criticisms that critique 'runs of steam' and is of little use for social and environmental politics when it does not offer alternatives.

He wants to avoid the nihilism and epistemic relativism that can result from a position that argues that all knowledge is constructed (and is thus equally valid), and to provide grounds for understanding how an affirmative critical politics based on scientific knowledge might best be 'composed'. Here, Latour develops his critique of the antipolitics of appeals to a singular Nature set outside of society (Figures 1.4 and 4.1). He argues that in a multinatural world, politics needs to nurture and affirm emergent processes, rather than aim to reveal transcendent principles.

In this manifesto and subsequent writings on the politics of climate change (Latour, 2018), he aims to establish political grounds for composing well: for building the necessary collective of actors who will

---

deliberate to decide on a problem through compromise. He encourages social scientists to attend to how claims about the world are assembled, tracing the robustness of the connections they draw, and the range of voices they consult. He is channelling the political imperative we reviewed above of bringing the sciences into democracy.

Latour's manifesto and his take on politics has been criticised from several different positions (which we review in the following chapter). Many of these share a concern that he fails to attend to the solidity of some actor-networks that lead to persistent structural disadvantages and inequality. While others argue that he has an insufficient grasp of the agonistic nature of the political and the limitations of deliberative democracy based on discussion and compromise (Wainwright, 2005).

persistent tone of cynical, pessimistic doom and a frequent failure to offer viable alternatives or even to 'read for difference' (Gibson-Graham, 2020). The geographers Tara Woodyer and Hilary Geoghegan (2013) argue that this negativity generates a 'dulling and deadening apprehension' of the world. Rather than inspiring action and the application of knowledge, this leaves us 'feeling helpless, depressed and defeated in the presence of unrelenting forces' (196). In response, they advocate cultivating a wider array of more 'affirmative' or 'playful' styles of knowing and engaging with the world. They draw on Bennett's work on enchantment to encourage: 'an open, ready-to-be-surprised "disposition" before, in, with the world' (195) and suggest that this shift would 'encourage a less repressed, more cheerful way of engaging' (195) with geographical relations.

This focus on affirmative styles of critique has been developed extensively by the cultural geographers we encountered above, who have studied, collaborated with, and in some cases become artists, to explore the political potential of artistic modes of experimentation (Hawkins, 2017; Hawkins, 2020). For Donna Haraway (2016), this focus on creativity and experimentation requires us to play close attention to questions of narrative and storytelling.[15] Here, Haraway and others in the environmental humanities have turned to science fiction, exploring the epistemic potential of existing work for imagining alternative futures, and engaging in their own creative experiments in what Haraway terms 'speculative fabulation': writing new stories to prefigure possible future social and ecological relations (for examples and reflections, see Whyte, 2018).

4.4.2 Less-than-human geographies

This affirmative focus on enchantment has been greeted with scepticism by geographers like Chris Philo (2017) who advocates a focus on 'less-than-human geographies', an approach not concerned with:

> What enhances the human, distributes it, grows its capacities, amplifying its affective reach and involvement, adding to the human in a manner that enchants, enthrals, enlivens. But, rather, it would be an approach alert to what diminishes the human, cribs and confines it, curtails or destroys its capacities, silencing its affective grip, banishing its involvements: not what renders it lively, but what cuts away at that life, to the point of, including and maybe beyond death.
>
> (2017, 258)

Philo's appeal has been taken up in more-than-human work examining the relations, processes, and affective experiences of range of health and social conditions, including addiction (Marković, 2019), boredom (Anderson, 2004), homelessness (Cloke et al., 2008), immobility (Waight and Yin, 2021), and pain (Bissell, 2011). It informs studies of the collective affective experiences of the 'slow violence' caused by chronic exposure to environmental toxicity as well as of the intergenerational transmission of harm (Lora-Wainwright, 2013). While political and feminist geographers have drawn on affect theory to critique the lived experience of 'cruel optimism' (Berlant, 2011) associated with precarious work in contemporary capitalism and the grief experienced by the losses associated with the biodiversity crisis (Head, 2016). The aim here is to recognise the transformative potential of negative affects, relegated by the ascendent focus on affirmation and enchantment (Dekeyser and Jellis, 2021; Falcon, 2023).

4.4.3 Ecological relations and the politics of biosecurity

A second literature shifts focus from human becomings to look at the ecological processes and relations that underpin political efforts to deliver biosecurity. Here, biosecurity refers to the protection of human, animal, and environmental health through interventions into the dynamics of ecological systems (Barker, 2015). This work builds from the literatures on animal biopolitics and plants as agents of history that we explored above, but here the target of biopolitics shifts from optimising animal breeds or populations towards securing the desired circulation of life and energy in ecological systems.

Much of this work has focused on political responses to the social and ecological harms that emerge from within the relations of intensive modern agriculture, urbanisation, and the networks of globalisation that accelerate the movement of unwanted microbes, plants, and animals. Even before the COVID-19 pandemic, geographers were examining the governance of zoonotic disease, demonstrating the risks of globalised intensive animal agriculture and the deficiencies of models of biosecurity premised on securing national borders. Steve Hinchliffe argued that biosecurity policy needs to focus on the networked geographies of disease and the promiscuous circulation of microbes along both the vectors of host organisms – like migratory birds or mobile wild boar – as well as along the routes of global trade and airplane travel. He argues that biosecurity needs to work in the topologically varied 'borderlands' (Hinchliffe et al., 2013), rather than only at the frontiers of the bounded nation state.

Similar arguments have been developed by geographers examining efforts to control the growing emergence and proliferation of agricultural pests and invasive species. Important strands of this work have focused on the multispecies politics of the industrial plantations that produce a substantial quantity of the world's food. Anna Tsing (2017) and Julie Guthman (2019) have traced how the ecological simplification associated with these monocultures, coupled with their dependence on artificial fertilisers, herbicides, and pesticides, not only reduces biological diversity and ecological functionality but creates ideal conditions for the emergence of drug-resistant organisms. They explore how the degraded ecologies of the plantation and the networks of agricultural trade enable 'invasive' species to proliferate and become established in different parts of the world. They link these processes to the anthropocentrism of modern agriculture and to the ecological irrationality of capitalist agri-business, and they flag the shared suffering inflicted on the often extremely politically and economically marginalised people employed as workers on these plantations, tracing the extractive relations of the plantation to longer colonial histories of forced migration and slavery.

A further literature has focused on the biosecurity practices associated with varied processes of ecological restoration, recovery, or rewilding. Jamie has documented a wider 'probiotic turn' (Lorimer, 2020) that is underway in the management of life across different domains of health and environmental management (see Table 4.2). In different ways, these interventions seek to restore degraded or 'dysbiotic' ecologies by intervening into their dynamics. Often this involves 'using life to manage life' by returning specific 'keystone species' and nonhuman 'ecological engineers' like fast-growing trees, cattle, and beavers or beneficial microbes that have the leverage to modulate ecosystem functions. These interventions span agriculture, conservation, as well as human and animal health. They seek to deliver a diverse range of ecosystem functions and services, including carbon sequestration and water and waste management in the wider environment, to immunity or digestion in the human body.

Taken together, this work identifies the emergence of an 'environmental' mode of biopower that seeks to govern the dynamics of ecological processes (Anderson, 2012; Lorimer, 2017). It explores how environmental management in the Anthropocene involves the choreography of ecological relations, tracing the risks of an antibiotic model and critically examining the merits of probiotic alternatives that seek to deliver political ecological resurgence. It links this interest to a wider enthusiasm for One Health and Planetary Health amongst policymakers looking to fold together human, animal, and environmental security (for critical discussions, see Hinchliffe, 2015; Lezaun and Porter, 2015). Work on biosecurity identifies a multispecies politics in the probiotic turn: it traces how these interventions into the circulation of life involve a great deal of killing, alongside sophisticated models for restricting the movement and reproduction of a small number of keystone and pathological organisms. It cautions that although 'nature-based solutions' (Seddon, 2022) may lead to more abundant futures, they could also make the future of different lifeforms conditional on the ecological labour they perform (Lorimer, 2020). While Stephanie Wakefield (2020) has examined how the emerging political economy informed by this systems ontology enables powerful actors to put a price on ecological services such that they are made amenable for market modes of environmental governance.

4.4.4 Ontopolitics, radical asymmetry, and living in the ruins

A final strand of the more-than-human literature on politics and ethics shifts focus from the biological to human relations with the geological and the geomorphic. This work builds from the interest in geosocial formations, that we introduced in Section 4.2, to explore situations where people are forced

Table 4.2 The probiotic turn (from Lorimer, 2020)

		Antibiotic model	Blowback	Probiotic alternative
Micro	Health	Antibiotic drugs, Caesarean sections, low rates of breast feeding	Loss of microbial diversity. Dysbiosis and epidemics of absence: rise in allergic, inflammatory, and auto-immune disease. Antibiotic resistance and new pathogens.	Probiotic and prebiotic supplements, new birthing practices, biome restoration, faecal microbiota transplant.
	Hygiene	Water purification, urbanisation, antimicrobials, limited contact with animals, smaller families, clean-living		Probiotic cleaning products, the promotion of dirt, and contact with domestic animals
	Diet	Pasteurisation, ultra-processed food, demise of live food		Raw, live, fermented, and paleo diets and forms of food processing
Macro	Agriculture and forestry	Use of pesticides and herbicides, artificial fertilisers, antibiotics in livestock, intensive management systems	Biodiversity loss, invasive species, zoonotic and other diseases, loss of soil fertility, loss of crop diversity, loss of ecosystem services, pesticide resistance, inability to adapt to climate change.	Biological pest control, regenerative agriculture, bioremediation, animal probiotics.
	Conservation	Preservation of low-intensity agricultural systems in small nature reserves	Habitat fragmentation, loss of adaptive capacity, trophic downgrading, extinction.	Rewilding, back-breeding, de-domestication. De-extinction.
	Environmental management	Rationalisation of environmental processes and disturbance regimes e.g. in rivers, coasts, fire, pest control	Loss of resilience, increased risks of natural disaster. Extreme events.	Rewetting, managed retreat, naturalistic erosion, and fire management
	Planetary management	Resource use that exceeds planetary boundaries: carbon, nitrogen, water	Climate change: global warming, extreme weather, sea level rise, positive feedbacks	Geo-engineering and nature-based climate solutions: ocean seeding, forest planting, rewilding the tundra and other systems

to come to terms with the radical asymmetry of the Earth. Much of this work starts from a critique of the Anthropocene visions for planetary steward-ship through acts of geo-engineering that are advocated by ecomodernists (Box 4.1). Critics like Nigel Clark and Anna Tsing see these as both anthro-pocentric and hubristic, too linked to modern dreams of mastery and at risk of ignoring the lived experience of those already living in the ruins of the modern humanist project. Instead, they see the apocalyptic futures pre-dicted to accompany climate change and ecological collapse as inevitable and develop politics and ethics for surviving in the ruins or even 'learning to die' (Scranton, 2015) in the Anthropocene.

As such, the emphasis shifts from different models of biopolitics and dreams of the control over life to 'ontopolitics' (Chandler, 2018): ways of learning to adapt to the unruly and unpredictable changes of an unravelling planetary system. An example of this work is given by Nigel Clark (2011) in his book *Inhuman Nature,* which explores the lived experience of a range of often marginalised peoples living through, and in the aftermath of, geologi-cal events like earthquakes, tsunamis, and hurricanes. Clark traces how those living in the ruins left by these disasters cope with their vulnerability to the radical asymmetry of the earth, and how, in some cases, develop new forms of generosity and hospitality with fellow survivors. Clark's example resonates with the writings of Anna Tsing (2015) who explores the precarious lives of the marginal labourers who make a living picking matsutake mushrooms (for a lucrative market in Japan) that often flourish in the ruined landscapes left in the aftermath of industrial forestry in different parts of the world. Elizabeth Povinelli (2016) helps connect this interest in ontopolitics with indigenous experiences in her writings on the survival strategies of Aboriginal peo-ples living under violent regimes of resource extraction in Australia. While Kathryn Yusoff examines the intersections between race, the geological and resource extraction in her writings on the inhumanities (Box 4.5).

Box 4.5   The inhumanities (2021)

The British geographer Kathryn Yusoff (2021) offers the inhumanities as an approach that foregrounds the centrality of race to the politics of environmental transformation in the Anthropocene. She is concerned that discussions of the politics of the Anthropocene, of the elemental, and of geopower have not done enough to challenge the legacies of humanism which, in the words of Sylvia Wynter, lead to the 'systemic inferiorization of black and of other non-white peoples of the earth' (Wynter, 2000 in Yusoff, 2021, 663). Yusoff seeks to decolonise environmental politics.

She flags the degree to which the proceeds from slavery – and the money paid to slave owners when the slave trade was legally ended – funded the industrial capitalism that drove the Anthropocene Great Acceleration, as well as funding the scientific institutions that produced knowledge about the human and the geological. She argues that the coming into existence of the modern ideal of the human was often premised on the systematic dehumanisation of non-white peoples.

She outlines the aim of her project (to be expanded in a forthcoming book) as the

> Unearthing of the very ground that materially constitutes the figure of the human through an examination of what might be termed the geologies of race. Geologies of race is a way to understand the conjoined material praxis of colonial terra – and subject – forming, its geosocial relation … and its legacies in the present.
>
> (2021, 664)

To do so, she develops a theory of 'political geology' tracing how the science, economics, and practice of geology was entangled in histories of colonialism and slavery through the extractive economies of mining. She draws on the work of black geographers examining the extractive relations of mines and plantations and explains that

> As geologic classification of earth minerals made matter as value, it also captured enslaved subjects in the brutal calculative enclosure of the inhuman as chattel … technologies of race are equally geologies of race, whereby metaphysical designations have geophysical effects, establishing antiblack and brown gravities as the affective architecture of extraction.
>
> (2021, 666)

She explains that her approach is concerned with both social and ecological harm as 'the inhumanities puts the kinship between the extraction of bodies and the extraction of earth at the core of its concerns about the possibilities and potentialities of lives, conjoining genocide and ecocide as tenants in the colonial project' (2021, 667). And she sees the inhumanities as an intellectual project to be institutionalised in academic disciplines and universities, suggesting that

> Rather than the environmental and geohumanities ... "we" might better be organized around the institutes of the inhumanities. The inhumanities registers a commitment to dismantling the humanist subject and the white supremacy that characterized its geographic project of the differentiation of subjects and earth.
>
> (2021: 672)

Kathryn Yusoff holds the title of Professor of Inhuman Geography at Queen Mary, University of London.

David Chandler (2018) differentiates three types of ontopolitics in the Anthropocene, which he terms 'mapping', 'sensing', and 'hacking'. He identifies sensing as an approach focused on responding to emerging events through the collection and correlation of real-time data. Sensing is not concerned with causation or even prevention but with minimising impacts or disturbance. Chandler argues that its primary focus is on 'homeostasis' or the preservation of the status quo. He argues that this is the most established mode of governance in the Anthropocene found for example in data-driven approaches to wildlife conservation that focus on calculating and managing extinction risk or in approaches to biosecurity geared towards the surveillance of undesired viral, microbial, and animal movements and the anticipation of potential epidemic events.

For Chandler, mapping describes governance practices that seek to model the immanent drivers of complex, emergent events. Mapping approaches do not share sensing's turn away from causation. Instead, they assume that 'causality is non-linear and that knowledge is not universal' (2018, 21). Mapping does not abandon the possibility of explanation but shifts from the pursuit of universal laws to focus on how the same external stimulus can produce different responses depending on the internal relations of a particular ecology. In other words, mapping examines the topology – or the shape and intensity – of these internal relations. Chandler explicitly links the rise of mapping to the institutionalisation of systems biology and resilience thinking in policy making. Finally, for Chandler, hacking 'seeks to enable the creativity of the Anthropocene rather than merely resist it or limit its effects' (2018, 23). He suggests that hacking involves the 'experimental' approach to dealing with uncertainty that we introduced in Section 3.3, in which governing occurs in the absence of the reference conditions of a singular Nature.

4.5 The normative commitments of more-than-humanism

In this final section, we draw out three normative commitments that infuse many of the examples of more-than-human politics and ethics that we have reviewed in this chapter. We do not claim that all our authors would ascribe to all these claims. The commitments are:

- To an ethics of care for entangled relations;
- To conversing (carefully) with a diversity of subjects;
- To a politics of connecting (carefully) with a world of becoming.

4.5.1 An ethics of care

A commitment to care (and similar concepts, such as compassion, curiosity, enchantment, friendship, and love) has become common in more-than-human scholarship in the last two decades. Care is a word with several meanings: it describes an attachment, liking or concern for something or someone else; it means taking time and giving thought to a relationship; and it also means being curious and perhaps even troubled about an encounter with the world. We see concerns with care expressed in Donna Haraway's (2008) appeal for a sense of 'response-ability' towards nonhuman others, in Vincianne Despret's (2004) accounts of how ethologists 'learn to be affected' by the world, in Steve Hinchliffe's (2008) appeal for a care-full mode of political ecological research, and in Jane Bennett's (2001) popular manifesto for finding 'enchantment' in modern life.

163

Maria Puig de la Bellacasa is a central figure in this centring of care. In her book *Matters of Care* (2017), she borrows from the long tradition of feminist care ethics to develop a more-than-human care ethics. Thom van Dooren (2014) provides a helpful summary of her approach, suggesting that care is simultaneously 'a vital affective state, an ethical obligation and a practical labour' (de la Bellacasa, 2012 in van Dooren, 2014, 291), and he goes on to detail these three facets:

> As an *affective* state, caring is an embodied phenomenon, the product of intellectual and emotional competencies: to care is to be affected by another, to be emotionally at stake in them in some way. As an *ethical* obligation, to care is to become subject to another, to recognise an obligation to look after another. Finally, as a *practical* labour, caring requires more from us than abstract well wishing, it requires that we get involved in some concrete way, that we *do* something (wherever possible) to take care of another.
>
> (2014, 291)

Much more-than-human work affirms care as an alternative to the dispassionate and anthropocentric ethics that follows from the modern nature-society binary and the figure of the objective, rational human subject. Care is about recognising our entanglements with the world, about noticing how we are always and inescapably in relation with others, and about appreciating that these relations impose obligations towards living well to enable multispecies flourishing or conviviality.

But this work also acknowledges that an ethics of care is never innocent, that it can never be abstracted from often violent and unequal historical relations and from the antagonism that characterises everyday ecological interactions. As van Dooren puts it, in this framing, care is 'grounded in all of the "inescapable troubles of interdependent existences," and can offer no guarantee of a "smooth harmonious world"' (2014, 293). Analysis has focused on the 'violent care' involved in various modes of biopolitics geared towards securing the flourishing of some desired animal, species, or ecological configuration at the expense of those whose lives must be constrained or ended to make this flourishing possible.[16]

Here, van Dooren argues that an ethics of care becomes a mode of critique, where in the context of discussions of the Anthropocene, being care-full involves recognising the differential human responsibilities for the world as it is, and for the worlds to come. In so doing, Bruce Braun (2004) argues an ethics of care avoids the 'nostalgic politics of purity' associated with models of environmentalism grounded in the protection of wilderness that we introduced in Section 4.1, where the quality of wildness is solely linked to the degree of human absence, and which 'fights any and all transformations in the name of recovering a prior essence and a lost unity between humans and non-humans' (271). But care as critique also avoids the nihilism of some modes of posthumanism that assume that after the End of Nature anything goes, that 'any and all experimentation is acceptable' (271) regardless of its ethical or political connotations. Advocates suggest that care in this register offers an ethics and a politics better equipped for the novel ecologies of the Anthropocene. It provides the ethical grounds for Haraway's 'cyborg' and 'companion species' manifestoes and, in Latour's (2011) terms, it enables us to learn to 'love our monsters'.

4.5.2 Conversing (carefully)

The first commitment to care informs a second commitment to political processes that make room for listening to and conversing with a diversity of voices (or forms of nonhuman non-vocal expression). This normative political commitment flows from the participatory praxis of engaging publics and of redistributing expertise that we reviewed in Sections 3.4 and 4.3. This ethos is given concrete expression in the range of approaches to PEST (see Table 4.1), exemplified in Sarah Whatmore et al.'s competency groups, in which different scientific experts worked in collaboration with lay experts and relevant stakeholders to research and deliberate flood risk and to co-produce new management approaches. It is also given expression in the participatory approaches pioneered by Bawaka Country et al. in which social and natural scientists collaborate with indigenous experts, to learn to listen to and be informed by the nonhuman wisdom of 'Country'.

These empirical examples make common reference to two influential and connected strands of political thinking that have emerged at the interface of political philosophy with the field sciences of geography, anthropology, and science studies. The first is the idea of *cosmopolitics* developed by the philosopher Isabelle Stengers (2010). The second is the concept of *pluriversal politics* developed by Arturo Escobar (2020) and other indigenous studies scholars (de la Cadena and Blaser, 2018). In different ways, these two approaches offer a politics for the cosmos – where the cosmos includes the myriad diversity of human and nonhuman actors and process – and where the cosmos can be legitimately known through multiple forms of knowledge, that include science, alongside the other knowledge practices that we encountered in the previous chapter. Stengers is most interested in bringing the sciences into Western models of democracy, providing methodologies for strengthening the objectivity of science by requiring scientists to disclose their interests and working methods. While Latour grounds Stengers' approach in Anthropocene concerns about the instability and potential hostility of a disturbed Earth System. Both Stengers and Latour aim to shore up the role of deliberative democracy in the face of the rise of authoritarian and fascist alternatives, while rethinking its methods to imagine an expansive 'parliament of things' (Latour, 1993).

Advocates for a pluriversal politics start from a centring of indigenous ontologies and learning from the political activities of social movements who mobilised to defend territories against large-scale resource extraction, especially in Latin America. They take issue with modern ideas of development and progress and the power of colonial capitalism buttressed by natural science. For example, Arturo Escobar follows how these movements engage in a politics that aim to bring about the 'pluriverse', defined as 'a world consisting of many worlds, each with its own ontological and epistemic grounding'. Escobar proposes that such a politics is 'key to crafting myriad world-making stories telling of different possible futures that could bring about the profound social transformations that are needed to address planetary crises' (Escobar, 2020). He defends a politics premised on indigenous knowledge practices against accusations of Romanticism and argues that they provide grounds for imagining and enacting alternative possible worlds.

4.5.3 Connecting (carefully)

The third normative commitment is to *connecting (with care)* to the emergence of desired political and ecological developments in a world of becoming. This commitment stems from the broad (though not universal) support for forms of affirmative critique in more-than-human geography, which flows from asserting that the relations through which beings (including humans) are positioned and governed are neither fixed, universal, nor necessary. It suggests that if societies are shaped through relations between actors, then those relations might be re-made in more just, care-full, and inclusive ways. This commitment emerges from the first two. It is based on the model of care as critique, where critique has an awareness of historical contingency such that, as Thom van Dooren (2014) puts it, 'things might have been and so might yet still be, otherwise'. It gives expression to the belief that is central to pluriversal politics that 'another world is possible' (Escobar, 2020).

We find expression of this commitment to connecting in work on the ethics and politics of affect. A key direction has been to take issue with the general negativity in prevalent left social and environmental politics, in which a wide range of problems are linked to a seemingly totalising model of colonial, patriarchal neoliberal capitalism, whose power and reach are beyond challenge, and to which no alternative can be imagined. Instead, a range of authors encourage us to 'read for difference' (Gibson-Graham, 2020), mapping the heterogeneity inherent within contemporary politics. And out of this reading for difference, they encourage us to seek out and amplify moments and models for political and ethical action. Strands of this work engage in speculative experiments that seek to prefigure possible political futures, imagining worlds with such appeal that they will be brought into existence (Jeffrey and Dyson, 2021).

This has led more-than-human geographers to collaborate with diverse publics, citizens, and vernacular experts to recognise their political claims, to engage them in the production of knowledge and, in some cases, to empower their political programmes. This move is founded on an understanding that politics is a universal, necessary, and generative dimension of contemporary life, not something that can be foreclosed or avoided by deference to powerful forms of expertise. It has required some to make an alliance with science, setting aside epistemic differences to forge transdisciplinary research frameworks that help scientists legitimate, apply, and communicate their research. For others, it has motivated creative experiments in artistic practice and speculative storytelling, alongside collaborations with experts in these modes of representation. For Bruce Braun (2015), this desire to connect is best evidenced in the experimental turn in political ecology and nature-society studies that are focused on the detection and generation of difference that we reviewed in the previous chapter.

4.6 Conclusions

This chapter has summarised the key dimensions to a more-than-human approach to politics and ethics. It has explored how commitments to material agency, multiple knowledges, and relations and processes help depart from the anthropocentrism of humanism and the impossible political settlement offered by the modern ideal of a singular Science set outside of society. We have reviewed diverse and ongoing efforts to think politics and ethics differently and suggest that they share three normative commitments. Taken together, we might therefore see more-than-humanism as one generational inheritor of the counter-culture hippy movement that we introduced in Chapter 1. More-than-humanists still want to care (love), converse (listen), and connect (link) – not to slight, shout, and create schisms. In the next chapter, we explore how these commitments have been critiqued by other critical social scientists, especially those who see themselves and their work as the rightful heirs to the left green political movements that were founded in response to the problems with humanism.

Questions for reflection

1   If you were to write your own manifesto for ecological politics, what would you include?
2   How do the material properties of oil or lithium shape your everyday life?
3   Can you identify any bureaucratic arrangements, cultural practices or governing technologies that shape plant-life where you live?
4   How do you think political decisions should take account of nonhuman animals or geological features?
5   Do you think public participation in shaping the objectives of scientific research is important? How could this occur?
6   Can politics be inclusive of multiple knowledges if some of those belong to extremist movements who seek to oppress minority groups?
7   How can you retain hope in the face of environmental crisis?
8   Is a 'politics of care' naïve in its hopefulness, or emancipatory in its possibilities?
9   How might you enact 'care' in your own lived relations?

Suggestions for reading

The following provide more discussion of the general principles of a more-than-human approach to politics and ethics:

Bennett J (2010) *Vibrant matter: A political ecology of things*. Durham, NC: Duke University Press.

Clark N and Szerszynski B (2020) *Planetary social thought: The Anthropocene challenge to the social sciences.* London: Wiley.

de la Bellacasa MP (2017) *Matters of care: Speculative ethics in more than human worlds.* Minneapolis: University of Minnesota Press.

Escobar A (2020) *Pluriversal politics: The real and the possible.* Durham: Duke University Press.

Haraway DJ (2008) *When species meet.* Minneapolis: University of Minnesota Press.

Lorimer J (2020) *The probiotic planet: Using life to manage life.* Minneapolis: University of Minnesota Press.

Nixon R (2011) *Slow violence.* Cambridge: Harvard University Press.

Whatmore S and Braun B (2010) *Political matter: Technoscience, democracy and public life.* Oxford: Oxford University Press.

Yusoff K (2018) *A billion black anthropocenes or none.* Minneapolis: University of Minnesota Press.

These references offer case study examples of more-than-human political analysis:

Barry A (2013) *Material politics: Disputes along the pipeline.* London: Wiley.

Barua M (2024) *Lively cities: Reconfiguring urban ecology.* Minneapolis: University of Minnesota Press.

Chao S (2022) *In the shadow of the palms: More-than-human becomings in West Papua.* Durham: Duke University Press.

Kimmerer RW (2013) *Braiding sweetgrass: Indigenous wisdom, scientific knowledge and the teachings of plants.* Minneapolis: Milkweed Editions.

Stephens AC (2022) *National affects: The everyday atmospheres of being political.* New York: Bloomsbury Publishing.

Tsing AL (2015) *The mushroom at the end of the world: On the possibility of life in capitalist ruins.* Princeton, NJ: Princeton University Press.

van Dooren T (2014b) *Flight ways: Life and loss at the edge of extinction.* New York: Columbia University Press.

Notes

1   Politics and ethics are complex and foundational philosophical terms, and most theorists see them as closely related. In this chapter, we use ethics to describe normative commitments (claims about what should be done), especially as they manifest in relations between humans and other organisms. We use politics to describe relations between people and a subset of animals that are elevated to quasi-human status. Politics also describes the collective organisation and institutions of power, and the art of government, which is the sole preserve of human action.

2   For introductions to the work of the French social theorist Michel Foucault, whose writings have had a significant influence on human geography, see Dean (2010), Elden and Crampton (2012), Lemke (2011), and Philo (2010, 2012).

3 Haraway first published her manifesto in the Socialist Review. It was republished in Simians, Cyborgs and Women in 1991.

4 Writing with Joshua Evans, Jamie has explored the agencies of food-related microbes – like the koji fungus – to generate tasty flavours and thus make humans work in their interests by propagating their spores and dedicating large areas of land to cultivating crops – like soy beans which they ferment (Evans and Lorimer, 2021). This work on the affirmative role of microbes stands in contrast to the majority of analyses that explore the harmful historical agencies of insects, bacteria, and viruses. See for example Mitchell (1988), and Diamond (1998).

5 We can read Scott alongside Paul Robbins' book Lawn People (Robbins, 2012), which provides a compelling account of the rise of the American lawn as a culturally and economically valued land use. Robbins documents how a small number of grass species domesticated a large number of affluent suburban Americans, entraining them into tending and propagating their seeds and stalks, at the expense of other species.

6 Nortje Marres (2005) suggests that there is no such thing as 'the public' as a singular or pregiven entity. Instead, she argues that there are multiple publics, which are brought into being around specific technologies or scientific topics. In light of this insight, Sarah Whatmore advises those seeking to counter distrust in science to engage publics with scientific decision-making 'to avoid equating democratic politics with the institutions of representative government and the machinery of policy-making, and to be more attentive to the multiple and emergent constitution of publics and their political capabilities' (2009, 592).

7 Urban geographers have revisited the practices of the Situationists, a group of mid-20th-century performance artists who used disconcerting arrangements of bodies and bodily practices to sense, disrupt, and circumvent powerful and normative understandings of urban spatial practice (Pyyry, 2019).

8 Sarah Wright presents their political commitment as follows: 'The Collective promotes a deeply collaborative Indigenous-led understanding of time/place, extending more-than-human methodologies and challenging human centred, non-Indigenous and Western understandings (and practices) within the academy and beyond it. Together they have explored what it might mean to take Indigenous ontologies of co-becoming seriously, in ways that might help better understand theoretical concepts such as space and place, and also to move towards a de-colonised, Indigenous-led practice in development studies and natural resource management'. https://www.newcastle.edu.au/profile/sarah-wright#career. These collaborations sometimes aim to include nonhumans as political subjects. The Bawaka Collective include Country as a co-author in its publications to acknowledge how it 'guided, inspired and enabled' and how 'it empowered learning, opened avenues of discussion and made us – human and more-than-human – who we are' (2016, 468). The wider aim is to grant political status to the land and those nonhumans – living, dead, and spiritual – from which it is comprised.

9 See also Dawn Prince-Hughes' (2004) Songs of the Gorilla Nation as well as Cary Wolfe's (2008) analysis of the politics of Temple Grandin's linkage between disability and animal studies.

10 The Economist reports that in 2015 at least 35% of all the cattle killed for meat in the US pass through a facility designed by Grandin (Economist, 2015).

Grandin's life story was brought to the big screen in 2010 in the HBO film *Temple Grandin* featuring Clare Danes.

11 Further ethnographic work in animal laboratories has described the care and emotional labour performed by animal technicians who seek to minimise the harm done to captive animals (Greenhough and Roe, 2011, 2019).

12 Compelling examples of this approach are given by Baptiste Morizot (2022) in his reports of his research developing interventions to ensure convivial relations between wolves, sheep, and pastoralists in France. See also the work of Marcus Baynes-Rock (2015) on ways of living with hyenas in urban Ethiopia.

13 For example, in his writing about cities, Nigel Thrift argues that: 'systematic knowledge of the creation and mobilisation of affect have become an integral part of the everyday day urban landscape: affect has become part of the reflexive loop which allows more and more sophisticated interventions in various registers of urban life ... these knowledges are not only being deployed knowingly, they are also being deployed politically (mainly, but not only, by the rich and powerful) to political ends: what might have been presented as aesthetic is increasingly instrumental ... Affect has always of course been a constant of urban experience, now affect is more and more likely to be actively engineered' (2004, 58).

14 Jamie has developed this concept of affective logics in a review of animal representations on film and other moving imagery. He distinguishes four different affective logics and explores their political and ethical implications for how animals are understood and thus how they might be treated. These range from a sentimental and anthropomorphic logic that make charismatic animals like elephants into lesser humans to a logic of disconcertion that aims to sensitise viewers to the radical alterity of animal life (Lorimer, 2010).

15 Haraway cautions that: It matters what matters we use to think other matters with; it matters what stories we tell to tell other stories with; it matters what knots knot knots, what thoughts think thoughts, what descriptions describe descriptions, what ties tie ties. It matters what stories make worlds, what worlds make stories (2016, 12).

16 For example, van Dooren (2011) examines the lethal practices of invasive species management in Australian nature conservation for the protection of a rare penguin from predation by nonnative species like foxes. He draws attention to the prevalence of killing in the careful practices of preventing extinction. Likewise, Krithika Srinivasan traces the tensions and paradoxes between forms of care that focus on individual welfare and those caring for wider collective and ecological flourishing in her analysis of the management of feral 'street dogs' in India and the UK. She argues that the supposedly civilised and high welfare regime that is common in the UK actually restricts the freedoms of dogs, in comparison to what is seen by some in the international animal welfare movement to be the 'backward' model in India. Dogs are property in the UK and are not allowed to live in the streets. Those that escape domestic life are rounded up, incarcerated, rehomed, or killed. They are not allowed to breed at will. Instead, they are subject to forced sterilisation. In contrast, dogs roam the streets in many cities in India. They are often nominally attached to a household that feeds them, but they are rarely owned. They breed at will and do suffer from hunger and diseases, but they do have greater autonomy (Srinivasan, 2013).

References

Adams WM (2019) Geographies of conservation II: Technology, surveillance and conservation by algorithm. *Progress in Human Geography* 43(2): 337–350.

Adams WM and Mulligan M (2003) *Decolonizing nature: Strategies for conservation in a post-colonial era.* London: Earthscan.

Akrich M (1992) The de-scription of technical objects. In: Bijker W and Law J (eds) *Shaping technology/building society. Studies in sociotechnical change.* Cambridge, MA: MIT Press, pp. 205–224.

Amoore L (2020) *Cloud ethics: Algorithms and the attributes of ourselves and others.* Durham: Duke University Press.

Anderson B (2004) Time-stilled space-slowed: How boredom matters. *Geoforum* 35(6): 739–754.

Anderson B (2012) Affect and biopower: Towards a politics of life. *Transactions of the Institute of British Geographers* 37(1): 28–43.

Asafu-Adjaye J, Blomqvist L, Brand S, Brook B, Defries R, Ellis E, Foreman C, Keith D, Lewis M, Lynas M, Nordhaus T, Pielke R, Pritzker R, Roy J, Sagoff M, Shellenberger M, Stone R and Teague P (2015) *An ecomodernist manifesto.* Oakland: Breakthrough Institute.

Atchison J and Head L (2013) Eradicating bodies in invasive plant management. *Environment and Planning D: Society and Space* 31(6): 951–968.

Bakker K and Bridge G (2006) Material worlds? Resource geographies and the 'matter of nature'. *Progress in Human Geography* 30(1): 5–27.

Bakker KJ (2003) *An uncooperative commodity: Privatizing water in England and Wales.* Oxford: Oxford University Press.

Barad K (2003) Posthumanist performativity: Toward an understanding of how matter comes to matter. *Signs: Journal of Women in Culture and Society* 28(3): 801–831.

Barker K (2010) Biosecure citizenship: Politicising symbiotic associations and the construction of biological threat. *Transactions of the Institute of British Geographers* 35(3): 350–363.

Barker K (2015) Biosecurity: Securing circulations from the microbe to the macrocosm. *The Geographical Journal* 181(4): 357–365.

Barua M (2020) Animating capital: Work, commodities, circulation. *Progress in Human Geography* 0(0): 0309132518819057.

Barua M (2022) Feral ecologies: The making of postcolonial nature in London. *Journal of the Royal Anthropological Institute* 28(3): 896–919.

Barua M and Sinha A (2017) Animating the urban: An ethological and geographical conversation. *Social & Cultural Geography* 20(8): 1160–1180. DOI: 10.1080/14649365.2017.1409908.

Barua M and Sinha A (2022) Cultivated, feral, wild: The urban as an ecological formation. *Urban Geography:* 1–22. DOI: 10.1080/02723638.2022.2055924.

Baynes-Rock M (2015) *Among the bone eaters: Encounters with hyenas in Harar.* Philadephia: Penn State University Press.

Bennett J (2001) *The enchantment of modern life: Attachments, crossings, and ethics.* Princeton, NJ: Princeton University Press.

Berlant L (2011) *Cruel optimism.* Durham: Duke University Press.

Biermann C and Mansfield B (2014) Biodiversity, purity, and death: Conservation biology as biopolitics. *Environment and Planning D: Society and Space* 32(2): 257–273.

Bingham N and Hinchliffe S (2008) Reconstituting natures: Articulating other modes of living together. *Geoforum* 39(1): 83–87.

Bissell D (2011) Placing affective relations: Uncertain geographies of pain. In: Harrison P and Anderson B (eds) *Taking-place: Non-representational theories and geography.* London: Routledge, pp. 93–112.

Blomqvist L, Nordhaus T and Shellenberger M (2015) *Nature unbound: Decoupling for conservation.* Oakland: Breakthrough Institute.

Bowker GC (2000) Mapping biodiversity. *International Journal of Geographical Information Science* 14(8): 739–754.

Bowker GC and Star S, Leigh (1999) *Sorting things out: Classification and its consequences.* Cambridge, MA: MIT Press.

Braun B (2004) Querying posthumanisms. *Geoforum* 35(3): 269–273.

Braun B (2015) From critique to experiment? Rethinking political ecology for the Anthropocene. In: Perreault T, Bridge G and McCarthy J (eds) *The Routledge handbook of political ecology.* London: Taylor and Francis, pp. 102–114.

Braverman I (2012) Zooveillance: Foucault goes to the zoo. *Surveillance & Society* 10(2): 119–133.

Braverman I (2014) Governing the wild: Databases, algorithms, and population models as biopolitics. *Surveillance & Society* 12(1): 15–37.

Breewood H and Garnett T (2022) *What is ecomodernism?* Report, London: TABLE Explainer Series.

Brockington D (2002) *Fortress conservation: The preservation of the Mkomazi game reserve, Tanzania.* Bloomington: Indiana University Press.

Callon M, Lascoumes P and Barthe Y (2009) *Acting in an uncertain world: An essay on technical democracy.* Cambridge, MA: MIT Press.

Carter S and McCormack DP (2006) Film, geopolitics and the affective logics of intervention. *Political Geography* 25(2): 228–245.

Cassidy R and Mullin MH (2007) *Where the wild things are now: Domestication reconsidered.* Oxford: Berg.

Castree N (2005) *Nature.* London: Routledge.

Chakrabarty D (2009) The climate of history: Four theses. *Critical Inquiry* 35(2): 197–222.

Chandler D (2018) *Ontopolitics in the Anthropocene: An introduction to mapping, sensing and hacking.* Abingdon: Taylor & Francis.

Chao S (2022) *In the shadow of the palms: More-than-human becomings in West Papua.* Durham: Duke University Press.

Chilvers J and Kearnes M (2015) *Remaking participation: Science, environment and emergent publics.* Abingdon: Taylor & Francis.

Chrulew M and Wadiwel DJ (2016) *Foucault and animals.* New York: Brill.

Clark N (2011) *Inhuman Nature: Sociable Living on a Dynamic Planet.* Thousand Oaks, CA: SAGE Publications.

Clark N and Yusoff K (2017) Geosocial formations and the Anthropocene. *Theory, Culture & Society* 34(2–3): 3–23.

Cloke P, May J and Johnsen S (2008) Performativity and affect in the homeless city. *Environment and Planning D-Society & Space* 26(2): 241–263.

Clutton-Brock J (1999) *A natural history of domesticated mammals.* Cambridge: Cambridge University Press.

Collard R-C, Dempsey J and Sundberg J (2016) The moderns' amnesia in two registers. *Environmental Humanities* 7(1): 227–232.

Collard RC (2020) *Animal traffic: Lively capital in the global exotic pet trade.* Durham: Duke University Press.

Collard RC and Dempsey J (2013) Life for sale? The politics of lively commodities. *Environment and Planning A* 45(11): 2682–2699.

Collective AO, Vemuri A and Barney D (2022) *Solarities: Seeking energy justice.* Minneapolis: University of Minnesota Press.

Crist E (2016) The reaches of freedom: A response to an ecomodernist manifesto. *Environmental Humanities* 7(1): 245–254.

Cronon W (1996) The trouble with wilderness; or, getting back to the wrong nature. In: Cronon W (ed) *Uncommon ground: Rethinking the human place in nature.* New York: Norton, pp. 69–90.

da Costa B and Philip K (2008) *Tactical biopolitics: Art, activism, and technoscience.* Cambridge, MA: The MIT Press.

Davidson J and Smith M (2009) Autistic autobiographies and more-than-human emotional geographies. *Environment and Planning D: Society and Space* 27(5): 898–916.

Davies G, Gorman R, Greenhough B, Hobson-West P, Kirk RGW, Message R, Myelnikov D, Palmer A, Roe E, Ashall V, Crudgington B, McGlacken R, Peres S and Skidmore T (2020) Animal research nexus: A new approach to the connections between science, health and animal welfare. *Medical Humanities* 46(4): 499–511.

Davis M (2001) *Late Victorian holocausts: El Niño famines and the making of the third world.* New York: Verso.

de la Bellacasa MP (2012) 'Nothing comes without its world': Thinking with care. *The Sociological Review* 60(2): 197–216.

de la Bellacasa MP (2017) *Matters of care: Speculative ethics in more than human worlds.* Minneapolis: University of Minnesota Press.

de la Cadena M and Blaser M (2018) *A world of many worlds.* Durham: Duke University Press.

Dean M (2010) *Governmentality: Power and rule in modern society.* London: SAGE Publications.

Dekeyser T and Jellis T (2021) Besides affirmationism? On geography and negativity. *Area* 53(2): 318–325.

Demeritt D (2002) What is the 'social construction of nature'? A typology and sympathetic critique. *Progress in Human Geography* 26(6): 767–790.

Despret V (2004) The body we care for: Figures of anthropo-zoo-genesis. *Body & Society* 10(2–3): 111–134.

Diamond JM (1998) *Guns, germs and steel: A short history of everybody for the last 13,000 years.* London: Vintage.

Dodsworth J (2024) *Locating communities in digital natures: Exploring the politics of national parks, identity and visual social media in the lake district.* Oxford: University of Oxford.

Economist (2015) A jungle no more. *The Economist* October.

Elden S (2013) Secure the volume: Vertical geopolitics and the depth of power. *Political Geography* 34: 35–51.

Elden S and Crampton JW (2012) *Space, knowledge and power: Foucault and geography.* London: Ashgate Publishing Limited.

Engelmann S (2020) *Sensing art in the atmosphere: Elemental lures and aerosolar practices.* Abingdon: Taylor & Francis.

Escobar A (2020) *Pluriversal politics: The real and the possible.* Durham: Duke University Press.

Evans J and Lorimer J (2021) Taste-shaping-natures: Making novel miso with charismatic microbes and New Nordic fermenters in Copenhagen. *Current Anthropology* 62(S24): S361–S375.

Falcon J (2023) Toward a critical posthuman geography. *Cultural Geographies* 30(1): 19–34.

Foucault M (2010) *The birth of biopolitics: Lectures at the College de France, 1978–1979.* New York: Picador.

Gabrys J (2022) *Citizens of worlds: Open-air toolkits for environmental struggle.* Minneapolis: University of Minnesota Press.

Gibson-Graham JK (2020) Reading for economic difference. In: Dombroski K and Gibson-Graham JK (eds) *The handbook of diverse economies.* Cheltenham: Edward Elgar Publishing.

Gillespie K (2018) *The cow with ear tag #1389.* Chicago: University of Chicago Press.

Gillespie K and Collard RC (2015) *Critical animal geographies: Politics, intersections and hierarchies in a multispecies world.* Abingdon: Taylor & Francis.

Ginn F (2014) Sticky lives: Slugs, detachment and more-than-human ethics in the garden. *Transactions of the Institute of British Geographers* 39(4): 532–544.

Ginn F, Beisel U and Barua M (2014) Flourishing with awkward creatures: Togetherness, vulnerability, killing. *Environmental Humanities* 4: 113–123.

Giraud EH (2019) *What comes after entanglement? Activism, anthropocentrism, and an ethics of exclusion.* Durham: Duke University Press.

Grandin T and Johnson C (2006) *Animals in translation: Using the mysteries of autism to decode animal behavior.* Orlando: Harcourt.

Granjou C and Phillips C (2019) Living and labouring soils: Metagenomic ecology and a new agricultural revolution? *BioSocieties* 14(3): 393–415.

Greenhough B, Dwyer A, Grenyer R, Hodgetts T, McLeod C and Lorimer J (2018) Unsettling antibiosis: How might interdisciplinary researchers generate a feeling for the microbiome and to what effect? *Palgrave Communications* 4(1): 149.

Greenhough B and Roe E (2011) Ethics, space, and somatic sensibilities: Comparing relationships between scientific researchers and their human and animal experimental subjects. *Environment and Planning D: Society and Space* 29(1): 47–66.

Greenhough B and Roe E (2019) Attuning to laboratory animals and telling stories: Learning animal geography research skills from animal technologists. *Environment and Planning D: Society and Space* 37(2): 367–384.

Guthman J (2019) *Wilted: Pathogens, chemicals, and the fragile future of the strawberry industry.* Oakland: University of California Press.

Hall E and Wilton R (2017) Towards a relational geography of disability. *Progress in Human Geography* 41(6): 727–744.

Hamilton C (2016) The anthropocene as rupture. *The Anthropocene Review* 3(2): 93–106. https://doi.org/10.1177/2053019616634741. DOI: 10.1177/2053019616634741.

Haraway DJ (1991) *Simians, cyborgs, and women: The reinvention of nature.* New York: Routledge.

Haraway DJ (2008) *When species meet.* Minneapolis: University of Minnesota Press.

Haraway DJ (2016) *Staying with the trouble: Making kin in the Chthulucene.* Durham, NC: Duke University Press.

Hawkins H (2015) Creative geographic methods: Knowing, representing, intervening. On composing place and page. *Cultural Geographies* 22(2): 247–268.

Hawkins H (2017) *Creativity.* London: Routledge.

Hawkins H (2020) *Geography, art, research: Artistic research in the geohumanities.* London: Taylor & Francis.

Head L (2016) *Hope and grief in the anthropocene: Re-conceptualising human–nature relations.* Abingdon: Taylor & Francis.

Hetherington K (2020) Agribiopolitics: The health of plants and humans in the age of monocrops. *Environment and Planning D: Society and Space* 38(4): 682–698.

Hinchliffe S (2007) *Geographies of nature: Societies, environments, ecologies.* London: Sage.

Hinchliffe S (2008) Reconstituting nature conservation: Towards a careful political ecology. *Geoforum* 39(1): 88–97.

Hinchliffe S (2015) More than one world, more than one health: Re-configuring interspecies health. *Social Science & Medicine* 129(0): 28–35.

Hinchliffe S, Allen J, Lavau S, Bingham N and Carter S (2013) Biosecurity and the topologies of infected life: From borderlines to borderlands. *Transactions of the Institute of British Geographers* 38(4): 531–543.

Hinchliffe S, Bingham N, Allen J and Carter S (2016) *Pathological lives: Disease, space and biopolitics.* London: Blackwell.

Holloway L (2007) Subjecting cows to robots: Farming technologies and the making of animal subjects. *Environment and Planning D-Society & Space* 25(6): 1041–1060.

Holloway L, Morris C, Gilna B and Gibbs D (2009) Biopower, genetics and livestock breeding: (re)constituting animal populations and heterogeneous biosocial collectivities. *Transactions of the Institute of British Geographers* 34(3): 394–407.

Jeffrey C and Dyson J (2021) Geographies of the future: Prefigurative politics. *Progress in Human Geography* 45(4): 641–658.

Judge SM (2018) Languages of sensing: Bringing neurodiversity into more-than-human geography. *Environment and Planning D: Society and Space* 36(6): 1101–1119.

Kirksey E (2014) *The multispecies salon*. Durham: Duke University Press.

Kirksey E, Munro P, van Dooren T, Emery D, Maree Kreller A, Kwok J, Lau K, Miller M, Morris K, Newson S, Olejniczak E, Ow A, Tuckson K, Sannen S and Martin J (2018) Feeding the flock: Wild cockatoos and their facebook friends. *Environment and Planning E: Nature and Space* 1(4): 602–620.

Klauser F (2016) *Surveillance and space*. London: SAGE Publications.

Latour B (1993) *We have never been modern*. Cambridge, MA: Harvard University Press.

Latour B (2004a) *Politics of nature: How to bring the sciences into democracy*. Cambridge, MA: Harvard University Press.

Latour B (2004b) Why has critique run out of steam? From matters of fact to matters of concern. *Critical Inquiry* 30(2): 225–248.

Latour B (2010) An attempt at a "compositionist manifesto". *New Literary History* 41(3): 471–490.

Latour B (2011) Love your monsters. In: Shellenberger M and Nordhaus T (eds) *Love your monsters: Postenvironmentalism and the Anthropocene*. San Francisco: Breakthrough Institute, 23–45.

Latour B (2018) *Down to earth: Politics in the new climatic regime*. Wiley.

Law J (1994) *Organizing modernity*. Oxford; Cambridge, MA: Blackwell.

Lemke T (2011) *Biopolitics: An advanced introduction*. New York: New York University Press.

Lezaun J and Porter N (2015) Containment and competition: Transgenic animals in the one health agenda. *Social Science & Medicine* 129: 96–105.

Lora-Wainwright A (2013) *Fighting for breath: Living morally and dying of cancer in a Chinese village*. Mānoa Valley, O'ahu: University of Hawaii Press.

Lorimer J (2007) Nonhuman charisma. *Environment and Planning D-Society & Space* 25(5): 911–932.

Lorimer J (2010) Moving image methodologies for more-than-human geographies. *Cultural Geographies* 17(2): 237–258.

Lorimer J (2015) *Wildlife in the anthropocene: Conservation after nature*. Minneapolis: University of Minnesota Press.

Lorimer J (2016) Gut buddies: Multispecies studies and the microbiome. *Environmental Humanities* 8(1): 57–76.

Lorimer J (2017) Probiotic environmentalities: Rewilding with wolves and worms. *Theory, Culture & Society* 34(4): 27–48.

Lorimer J (2020) *The probiotic planet: Using life to manage life*. Minneapolis: University of Minnesota Press.

Lorimer J and Driessen C (2013) Bovine biopolitics and the promise of monsters in the rewilding of Heck cattle. *Geoforum* 48: 249–259.

Lorimer J, Hodgetts T, Grenyer R, Greenhough B, McLeod C and Dwyer A (2019) Making the microbiome public: Participatory experiments with DNA sequencing in domestic kitchens. *Transactions of the Institute of British Geographers* 44(3): 524–541.

Lynas M (2011) *The god species: How the planet can survive the age of humans*. London: Fourth Estate.

Margulies JD (2019) Making the 'man-eater': Tiger conservation as necropolitics. *Political Geography* 69: 150–161.

Marković I (2019) Out of place, out of time: Towards a more-than-human rhythmanalysis of smoking. *Cultural Geographies* 26(4): 487–503.

Marres N (2005) Issues spark a public into being: A key but often forgotten point of the Lippmann-Dewey debate. In: Latour B and Weibel P (eds) *Making things public*. Cambridge: MIT Press, pp. 208–217.

McCance D (2013) *Critical animal studies: An introduction*. New York: State University of New York Press.

Mitchell T (1988) *Colonising Egypt*. Cambridge: Cambridge University Press.

Mitchell T (2011) *Carbon democracy: Political power in the age of oil*. New York: Verso Books.

Mol A (1999) Ontological politics: A word and some questions. In: Law J and Hassard J (eds) *Actor-network theory and after*. Oxford: Blackwell, pp. 74–89.

Morizot B (2022) *Wild diplomacy: Cohabiting with wolves on a new ontological map*. New York: State University of New York Press.

Mouffe C (2011) *On the political*. London: Taylor & Francis.

Nast HJ (2005) Book review: The companion species manifesto: Dogs, people, and significant otherness. *Cultural Geographies* 12(1): 118–120.

Philo C (1995) Animals, geography, and the city: Notes on inclusions and exclusions. *Environment and Planning D: Society & Space* 13(6): 655–681.

Philo C (2010) Foucault. In: Hubbard P and Kitchin R (eds) *Key thinkers on space and place*. 2nd ed. London: SAGE, pp. 45–67.

Philo C (2012) A 'new Foucault' with lively implications – or 'the crawfish advances sideways'. *Transactions of the Institute of British Geographers* 37(4): 496–514.

Philo C (2017) Less-than-human geographies. *Political Geography* 60: 256–258.

Philo C and Wilbert C (2000) *Animal spaces, beastly places: New geographies of human-animal relations*. London: Routledge.

Pollan M (2001) *The botany of desire: A plant's-eye view of the world*. New York: Random House.

Povinelli EA (2016) *Geontologies: A requiem to late liberalism*. Durham: Duke University Press.

Price L and Hawkins H (2018) *Geographies of making, craft and creativity*. Abingdon: Taylor & Francis.

Prince-Hughes D (2004) *Songs of the gorilla nation: My journey through autism*. Bancyfelin, Carmarthen: Crown.

Pyyry N (2019) From psychogeography to hanging-out-knowing: Situationist dérive in nonrepresentational urban research. *Area* 51(2): 315–323.

Rice T, Badman-King A, Hurn S, Rose P and Reed A (2021) Listening after the animals: Sound and pastoral care in the zoo. *Journal of the Royal Anthropological Institute* 27(4): 850–869.

Robbins P (2012) *Lawn people: How grasses, weeds, and chemicals make us who we are.* Philadelphia: Temple University Press.

Sariola S (2021) Fermentation in post-antibiotic worlds. *Current Anthropology* 62(S24): S388–S398. DOI: 10.1086/715208.

Scott JC (2017) *Against the grain: A deep history of the earliest states.* New Haven: Yale University Press.

Scranton R (2015) *Learning to die in the Anthropocene: Reflections on the end of a civilization.* San Francisco, CA: City Lights Publishers.

Seddon N (2022) Harnessing the potential of nature-based solutions for mitigating and adapting to climate change. *Science* 376(6600): 1410–1416.

Smith A, Shah S and Blaustein-Rejto D (2021a) *The case for public investment in alternative proteins. Report,* San Francisco, CA: Breakthrough Institute.

Smith H, Miele M, Charles N and Fox R (2021b) Becoming with a police dog: Training technologies for bonding. *Transactions of the Institute of British Geographers* 46(2): 478–494.

Sneegas G (2022) Producing (extra)ordinary death on the farm: Unruly encounters and contaminated calves. *Social & Cultural Geography* 23(1): 63–82.

Srinivasan K (2013) The biopolitics of animal being and welfare: Dog control and care in the uk and india. *Transactions of the Institute of British Geographers* 38(1): 106–119.

Srinivasan K, Kasturirangan R and Driessen C (2020) Biopolitics. In: Kobayashi A (ed) *International encyclopedia of human geography.* 2nd ed. Oxford: Elsevier, pp. 339–345.

Stein A, Messinger J, Wang S, Lloyd J, McBride J and Franovich R (2022) *Advancing nuclear energy: Evaluating deployment, investment, and impact in America's clean energy future.* Report, San Francisco, CA: Breakthrough Institute.

Stengers I (2010) *Cosmopolitics.* Minneapolis: University of Minnesota Press.

Stephens AC (2022) *National affects: The everyday atmospheres of being political.* New York: Bloomsbury Publishing.

Swanson HA, Lien ME and Ween GB (2018) *Domestication gone wild: Politics and practices of multispecies relations.* Durham: Duke University Press.

Thrift N (2004) Intensities of feeling: Towards a spatial politics of affect. *Geografiska Annaler: Series B, Human Geography* 86(1): 57–78.

Thrift N and French S (2002) The automatic production of space. *Transactions of the Institute of British Geographers* 27(3): 309–335.

Tsing A (2017) A threat to Holocene resurgence is a threat to livability. In: Brightman M and Lewis J (eds) *The anthropology of sustainability: Beyond development and progress.* New York: Palgrave Macmillan, pp. 51–65.

Tsing AL (2015) *The mushroom at the end of the world: On the possibility of life in capitalist ruins.* Princeton, NJ: Princeton University Press.

Tsing AL, Mathews AS and Bubandt N (2019) Patchy Anthropocene: Landscape structure, multispecies history, and the retooling of anthropology: An introduction to supplement 20. *Current Anthropology* 60(S20): S186–S197.

Turnbull J, Searle A and Lorimer J (2023) Anthropause environmentalisms: Noticing natures with the self-isolating bird club. *Transactions of the Institute of British Geographers* 48: 232–248. Available from: https://doi.org/10.1111/tran.12569.

van Dooren T (2011) Invasive species in penguin worlds: An ethical taxonomy of killing for conservation. *Conservation and Society* 9(4): 286–298.

van Dooren T (2014) Care. *Environmental Humanities* 5(1): 291–294.

Wainwright J (2005) Politics of nature: A review of three recent works by Bruno Latour. *Capitalism Nature Socialism* 16(1): 115–127.

Waight E and Yin Y (2021) Using non-representational theory to explore older people's travel to and from the supermarket. *Mobilities* 16(4): 537–552.

Wakefield S (2020) *Anthropocene back loop.* Oxford: Saint Philip Street Press.

Weisberg Z (2009) The broken promises of monsters: Haraway, animals and the humanist legacy. *Journal for Critical Animal Studies* 7(2): 23–64.

Whatmore S (2002) *Hybrid geographies: Natures, cultures, spaces.* London: Sage.

Whatmore S and Braun B (2010) *Political matter: Technoscience, democracy and public life.* Oxford: Oxford University Press.

Whatmore SJ (2009) Mapping knowledge controversies: Science, democracy and the redistribution of expertise. *Progress in Human Geography* 33(5): 587–598.

Whyte KP (2018) Indigenous science (fiction) for the Anthropocene: Ancestral dystopias and fantasies of climate change crises. *Environment and Planning E: Nature and Space* 1(1–2): 224–242.

Wolch J (1998) Zoopolis. In: Wolch J and Emel J (eds) *Animal geographies: Place, politics and identity in the nature-culture borderlands.* London: Verso, pp. 119–138.

Wolfe C (2008) Learning from Temple Grandin, or, animal studies, disability studies, and who comes after the subject. *New Formations* 64: 110.

Woodyer T and Geoghegan H (2013) (Re)enchanting geography? The nature of being critical and the character of critique in human geography. *Progress in Human Geography* 37(2): 195–214.

Youatt R (2008) Counting species: Biopower and the global biodiversity census. *Environmental Values* 17(3): 393–417.

Yusoff K (2013) Geologic life: Prehistory, climate, futures in the Anthropocene. *Environment and Planning D: Society and Space* 31(5): 779–795.

Yusoff K (2018) *A billion black anthropocenes or none.* Minneapolis: University of Minnesota Press.

Yusoff K (2021) The inhumanities. *Annals of the American Association of Geographers* 111(3): 663–676.

5 The tensions within and prospects for more-than-humanism

More-than-humanism is a live field of academic enquiry. Like other areas of scholarship, it is subject to internal debate and external criticism. Many of the developments that we have covered so far in this book have been generated by the standard academic processes of reflection and critique. But the story we have told is largely one of consensus. We have traced a chronology of evolving ideas, attending mainly to points of agreement. As a result, we have spent less time on the internal differences between those who describe themselves as more-than-humanists, as well as on the criticisms offered by those who disagree with the central tenets of the more-than-human project.

In this final chapter, we shift focus to examine these points of tension within more-than-humanism and between more-than-humanism and several other academic approaches concerned with similar questions. We outline the substance of the criticisms they have made of more-than-human approaches, reflect on emerging points of synthesis with the potential for future development, and in some cases, recognise the incommensurability between more-than-humanism and the alternatives that they offer.

In the sections that follow, we explore points of tension between more-than-humanism and four proximal fields of academic enquiry: Marxist political ecology, indigenous and black studies, critical animal studies, and science studies. These fields sit broadly within the tradition of critical social theory, in that they are concerned with the social and environmental justice implications of status quo modes of political and economic order. In different ways they take issue with the shifts they see more-than-humanists making away from the central conceptual and political tenets of critical theory. Three main criticisms emerge (for a helpful review, see Falcon, 2023):

DOI: 10.4324/9781315164304-6

1   That the 'flat ontologies' of more-than-humanism, that we outlined in Chapter 2, fold the human into the nonhuman and are thus unable to describe and account for important forms of interspecies and intraspecies difference. They suggest that more-than-humanism cannot account for what makes humans (and some animals) different, important, and responsible. They argue for maintaining the analytical and political distinctions between subjects and objects and between Nature and Society.

2   That the more-than-human knowledge practices we reviewed in Chapter 3 have either become too close to science, by suspending critical attention to the social construction of scientific knowledge, or that they have too readily given up on science, technology, reason, and the idea of progress in turning to non-Western, non-scientific knowledges. They accuse more-than-humanism of betraying the Enlightenment project of human emancipation.

3   That the models of politics and ethics outlined in Chapter 4 pay insufficient attention to questions of historical and contemporary injustice, especially in relation to the operations of capitalism, colonialism, racism, patriarchy, and (to a lesser extent) anthropocentrism. They accuse more-than-humanism of political quietism or even complicity in the face of injustice.

We trace and evaluate these claims as they are made across the four fields we identify above, starting with Marxist political ecology.

5.1 With Marxist political ecology: dithering while the planet burns!

Political ecology is a diverse and well-established field that spans geography, anthropology, and development studies. It emerged in the 1970s from social science research on how natural scientific knowledge was being used to govern people and places, especially in (what was then known by some) as the 'Third World' (Bryant and Bailey, 1997). Concerns were expressed that Western natural scientists involved in agriculture, healthcare, resource extraction, and other modes of health and environmental management were deeply entangled in colonial, racist, capitalist, and patriarchal political projects of the type we encountered in Chapter 1. Political ecologists offered profound critiques of these entanglements between politics and natural science, from a wide range of conceptual and political positions, including feminism, antiracism and decolonialism, and Marxism. In the last 20 years, political ecology has expanded in geographic scope to include activities in the Global North, as well as in urban contexts (for introductions and overviews, see Robbins, 2019; Perreault et al., 2015).

The Marxist strand of political ecology has been most influential in geography, and eco-Marxists have been most fulsome in critiquing more-than-humanism. This field is founded on Karl Marx's 19th-century theories of how liberal capitalism transforms the human and nonhuman world and unequally distributes the benefits of economic activity. 'Neo-'Marxist geographers like David Harvey, Neil Smith, and Eric Swyngedouw updated Marx's writings for the 21st century to critically examine: (i) the material transformation of the nonhuman world under neoliberal capitalism; (ii) the ways in which ideas of Nature are used to naturalise capitalism; and (iii) how capitalism is adapting to the environmental crisis through the rise of 'free market' environmentalism (Castree, 2001). These and other geographers' engagements with Marx in the 1980s and 1990s were central to the diagnosis of many of the social and environmental problems that continue to concern more-than-humanists. It was through the Marxist interest in 'historical materialism' that many geographers first got interested in the material 'production of Nature' (Smith, 2010) under capitalism and the ways in which different plants, animals, and landscapes are modified or 'subsumed' (Boyd et al., 2001) according to the unjust and 'ecologically irrational' logics of capitalist production (O'Connor, 1998).[1]

Some Marxist political ecologists were receptive to the more-than-human approaches that emerged in the 1990s and 2000s, seeing the potential in the hybrid ontology offered by ANT to rethink the material operations of capitalism. For example, Eric Swyngedouw borrowed from Bruno Latour and Donna Haraway in developing the field of urban political ecology, presenting the 'city as hybrid' (1996) and exploring what he termed the 'socionatures' (2004) produced through practices like urban water management. In an early review article exploring the possibility of drawing together insights from ANT and Marxism, Noel Castree (2002) cautioned against establishing 'false antitheses' between the two approaches. He encouraged Marxist geographers to embrace some elements of the new materialisms being offered by this nascent field, expressing hope that his synthesis of the two: 'offers conceptual tools with which Marxists can still critique a perva-sive mode of human relationality to nature—namely, capitalist—while mul-tiplying the actors and complicating the politics involved in approaching the society-environment nexus' (111).

While this spirit of synthesis lives on, it has not been shared by all Marxist political ecologists. As Margulies and Bersaglio (2018) argue in a recent review: 'while some political ecologists are apt to recognize that there is something theoretically cutting edge about post-human geographies, some are also apt to question whether this edge is sharp (i.e. political) enough for political ecology' (2018, 104). This is especially true for Andreas Malm and Alf Hornborg, two Scandinavian Marxists who in their recent polemical writings express strong concerns that: (i) the flat ontologies of more-than-humanism downplay important differences between humans and nonhu-man; and (ii) that the focus on relations makes more-than-humanism ill equipped to diagnose and critique the structures of neoliberal capitalism.

Hornborg (2017) advocates retaining what he terms the 'much-maligned "Cartesian" categories such as the distinctions between subject and object, society and nature, and human and non-human' that we sketched at the end of Chapter 2 (see also Malm, 2018). He suggests that researchers need to be able to distinguish between humans and other organisms and between organisms and inorganic matter (like rocks) so that they can provide clear and critical analysis of social and environmental problems. He argues that theorists need to be able to recognise what makes humans special and important, so that they can identify specific human forms of agency, attri-bute responsibility for social and ecological changes, and devise transfor-mative political models. Hornborg warns that 'the undeniable uniqueness of human responsibility—which simply cannot be extended to rivers, volca-noes, or even dogs—remains an insurmountable dilemma for posthuman-ism' (2017, 72–73). He maintains that social science needs to define and defend a domain termed Society that is separated from Nature.[2]

Marxist critiques of the ontology of more-than-humanism underpin a more profound dissatisfaction with how they feel it undermines the political imperative of critical theory. They focus on Latour's reluctance to attribute social and environmental problems to the operations of capitalism, argu-ing that the focus in ANT on fluid relations neglects the persistence and power of political economic structures (Wainwright, 2005). They caution that all relations are not equal, that some networks seem remarkably fixed and permanent, and that the ANT focus on the agency of technologies and infrastructure masks the unequal human social relations mediated by such technologies. Hornborg accuses Latour of 'technological fetishism' (2014).[3] In a withering article, he lambasts Latour, Haraway, and others for 'abandoning serious analysis altogether' (2017, 66), of 'dithering while the planet burns', and ultimately of being complicit in the neoliberal project:

> Unfortunately, however, the growth enthusiasts and ecomodernists who are promoting this civilization are unlikely to be the least perturbed by posthumanism. In keeping critical human science defused—preoccupied with crochet artwork, leaking dogs, and expensive mushrooms—the promotion of posthumanist discourse is ultimately tantamount to looking away while neoliberal capitalism continues to destroy the planet. In other words, it can only serve as a convenient accomplice of neoliberalism.
>
> (2017, 66)

Malm and Hornborg offer polemics, which are useful, in that they clearly identify the problems with an extreme version of a flat ontology, but they tend towards parody and caricature. Many of the problems they identify with more-than-humanism were anticipated by geographers and others in science studies as they first engaged with ANT, with figures like Thrift (2000) and Whatmore (2002) being ambivalent about its failure to capture specific human competencies while Susan Leigh Star (1991) cautioned about the inability of ANT to differentiate between the durability of different networks as well as account for how some are excluded from processes of ordering.

5.1.1 Reconciling more-than-human geography and political ecology

More recent work has again sought to reconcile the concerns of Marxist political ecology with the unequal and unsustainable operations of neoliberal capitalism, with more-than-human geography. Three moves towards synthesis stand out here. The first is found in research that explores how human and animal life is managed in the intensive practices of modern capitalist agriculture and through the globalised networks of international trade. For example, as we traced in Section 2.3, Steve Hinchliffe and his collaborators (2016) have traced the emergence and proliferation of zoonotic disease in the intensive livestock systems that produce much of the world's pork, chicken, and prawns. These diseases include avian flu, campylobacter (a bacteria that causes food poisoning), and antimicrobial resistance. They suggest that the simplified ecologies of such farms, coupled with the concentration of stressed and immuno-compromised animal bodies, animal waste, and high levels of pharmaceutical use create 'disease hotspots': ideal situations for the emergence of new and highly virulent strains of pathogenic microbes. As we saw with COVID, these diseases easily cross over into human bodies and become highly mobile, travelling in human passengers and along the supply chains of the global food system.

Engaging with approaches from political economy, Hinchliffe et al. suggest that we see these as 'industrial diseases' generated by the logics of the 'just in time' production systems that are now common in globalised agriculture, and which have radically changed the biology of animal bodies, as well as further degrading the living and working conditions of agricultural labourers. Julie Guthman (2019) offers a comparable synthesis of political ecology and more-than-human approaches in her analysis of the emergence of plant disease in the Californian strawberry industry. She traces how the logics of capitalist agriculture drove process of automation, monoculture, fertiliser and pesticide dependence, and low pay and toxic working conditions which created the ideal conditions for the emergence and spread of pesticide-resistant pathogens as well as worker health problems. The high value of land makes it uneconomic for farmers to de-intensify and lower yields or to switch to organic models. The work of Guthman, Hinchliffe, and others couples an interest in political and economic practices with a close attention to the ecological and immunological relations that configure health and disease.

A second model of synthesis is offered by Jason Moore (2015) in his analysis of how global capitalism has transformed the 'web of life'. Moore is a Marxist political ecologist who once worked closely with Malm and Hornborg, but who is more sympathetic to more-than-humanist concepts and concerns. In his book *Capitalism and the Web of Life*, Moore traces the historical transformation of the nonhuman world under capitalism to argue that the Anthropocene is better described as the Capitalocene. He explains that 'the Capitalocene signifies capitalism as a way of organizing nature – as a multispecies, capitalist world-ecology, situated in the web of life' (2015, 6). He presents capitalism as a 'world ecology' or a 'way of organising nature' characterised by now-planetary scale modifications to earth systems. He focuses on how capitalism creates and appropriates 'cheap natures' by undervaluing food, energy, resources, and human labour to extract profit. He cautions that these cheap natures are coming to an end, with disastrous consequences and that we need to find other modes of valuing life and planetary systems. He suggests that 'global warming is not the accomplishment of an abstract humanity, the *Anthropos*. Global warming is capital's crowning achievement. Global warming is *capitalogenic*' (Moore, 2016; no page, *emphasis in original*). As an example of synthesis, Moore presents capital accumulation as an ecological process, arguing that we need to understand 'capitalism in nature', not capitalism as set apart from nature as in the work of Hornborg and others. He seeks to avoid the Nature-Society dualism that he detects in Marxist analysis and offer a relational ontology which grants some agency to the nonhuman world in both 'co-producing' and resisting capitalist economic relations.

A third and final strand of synthesis examines how more-than-human approaches help political ecologists understand the economic value provided by a range of plants and animals. The focus here is on the coupled concepts of 'nonhuman labour' and 'lively commodities'. Geographers like Maan Barua (2019), Rosemary Collard, and Jessica Dempsey (2013) develop Marx's labour theory of value, which traces how the labour of (indentured, enslaved, waged, or otherwise employed human) workers adds value to material inputs in the production of commodities. It follows how this value accrues unequally to capitalist employers at the expense of labour and seeks to find ways of organising the relations of production differently. Recent writing shares Jason Moore's concern with the consequences of cheap natures and explores what happens when we take animals, plants, and microbes not as objects and resources but as workers or labourers (Besky and Blanchette, 2019; Ernwein et al., 2021). This writing identifies a typology of forms of nonhuman labour that includes:

- the 'physical labour' performed by draught animals like donkeys and working animals like sheepdogs and horses (Coulter, 2016);
- the 'metabolic labour' (Beldo, 2017; Wadiwel, 2018) of chickens and other livestock that transform plants to meat and dairy products before they are killed and eaten. As well as of the microbes in their guts that do the metabolism (Cooper, 2017; Folkers and Opitz, 2022). Or of plants enrolled as biofuels or agents of carbon sequestration (Palmer, 2021);
- the 'body work' and 'affective labour' performed by both therapy animals like domestic pets and those providing entertainment in zoos and other captive settings (Barua, 2020).

187

- the 'ecological labour' of animals like beavers or valued ecosystems charged with delivering ecosystem services as part of 'nature-based solutions' to environmental problems (Lorimer, 2020) or as inspirations for military-industrial projects of biomimicry (Goldstein and Johnson, 2015).

This literature applies the labour theory of value to better understand the 'work of nature' (Battistoni, 2016). It helps specify the forms of value that some nonhumans provide in a capitalist economy. It also raises important political questions about how animals and other nonhumans might be empowered and emancipated through a redistribution of the ownership of the means of production, that we discuss in Section 5.3 below.

5.2 With black and indigenous studies: provincialising and decolonising more-than-humanism

A second set of criticisms of more-than-humanism comes from decolonial, black, and indigenous studies. These connected fields are concerned with revealing the history of racism and colonialism and critiquing their continuity, both in the world at large and in academia (for introductions, see Jazeel, 2019; Hawthorne, 2019; Noxolo, 2022; de Leeuw and Hunt, 2018). As we explained in Chapter 1, key thinkers in these fields like Franz Fanon, Sylvia Winter, and Edward Said were central to the deconstruction of the modern figure of the human. They revealed how the human has often been defined in relation to a racialised or primitive other, who was rendered subhuman or inhuman. And they traced how the contemporary circle of humanist concern rarely extends to equally encompass all forms of racial and ethnic difference. As we have seen in the previous chapters, there is already a vibrant conversation between more-than-humanism and black and indigenous studies, with the rise of Black Geographies and anthropologists and geographers increasingly recognising the more-than-human character of non-Western cosmologies and seeking to engage and collaborate with indigenous people in their research. These developments have come in part as a response to the criticisms that we outline below, but critics maintain that more-than-humanism remains insufficiently attuned to the history and politics of racism and colonialism. We can divide these criticisms into two related themes.

5.2.1 Provincialising more-than-humanism

In the first line of criticism, indigenous scholars have sought to provincialise more-than-humanism. The idea of 'provincialising' was developed by the postcolonial theorist Dipesh Chakrabarty (2009) in his book *Provincialising Europe*. He argued that Western social science accounts of a universal human experience and condition, of rationality, and of a secular modernity do not hold everywhere. Instead, they are produced in particular places at particular times and then exported, often violently, to other locations which are made to fit these accounts (e.g. race, development, nature). Chakrabarty argues that we need to provincialise Western theory to acknowledge that it is produced somewhere, might not apply everywhere, and thus to make space for theory from what were once seen as the margins. He is not proposing that we reject Western social theory but that it will be renewed through an engagement with other accounts of the world.

This idea of provincialising helps describe an insistent and growing concern amongst indigenous and decolonial scholars with the orthodox origin story of more-than-humanism that we related in Chapter 1. In this account: (i) humanism is a uniquely European intellectual and political achievement that begins in the Renaissance rediscovery of the values of classical European civilisation and proceeds through their development by European scholars associated with the Enlightenment and the Scientific Revolution; and (ii) that the problems with the model of humanism to which this gave rise have only been diagnosed by a small number of perceptive European social scientists, especially anthropologists like Latour and Haraway, who argue that 'we' have never been modern or human. Decolonial historians have addressed the deficiencies with the first strand of this narrative by tracing the spatially complex intellectual histories of humanism and noting the international geographies of knowledge exchange between Europe, China, India, Africa, and the Arab world that underpinned the Renaissance and the Enlightenment. They convincingly show that the Enlightenment was not solely a European achievement (Conrad, 2012).

Meanwhile, critics of the standard origin story of more-than-humanism argue that there are important silences in how it is told and in how its intellectual foundations are presented. For example, Métis[4] anthropologist and scholar of indigenous studies Zoe Todd (2016) provides a compelling account of her disappointment on attending her first anthropology conference and hearing Bruno Latour speak about climate change and the need to establish new relations to the Earth. She relates how:

> I waited through the whole talk, to hear the Great Latour credit Indigenous thinkers for their millennia of engagement with sentient environments, with cosmologies that enmesh people into complex relationships between themselves and all relations, and with climates and atmospheres as important points of organization and action. I waited. I waited, with baited breath ... It never came. He did not mention Inuit. Or Anishinaabeg. Or Nehiyawak. Or any Indigenous thinkers at all.
>
> (2016, 7)

Todd uses this anecdote to develop a broader argument that the more-than-human turn:

> Was spinning itself on the backs of non-European thinkers. And again, the ones we credited for these incredible insights into the 'more-than-human', sentience and agency, and the ways through which to imagine our 'common cosmopolitical concerns' were not the people who built and maintain the knowledge systems that European and North American anthropologists and philosophers have been studying for well over a hundred years, and predicating many of their current 'aha' ontological moments (or re-imaginings of the discipline) upon. No, here we were celebrating and worshipping a European thinker for 'discovering', or newly articulating by drawing on a European intellectual heritage, what many an Indigenous thinker around the world could have told you for millennia.
>
> (2016, 7–8)

Todd accuses Latour, and the wider field of anthropology in which she is based, of intellectual 'extractivism': of taking the knowledges of indigenous people without attribution and without ensuring that they benefit from their incorporation into the academic canon.[5]

5.2.2 Decolonising more-than-humanism

A second, connected strand of critical work from black and indigenous studies aims to decolonise more-than-humanism. It critiques the efforts by more-than-human scholars that we outlined in previous chapters to engage with indigenous and black scholars, communities, and their ideas, suggesting that these collaborations do not sufficiently decolonise academic relations of knowledge production; nor do they address the structural violence of contemporary racism and the persistence of neo-colonial political and economic relations in agriculture, conservation, resource extraction, and other modes of environmental management. They accuse more-than-humanism of being complicit in colonial modes of violence.

One example is provided by African American geographer and 'scholar-activist'[6] Janae Davis and her co-authors (2019). In a critique of the writings of Donna Haraway, Anna Tsing, and others on the plantation and on the rise of the Plantationocene that we encountered in Section 4.4, they note 'the unmarked whiteness and Eurocentricity of Anthropocene discourses' and suggest that: 'their multispecies framing minimizes the role of racial politics and leads to a flattened notion of "making kin" that is inadequate for the creation of more just ecologies in the plantation present' (3). Critics suggest that more-than-human geography, as part of wider initiatives in the discipline to engage with indigenous and black studies, still tends to essentialise, dilute, or extract non-Western knowledges.[7] For example, in a reflection on her hostile experience of presenting at the 2011 annual conference of the Association of American Geographers, the indigenous Kwakwaka'wakw[8] scholar Sarah Hunt (2014) argues that

> Indigenous knowledge is rarely seen as legitimate on its own terms, but must be negotiated in relation to pre-established modes of inquiry. The heterogeneity of Indigenous voices and world-views can easily become lost in efforts to understand Indigeneity in ways that fix Indigenous knowledge, suppressing its dynamic nature.
>
> (2014, 29, in Barker and Pickerill, 2020, 645)

Critics like Hunt are sceptical as to whether it is possible to fully decolonise a discipline that was so central to the colonial project, cautioning that 'the master's tools of colonization will not work to decolonize what the master built'.[9] They suggest that the moves to decentre Western science and to recentre marginal, vernacular, and indigenous thought, that we outlined in Chapter 4, are not sufficient (Loftus, 2019). Instead, they serve as what Tuck and Yang (2012) describe as 'settler moves to innocence', which they define as

> Those strategies or positionings that attempt to relieve the settler of feelings of guilt or responsibility without giving up land or power or privilege, without having to change much at all. In fact, settler scholars may gain professional kudos or a boost in their reputations for being so sensitive or self-aware. Yet settler moves to innocence are hollow, they only serve the settler.
>
> (2012, 10)

A comparable critique is offered by David Chandler and Julian Reid (2019) in their book *Becoming Indigenous*, which presents a critical analysis of the turn to indigeneity in both more-than-human scholarship and contemporary Western approaches to environmental or Anthropocene governance. They are critical of Latour and others' claims, that we reviewed in Chapter 4, that we have all 'become indigenous' in the Anthropocene as we all experience the 'universal condition of dispossession' of which indigenous people are the experts due to 400 years of colonisation. They suggest that this interest in indigeneity is insincere, arguing that

> The interests of the West in indigeneity today appears to us to have arisen less out of any genuine concern for appreciating the diverse realities and powers of indigenous ways of being and more about the crisis that is afflicting the West's confidence in its own future and survivability.
>
> (2019, 150)

They suggest this forms part of the wider neoliberal shift in governance that prioritises resilience or 'ways of coping in the Anthropocene' (2019, 17) that we reviewed in Section 4.4, so that

The ontopolitical imaginary of indigeneity is less concerned with contributing to existing struggles against white supremacy or other racialised structures, with discourses of equality or inclusion, or with liberal or modernist rights struggles, but with learning ways of becoming responsible and adaptive.

(2019, 17)[10]

5.2.3 Reconciling more-than-human geography with indigenous and black studies

More-than-human geographers take these criticisms seriously, and many would dispute the accusation that they are complicit in colonialism or guilty of settler moves to innocence. But in the spirit of reconciliation, all share in the growing awareness of the wider need to decolonialise the discipline of geography at large. The growing public awareness of contemporary racism that followed the Black Lives Matter campaign, powered up existing moves to attend to how the discipline was historically entangled with racism and settler colonialism, and to address the persistence of extractive models of academic practice in the colonial present.[11] We see evidence of this decolonial move in the work of Bawaka Country et al., that we encountered in previous chapters, whose writings aim to counter extractive academic relationships and to centre indigenous participants and Country itself as authors and beneficiaries of the research collaboration. Two further moves towards reconciliation are worth noting here.

The first is found in efforts to decolonise animal geography by centring analysis on human-animal relationships from the Global South (Hovorka, 2016). One example is given by Krithika Srinivasan and her co-authors (2019) in their work on decolonising public health approaches to the management of rabies in India. They trace how dominant approaches focus on the eradication or vaccination of the street dogs that are the primary vector for the disease. But they caution that this model is premised on a (neo)colonial, Western model of dogs as pets and property. Drawing on participatory, ethnographic research with different urban residents, including marginal pavement dwellers and waste workers, they instead note how 'as the Tamil term "theru nai" (street dog) conveys, these animals are seen as rightfully belonging in public spaces—dogs that are not under human ownership are not automatically "stray"' (7). Instead, 'dogs are perceived as 'paavam', and as 'jeevan'—as vulnerable living beings who are susceptible to various harms and suffering, and who are a part of society' (7). They map the rich vernacular knowledge of their participants on how to live safely with dogs. Drawing on this work, they propose that:

> In the context of rabies, the decolonisation of public health agendas involves paying attention to, without reifying or essentialising, human-dog interactions that do not conform to Western norms of dog ownership. Decolonisation involves taking seriously the plurality of interrelations between street dogs, health and people. This generates fresh, perhaps counter-intuitive, ways of thinking about and approaching the emergent possibilities of healthy publics.
>
> (2019, 8)

Their analysis seeks to counter the persistence of colonial models of conceiving animals and of denigrating subaltern knowledges, while recognising the multispecies character of urban life and pushing the potential of a more generous, more-than-human model of One Health less premised on animal death.[12]

A second example is given in work emerging from the criticisms of the unmarked whiteness and Eurocentricity of Anthropocene discourses associated with the Plantationocene that we noted above. This seeks to reconcile a concern with racial politics with a multispecies and/or new materialist ontology and ethics. It maintains a close attention to interspecies and intraspecies difference to avoid the risks of what Davis et al. (2019) term the 'multispecies flattening' that we reviewed in Section 5.1. One example is given in the work of Kathryn Yusoff we reviewed in the previous chapter (see Box 4.4), who is informed by black geographers researching the historical 'Maroon ecologies' of freed slaves living in forests on the edges of colonial plantations in Jamaica and the USA (Moulton, 2023). These authors draw on the influential writings of the Jamaican philosopher Sylvia Wynter and her analysis of 'the plot': the spaces on the margins of the plantation where slaves grew their own food. As Davis et al. (2019) explain, for Wynter, the plot was a 'demonic ground': a site for the 'underlife of the plantation' which nurtured 'an oppositional mode of Black life'. They propose that:

> It is within the plot that we find relational modes of being, multiple forms of kinship, and non-binary ways of engaging the world that foster ethics of care, equity, resilience, creativity, and sustainability. It is

absolutely crucial to recognize that the ethics of the plot are forged in and articulated through grounded racial–political struggles … Thus, the plot offers a challenge to ethical visions that minimize or obscure unequal relations of difference, and it might help conceptualize multispecies assemblages that lead out of socioecological crises toward better futures – assemblages that are not just envisioned but lived and that simultaneously tend to the needs of social reproduction, social justice, and ecological care'.

(2019, 8)

This revisionist reading of the plantation is mirrored in contemporary research by the anthropologist Sophie Chao (2022) on palm oil plantations in West Papua, Indonesia. Chao traces how the indigenous Marind who live and work on these plantations attribute environmental destruction to humans, technologies, and capitalism but also to the actions of the oil palm plant itself. She presents the capitalist violence of the plantation as a multispecies act but also makes clear the creative ways in which the Marind fashion their own changing worlds on the margins of the plantation system.

5.3 With critical animal studies

A third set of criticisms come from those concerned with the rights and welfare of individual animals; a position broadly described as critical animal studies. While thinkers and activists involved in animal studies were central to the invention of more-than-human approaches – for example in the field of animal geographies (see Section 2.2) – key figures in this area have expressed a range of worries that their original, critical focus on animal harm and on improving the lives of animals has been diluted or even lost.

Some in critical animal studies share the concerns of the political ecologists we encountered above that more-than-human approaches struggle to account for the systemic drivers of land use change and animal exploitation. Most terrestrial mammals (who have always been the principal concern of critical animal studies) are kept in domestic and agricultural relations that are increasingly subject to the logics of capitalism. The lives of millions of chickens, pigs, cattle, and sheep are configured by the laws of supply and demand, by the investment strategies of large companies, and by government regulations (or their absence). In capitalist agriculture, many animals are exploited as 'cheap nature' (Patel and Moore, 2017), living short painful and isolated lives. Critical animal studies scholars concerned with industrial agriculture suggest that the more-than-human approaches we outlined in the previous chapter (Section 4.3) that advocate an ethics of response-ability in proximal relations between people and livestock do not sufficiently account for the political and economic drivers of agriculture and food consumption that cause both human and animal suffering. They argue that the ethics of intimate flourishing associated with multispecies approaches are insufficient for tackling animal abuse and for driving the large reductions they see as necessary in the production and consumption of meat. As Srinivasan (2016) puts it:

> The emphasis on situated and pragmatic ethics thus often results in *a favouring of the status quo* because it places the onus on individuals and their encounters with animals without attending adequately to larger processes and systems that mediate these encounters … animal ethics is viewed mostly as a matter for micro-scale decision making: it is largely seen as a *personal* – not *political* – matter'.
>
> (2016, 77)

Instead, they advocate for large-scale legal, political, and economic reforms designed to tackle animal exploitation (Gillespie and Collard, 2015).

A second set of criticisms come from critical animal theorists like Cary Wolfe (2012), who are concerned that some versions of the relational, affirmative environmental ethics associated with multispecies approaches give undue emphasis to biological processes (like evolution, wildness, or ecological functions like biodiversity, carbon sequestration, and resilience) over the lived experience of individual animals. They caution that this can lead to a mode of managing life that normalises and legitimises the large-scale killing and suffering of animals that are held to be out of place, or whose diets and ecological interactions harm valued others. We see examples in the literatures on biopolitics we reviewed in Section 4.3, including the commonplace ways in which conservationists and pest control authorities kill and control invasive species to secure the futures of valued native species.

We see similar tensions in efforts to restore ecological systems to enable processes of rewilding. Jamie explored this debate in collaborative writings with Clemens Driessen (Lorimer and Driessen, 2013) in the context of the Oostvaardersplassen, a nature reserve that hosts the flagship rewilding project in the Netherlands (see Box 3.3). Here, conservationists introduced 'back-bred' and 'de-domesticated' horses and cattle in order that they might perform 'naturalistic' models of grazing. But the Oostvaardersplassen does not contain wolves, or other predators who would control the populations of these herbivores in a more complete and fully functional ecology. Populations of cattle and horses expanded such that they put pressure on the food supply, go hungry, and even starve to death in the winter. While conservationists argue that starvation happens in the wild, those concerned with individual animal's welfare argue that the welfare of cattle and horses is being compromised or even sacrificed in the interests of the abstract idea of ecological functionality. They successfully campaigned to change the management of the reserve to allow the supplementary feeding of animals and to impose artificial controls on the growth of the herbivore population. These criticisms and the debates they have engendered make visible the differences and the tensions between approaches to individual animal and ecological ethics.

Critical animal studies scholars have voiced a third, connected set of concerns about the deficiencies of a relational ontology of entanglements. Krithika Srinivasan (2019) observes that a relational ontology does not necessarily lead to a relational ethics that takes seriously the interests of the nonhumans caught up in any entanglements. She analyses a range of situations in which ethical dualisms between humans and animals co-exist alongside nondualistic ontologies and sophisticated ways of attuning to the lifeworlds of animals. These situations include the control of street dogs and other practices of pest control in India that we discussed above. She shows how effective pest control requires a deep and detailed knowledge of the ecologies of the target organism in order to set traps, and to track and catch the target animal. Pest control, like hunting, animal testing, and other lethal modes of animal encounter requires the hunter, technician, or pest control officer to adopt and develop a relational ontology even as this is put to work to end nonhuman lives or to cause suffering. Often hunters, lab technicians, and pest controllers do care about their animals and seek to minimise animal suffering. But they ultimately work to secure an ethical dualism that holds animal lives to be inferior to those of humans.

Srinivasan's concerns about the ethical failures of more-than-human approaches resonate with those expressed by Eva Giraud (2019) in her book *What comes after Entanglement?* Giraud offers a critique of Haraway and multispecies studies, focusing on situations in which humans and animals are harmed by virtue of being entangled, and where their interests would best be served by selective processes of disentanglement. She outlines what she terms 'an ethics of exclusion', which 'pays attention to the entities, practices, and ways of being that are *foreclosed* when other entangled realities are materialized' (2, *emphasis in original*). And she identifies what she terms 'the paradox of relationality': 'that it struggles to accommodate things that are resistant to being in relation, including forms of politics that actively oppose particular relations' (7).

Rosemary Collard (2014, 2020) provides convincing examples of the problems with an ethics of entanglement and the merit of an ethics of exclusion in her analysis of the exotic pet trade and the practices through which animals rescued from this trade are rehabilitated for return to the wild. She shows how taking animals from the forests of Central America and training them for life in captivity involves violently severing social relations with kin and other animals in the habitats from which they are extracted. She follows how their rehabilitation for return to the wild involves making these animals distrustful of humans to which they have become accustomed in captivity, in order that they can adjust to the demands of living in the forest and avoid the risk of subsequent capture. For Collard, this involves selective acts of disentanglement and a deliberate ethics of exclusion.

5.3.1 Reconciling more-than-human geography with critical animal studies

The differences between critical animal studies and more-than-humanism are less stark than those reviewed in the two previous sections, and both share a great deal of common ground. Nonetheless, there are two areas of reconciliation we flag here in which animal studies scholars have sought to respond to these criticisms.

The first seeks to reconcile an interest in proximal human-animal encounters and individual animal experience with a broader critical analysis of the political economy of modern animal agriculture. Strands of this work develop the long-standing interest in animal studies in the 'shared suffering' (Haraway, 2008) of humans and animals employed in, or made subject to, factory farms, slaughterhouses, and animal testing facilities. This work reveals the conjoined exploitation of different species like pigs, cattle, and undocumented, migrant workers (Blanchette, 2020; Shukin, 2009). It also attends to how animal carers develop modes of 'embodied empathy' to try and understand and improve the captive animal experience (Greenhough and Roe, 2011, 2019), sometimes subjecting their own bodies to harm to better understand the experience or test subjects like the rats and mice that predominate the animal houses for scientific research.

Jocelyne Porcher (2017) develops this approach in her book *The Ethics of Animal Labour: A Collaborative Utopia*. This forms part of the wider interest in animal labour that we introduced above. But she takes it in a slightly different direction to focus on the lived experience, welfare, and rights of animals as labourers, rather than on their role in delivering forms of value under capitalism. For Porcher (and others like Kendra Coulter, 2016), the long history of animal domestication requires us to treat animals like horses, dogs, donkeys, and livestock as workers and to develop an ethics of labour as the basis for improving the welfare of agricultural animals. Unlike many in critical animal studies, she does not have a problem with the idea of animals as workers or of eating animals. Although she shares the horror of animal activists at the mistreatment associated with factory farming, she argues that good, interspecies working relations can be the foundation for an animal ethics, suggesting that working animals can enjoy mental and physical health. Her model of 'collaborative utopia' offers a critical appraisal of the political economy of modern industrial agriculture premised on a distinction between good and bad work. This is a provocative position that has been criticised by opponents of animal agriculture as well as by humanist scholars who dispute the idea of animal labour.

A second area of reconciliation aims to think through the tensions between the ecological and the individual animal ethics that we saw in the context of the Oostvaardersplassen above. Conceptually, this has led some to explore the ethical potential of concepts like hospitality and immunity, engaging the writings of philosophers like Jacques Derrida and Roberto Esposito (Hinchliffe and Ward, 2014). For example, Jamie has developed these concepts in an analysis of how a group of patients undergoing helminth therapy learn to live with parasitic worms to improve their own health and to gain remission from autoimmune disease. He explores how hosting worms requires them to endure the pain of infection and to modify their diets and lifestyles to care for their worms, taking seriously the welfare of individual worms in return for the benefits that the worms provide in recalibrating their immune systems to deliver a desired ecological function. Worms figure as 'gut buddies' (Lorimer, 2016); they are offered hospitality on condition that they provide mutual benefit. This somewhat bizarre story offers one example from a wider literature in animal studies and the environmental humanities that seeks to attend to the ethical complexities and trade-offs in human-animal relations.[13] In Donna Haraway's terms, this work 'stays with the trouble' (2016) and avoids making recourse to simple, pure, or final solutions to the inexorable challenges of human-nonhuman relations.

5.4 With advocates for science and progress

The final set of tensions are with a range of critical theorists concerned with how more-than-humanism engages with science and the degree to which it departs from or helps enable the Enlightenment project of human progress and emancipation. These criticisms build from those of the political ecologists and black and indigenous studies scholars reviewed above, as well as expressing internal tensions within more-than-humanism. They come in very contrasting forms including those who are concerned that some more-than-humanists have become insufficiently critical in making the new alliance with science (see Section 3.5) and in their optimism about biopolitics and planetary management. In contrast, others are concerned that some more-than-human approaches disavow science and reason so that it is rendered toothless and insufficient in the face of the political and environmental challenges of the Anthropocene. We explore these criticisms under the three themes of scientism, hubris, and transformation.

5.4.1 Scientism

As we explained in Chapter 1, more-than-human theory has origins in science studies and the work of geographers, sociologists, and anthropologists who studied science in action – tracing how scientists come to speak for the nonhuman world and how scientific knowledge is shaped by its social context. This work revealed the politics of Nature (Section 4.1), in which natural scientists appeal to a singular nature to shortcut the political processes expected in a deliberative democracy. More-than-humanists became wary of appeals to Science as objective and outside of politics, instead suggesting that we understand knowledge as situated, relational, and contingent on spatial and temporal location. Such interventions proved powerful in debunking scientific racism, in criticising the naturalisation of capitalism, gender, and sexuality, and for challenging anthropocentric models of resource extraction. But the diagnosis of the Anthropocene and the recognition of the key role science and scientists must play in securing habitable planetary futures pushed prominent more-than-humanists (like Donna Haraway, Bruno Latour, and Anna Tsing) to make new epistemic and political alliances with select fields of science and with some scientists.

In so doing, these scholars turned to fields of science that offer liberal, symbiotic, and ecological versions of the nonhuman world and of interspecies relations akin to the models of political and environmental interaction and organisation they advocate in their social theory. For example, Latour finds inspiration in holistic Earth System Science, while Haraway is drawn to ecological-evolutionary-developmental biology. Both see these sciences offering more palatable ontologies than the models of individual, violent, competition offered by Neo-Darwinism or the theories of genetic and environmental determinism that predominated in the 20th century. But critics suggest this risks 'scientism' – an excessive belief in the power of scientific knowledge based on a selective and unreflective borrowing of scientific theories. As Bruce Braun (2015) argues in a critique of new materialism

> In looking to the natural sciences, the [new materialist] literature too often takes "science" to speak in one voice, or in what often amounts to the same thing, draws selectively from the natural sciences in order to find the ideas and concepts it needs, ignoring science's heterogeneity and side-stepping vibrant internal debate over models and paradigms.
>
> (2015, 2–3)

Critics argue that this scientism is often coupled with an 'ahistoricism' (Buscher, 2022): the failure to see how specific scientific theories rise to prominence in response to historical conditions. For example, that the scientific accounts favoured by more-than-humanists emerge from the 'crisis disciplines' like Earth System Science, conservation biology, or immunology that are charged with addressing the bundled problems of the Anthropocene, and which sit within the wider environmental zeitgeist that has gripped the Western academy (Hörl and Burton, 2017). For Braun, it is ironic that a conceptual paradigm that is otherwise so committed to understanding things in relation fails to appreciate the historical contingencies associated with the rise to prominence of the scientific theories upon which it founds its approach. He notes:

There is an irony here, for even as many new materialists propose an ontology that is non-deterministic and non-teleological, they often deploy a very different epistemological position when it comes to the emergence of their ideas, which are viewed as universal rather than particular, and necessary rather than contingent: the world is marked by indeterminacy and contingency, except when it comes to theories of indeterminacy and contingency!

(2015, 4–5)

In response, Braun and others advocate continued analysis of science in its social, political, historical, and geographical contexts.

5.4.2 Hubris and ruination

A different set of tensions come from those like Nigel Clark (2011) who are concerned that some strands of more-than-humanism do not go far enough; that they do not acknowledge the radical asymmetry of nonhumans, especially geological forces, and that they are too optimistic about the ability of modern science and technology to understand and control nonhuman processes. These critics are most interested in the agencies of the elemental (see Section 2.5) and focus their criticisms on more-than-humanists concerned with the agency of human artefacts (like Latour) or with developing models of biopolitics to secure the circulation of life or to geoengineer planetary management. We encountered these figures in Section 4.4 in the discussion of nature recovery and biosecurity.

Clark cautions that the earth is 'indifferent': it does not need us, in the way that we need it. Like Eva Giraud (see above), he is interested in processes and entities not in direct relation to us. And he is most concerned that the disruptions that are predicted to accompany our passage into the Anthropocene have the potential to destroy civilisation. He suggests that a more-than-humanism seeking biopolitics smacks of hubris, or the excessive pride and self-confidence in human abilities (that in Greek tragedy leads to nemesis). He suggests that encounters with the powers of the Earth require theorists to be humbler and more cautious with their hopes and dreams of human mastery, pivoting instead to modes of 'ontopolitics' (rather than biopolitics) concerned with adapting to and living with worlds in ruins, including by learning from indigenous peoples and others already living in them (Clark and Szerszynski, 2020). An appeal to learning from those living in the ruins is most associated with Anna Tsing (2015) and her book *The Mushroom at the End of World*. Tsing follows the economic survival strategies of those who make a living from the matsutake mushroom trade, tracing how they generate value foraging for mushrooms in the secondary forests that regrow in various temperature regions in the ruins of industrial capitalist resource extraction.

5.4.3 Quietism and transformation

We explained in Sections 5.1 and 5.2 how the focus on 'becoming indige-nous' and on 'surviving in the ruins of capitalism' advocated by figures like Clark, Tsing, and Latour has been criticised by political ecologists and black and indigenous studies for the insufficient attention it pays to capitalism and colonialism. Here, we flag a further set of criticisms that come from philos-ophers and political theorists concerned that a focus on ruination leads to political quietism, a lack of ambition to tackle the planetary condition, and ultimately a betrayal of the Humanist, Enlightenment project. For example, the political theorists David Chandler and Julian Reid ask:

> If there is to be a flight from modernity, why should this lead to a 'return' to indigeneity? Perhaps it could be argued that the flight to indigeneity or the inculcation to become indigenous is a useful fram-ing, enabling a substantial lowering of policy-horizons to merely sur-viving or coping in the present. What is particularly attractive about this framing of the rolling back of aspirations is that it can be legit-imised and rationalised on the basis that retrenchment is actually a more 'authentic', more 'natural', more 'organic', more 'community'-oriented, more 'caring' approach, than the consumerist, extractivist, individualist, competitive approach of modernist demands for prog-ress and ever higher living standards. All those promises of a better future, which were given lip service by elites when there was com-petition between the alternatives of Left and Right, are seemingly now off the table in the times of coping, crises and constraint of the Anthropocene.
>
> (2019, 11)

They are suggesting that the focus on ruination, on coping, and on build-ing resilience is defeatist and apolitical, negating the potential of imagining and delivering more just and sustainable futures. Similarly, the geographer Stephanie Wakefield (writing with David Chandler and Kevin Grove) (2022) is critical of approaches to building resilience or coping with the asymmetric Anthropocene, suggesting that they dissolve the human into the flow of natural forces (with differing degrees of control), leaving no analytical or political space for visions of justice, progress, and human emancipation. She warns that in this formulation

> we must make a choice between two varieties of posthuman, either the human as suborned to the world – a world still 'for us' but one in which we are humbled into obeyance; the world of the adaptive imaginaries of recursivity offered by the advocates of resilience – or we must imagine a world that is not 'for us' and the dissolution of the subject itself; into the flows and abyssal flux of matter and meaninglessness.
>
> (2022, 398)

While authors like Chandler and Wakefield take on board some of the ontological and epistemic moves made by more-than-humanist theories, they call for a reassertion of the political and ethical foundations of the humanist project, shoring up a place for humans as a special category of life with distinct types of agency and unique responsibilities towards tackling contemporary environmental and social problems. In different ways, they seek to reimagine humanism for a transformative politics for the Anthropocene, calling for models of 'enlightened anthropocentrism' (Keulartz, 2012) or 'radical anthropocentrism' (Hamilton, 2017). Suggesting that, in the words of Chandler and Reid:

> The task is not one of losing the remnants of our human hubris to embrace our co-implications with the nonlinear circuitry of other resilient, adaptive living systems; it is to recover the image we once had of ourselves and are now in danger of losing—as a being with capacities different to other merely adaptive creatures, capable of saying no to mere nature, yes to human empowerment, existing free from the necessities of a mere life of endless toil, struggle and survival, which the blackmail of the Anthropocene would so happily reduce us to ... No discourse on modernity, however attuned to the violence, suffering and suppression which we moderns have done in

and to the world, should fail to arouse admiration and wonder at the immensity of the achievements, progression and breakthroughs made possible by the human guile, ingenuity and labour which the term evokes. If it does not arouse such then it is a bad and false discourse of little worth. It's time to say no to becoming indigenous and yes to the recovery of the hubris on which modernity was built and from which other worlds are yet to come, in destruction of the old, and in welcome of the new.

(2019, 152–153)

Stephanie Wakefield (2019) and Sara Nelson (2014) provide more concrete illustrations of this approach, in revisionist readings of resilience theory applied to the critical analysis of contemporary forms of environmental management like flood prevention. They are critical of the conservative tendencies of resilience theorists to shore up neoliberal order but suggest that the model of dynamic nonlinear systems marked by tipping points that is offered by resilience theory has the potential to imagine socio-ecological transformation towards more just and sustainable futures. Here Wakefield (2020) develops the concept of the 'back loop': the point in the dynamics of a system in which it moves from one condition to another. She suggests that we are now in 'the Anthropocene back loop' and that in harnessing the changes that are associated with a system in transition we might imagine and enact futures that depart radically from the status quo. She suggests that this involves working with nonhuman agencies – organic, technological, and inorganic – steering their interactions along a trajectory towards more desirable ends. She maintains a place for science and technology, holds the human in special regard, and shores up the humanist and Enlightenment teleology of progress and improvement.[14]

5.5 Conclusions

We began this book by identifying three core claims shared by various more-than-humanisms: extending agency beyond human actors, engaging with multiple ways of knowing, and turning attention to the relations and processes through which worlds cohere. In this chapter on tensions and prospects, we have seen each of these core assumptions challenged. We are reminded by political ecologists and decolonial scholars of the importance of humans in shaping economies and empires: humans might not be the only actors shaping worlds, but humans (both present and past) are of *particular importance* in shaping contemporary and future human lives. We are reminded by indigenous, decolonial, and science studies scholars that in the enthusiasm for multiple ways of knowing, some forms of knowledge are appropriated without adequate recognition, and others are reified without adequate attention being paid to how such knowledges are produced and transmitted. And we are reminded by all of this work, as well as by scholars in critical animal studies, that specific relations created *largely through the actions of people* indelibly shape the lived experiences of other people, other animals, and the ecologies of wider worlds.

In simple terms, more-than-humanism is thus critiqued for its apparent 'bluntness'. In widening its focus beyond the groups of people (and their institutions) whose actions do so much to create relations of inequality, violence, and destruction, more-than-humanists apparently lose the ability to produce incisive critical analyses. In seeking to celebrate emergent practices of living well within more-than-human worlds, more-than-humanists are seen as idealist dreamers too busy playing with critters while the world burns.

More-than-humanism is thus caricatured as both cuddly and apolitical. It is nothing of the sort. Instead, as we have outlined in the preceding chapters, the 'sharpness' of more-than-human analyses comes, first, from the attention given to the ways in which relational worlds cohere. Not all of the actors are human, and diverse actors do not all have the same importance in shaping worlds. What people do matters, often disproportionately; *and* there is often more afoot, too. The sharpness comes, second, through forms of affirmative critique (see Chapter 4) that create space for imagining alternative ways of living, often opposed to the status quo. The radical edge of more-than-humanism thus comes through both identifying harmful relations (between people, among ecologies) and engaging with emergent or long-standing cultural practices that offer alternatives. These alternative practices offer a different model of progress to the humanist teleology we encountered in Chapter 1 – progress that is more diverse, and less enslaved to a particular mode of scientific understanding and capitalist development. It is a politics of hope to imagine worlds otherwise.

Nevertheless, the tensions identified in this chapter are generative in their reminders. There can, indeed, be a tendency in some more-than-human work to over-emphasise nonhuman agency or to lose sight of today's struggles while straining to imagine utopian futures. The search for alternatives has sometimes led to expropriation of non-Western ontological theories without recognition or permission, often enacted through citational chains of secondary interlocutors. And an undoubted fetish for novelty, technology, and some forms of science can be traced through the field. More-than-human analyses are often 'sharper' when they engage with these concerns, as we have shown in the various prospects outlined above.

Questions for reflection

1   What are the risks of de-centring the human in human geography?

2   Is more-than-human geography extractivist and complicit in furthering colonialism?

3   What should be terms of engagement between more-than-human geography and natural science?

4   What are the risks to plants and animals of a more-than-human focus on making relations and enabling response-ability?

5   Are more-than-human geographers merely dithering while the planet burns?

6   Are plans for planetary stewardship inevitably hubristic?

Suggestions for reading

Key works that are critical of more-than-humanism:

Büscher B (2022) The nonhuman turn: Critical reflections on alienation, entanglement and nature under capitalism. *Dialogues in Human Geography* 12(1): 54–73.

Chandler D and Reid J (2019) *Becoming Indigenous: Governing imaginaries in the Anthropocene*. London: Rowman & Littlefield International.

Hornborg A (2017) Dithering while the planet burns: Anthropologists' approaches to the anthropocene. *Reviews in Anthropology* 46(2–3): 61–77.

Sundberg J (2014) Decolonizing posthumanist geographies. *Cultural Geographies* 21(1): 33–47.

Todd Z (2016) An indigenous feminist's take on the ontological turn: 'Ontology' is just another word for colonialism. *Journal of Historical Sociology* 29(1): 4–22.

Tuck E and Yang KW (2012) Decolonization is not a metaphor. *Decolonization: Indigeneity, Education & Society* 1(1): 1–40.

Summaries of these debate and attempts at synthesis:

Braun B (2015) New materialisms and neoliberal natures. *Antipode* 47(1): 1–14.

Davis J, Moulton AA, Van Sant L and Williams B (2019) Anthropocene, capitalo-cene, … plantationocene? A manifesto for ecological justice in an age of global crises. *Geography Compass* 13(5): e12438.

Falcon J (2023) Toward a critical posthuman geography. *Cultural Geographies* 30(1): 19–34.

Giraud EH (2019) *What comes after entanglement? Activism, anthropocentrism, and an ethics of exclusion.* Durham: Duke University Press.

Lorimer J (2020) *The probiotic planet: Using life to manage life.* Minneapolis: University of Minnesota Press.

Margulies JD and Bersaglio B (2018) Furthering post-human political ecologies. *Geoforum* 94: 103–106.

Srinivasan K (2019) Remaking more-than-human society: Thought experiments on street dogs as "nature". *Transactions of the Institute of British Geographers* 44(2): 376–391.

Notes

1   Several early more-than-human geographers cut their teeth as Marxist theorists. But it was also a dissatisfaction with Marxist approaches that led key figures like Sarah Whatmore, Doreen Massey, and Nigel Thrift to look elsewhere for their conceptual resources. In an important paper in 1989, Margaret Fitzsimmons took Marxist geographers to task for their failure to account for the 'matter of Nature' (Fitzsimmons, 1989), while in *Hybrid Geographies*, Sarah Whatmore (2002) expressed concerns that the Marxists' dialectics did not sufficiently escape the problems of the Nature-Society binary. For a wider discussion, see Castree (2005). Other critics of Marxist political ecology remain concerned about its prevalent anthropocentrism. Political ecology remains principally concerned with how Western efforts to protect nonhuman life impact on marginalised people. They argue that political ecology has not traditionally been concerned with animals or the environment – beyond their role as inputs for human livelihoods (Srinivasan and Kasturirangan, 2016).

2   Similar arguments are made in Büscher (2022) and Swyngedouw and Ernstson (2018).

3   Hornborg presents his theory of agency as follows. 'I hold that the distinction between living and non-living entities hinges on the occurrence of agency, that is, the capacity to act. Agency is propelled by purpose. All living organisms have purposes inscribed in their composition, whether the amoeba's absorption of nutrients from its surroundings, the tree's extension of branches into the sunlight and roots into the soil, or a human preparing and ingesting a meal. Such various processes are all examples of agency generated by purposes internal to living beings. When purposes are consciously reflected on, as is often the case among humans, we talk about intentions. To attribute agency, purposes, or intentions to

non-living objects is tantamount to fetishism. The purposes which define biotic entities presuppose a certain capacity for sentience and communication... Amoebas, trees and humans are all equipped to register specific aspects of their environments and to somehow respond to them. This capacity for sentience and communication is what defines a subject. Abiotic entities such as rocks or artifacts do not have such capacities. They are objects' (2007, 97).

4   The Métis are indigenous peoples whose historical homelands include parts of northwest Canada and northern United States.

5   In the case of geography, this argument was first outlined by Juanita Sundberg (2014), who argues (in the words of Margulies and Bersaglio, in a useful review of her work) that: 'an unqualified reliance on Anglo-European philosophy in post-human geographies privileges colonial and settler-colonial onto-epistemologies. When matched by a lack of reflexivity, post-humanist discourse risks re-enacting epistemic violence against Indigenous and other non-dualistic onto-epistemological traditions. Accordingly, these silences make post-humanism complicit in re-producing a colonial intellectual tradition that problematically appropriates, erases, or invalidates other ways of being and knowing' (2018, 104).

6   Davis describes herself in these terms on her researchgate.net page https://www.researchgate.net/profile/Janae-Davis

7   Davis et al. suggest that in coining the concept of the Plantationocene 'The scholars of the plantation and slave plot that Haraway (2015) alludes to remain unnamed. We see their nameless footnoting as part of a broader failure among initial Plantationocene scholarship to seriously attend to and ecological thought and practice' (2019, 5). See also Whyte (2018).

8   The Kwakwaka'wakw are one of the indigenous peoples of the Pacific Northwest Coast. Most live on their traditional territory on Vancouver Island.

9   I take this quotation from a tweet by the anthropologist Jairo Funez, who was referring to Smith (2021). The quotation is a reworking of the famous statement by the American writer, poet, and feminist and civil rights activist Audre Lorde: 'The Master's Tools Will Never Dismantle the Master's House'. For the original tweet, see https://twitter.com/Jairo_I_Funez/status/1546859441592700929

10 Chandler and Reid also pick up the criticism of the flat ontologies of more-than-humanism offered by political ecologists arguing that: 'The new forms of governing purporting to support, encourage and to draw from indigenous thought and practice are far too closely linked to contemporary philosophical and political trends in academic thought that equally seek to downplay the powers of human agency and the importance of political forms of subjectivity for transformative struggles and strategies. While leading international and domestic political institutions repeat mantras of resilience and adaptation, suborning human agency to the whims of market forces and 'natural' disasters, articulating the seeming stranglehold of neoliberal thinking, leading critical academic voices, from feminist and scientifically informed theorists like Donna Haraway and Anna Tsing to popular social and political philosophers like Bruno Latour and Timothy Morton, seek to diminish the human and celebrate non-human agency instead' (2019, 4).

11 'Decolonising geographical knowledges' was the theme of the 2017 RGS-IBG conference and the subject of many of the invited plenary talks and panels (for an introduction, see Radcliffe, 2017). It helped catalyse discussion in the

discipline about colonial histories. It also led to criticism from Black (and other BAME) geographers that it did not go far enough in that 'the emphasis on decolonising geographical knowledges rather than structures, institutions and praxis reproduces coloniality, because it recentres non-Indigenous, white and otherwise privileged groups in the global architecture of knowledge production' (Esson et al., 2017, 384).

12 See also the work of Steve Hinchliffe developing postcolonial approaches to antimicrobial resistance and multispecies health, drawing on ethnographic research with shrimp farmers in Bangladesh, which demonstrates the 'potential contribution that vernacular approaches to human and animal health can play in altering the milieu of resistance' Hinchliffe S (2022, 145). See also Margulies (2019) and Narayanan (2017).

13 In the case of the OVP, ethicists developed a practical model that tried to balance the claims of the individual animal with those of the wider ecology (Klaver et al., 2002).

14 For further examples of work in this register, see Buck (2019) and Lorimer (2020).

References

Barker AJ and Pickerill J (2020) Doings with the land and sea: Decolonising geographies, indigeneity, and enacting place-agency. *Progress in Human Geography* 44(4): 640–662.

Barua M (2019) Animating capital: Work, commodities, circulation. *Progress in Human Geography* 43(4): 650–669.

Barua M (2020) Affective economies, pandas, and the atmospheric politics of lively capital. *Transactions of the Institute of British Geographers* 45(3): 678–692.

Battistoni A (2016) Bringing in the work of nature: From natural capital to hybrid labor. *Political Theory* 45(1): 5–31.

Beldo L (2017) Metabolic labor: Broiler chickens and the exploitation of vitality. *Environmental Humanities* 9(1): 108–128.

Besky S and Blanchette A (2019) *How nature works: Rethinking labor on a troubled planet.* Albuquerque: University of New Mexico Press.

Blanchette A (2020) *Porkopolis: American animality, standardized life, and the factory farm.* Durham: Duke University Press.

Boyd W, Prudham WS and Schurman RA (2001) Industrial dynamics and the problem of nature. *Society & Natural Resources* 14(7): 555–570.

Braun B (2015) New materialisms and neoliberal natures. *Antipode* 47(1): 1–14.

Bryant RL and Bailey S (1997) *Third world political ecology.* London: Routledge.

Buck HJ (2019) *After geoengineering: Climate tragedy, repair, and restoration.* London: Verso Books.

Büscher B (2022) The nonhuman turn: Critical reflections on alienation, entanglement and nature under capitalism. *Dialogues in Human Geography* 12(1): 54–73.

Castree N (2001) Marxism, capitalism and the production of nature. In: Castree N and Braun B (eds) *Social nature.* Oxford: Blackwell, pp. 189–209.

Castree N (2002) False antitheses? Marxism, nature and actor-networks. *Antipode* 34(1): 111–146.

Castree N (2005) *Nature.* London: Routledge.

Chakrabarty D (2009) *Provincializing Europe: Postcolonial thought and historical difference - new edition.* Princeton, NJ: Princeton University Press.

Chandler D and Reid J (2019) *Becoming indigenous: Governing imaginaries in the Anthropocene.* London: Rowman & Littlefield International.

Chao S (2022) *In the shadow of the palms: More-than-human becomings in West Papua.* Durham: Duke University Press.

Clark N (2011) *Inhuman nature: Sociable living on a dynamic planet.* Thousand Oaks, CA: SAGE Publications.

Clark N and Szerszynski B (2020) *Planetary social thought: The Anthropocene challenge to the social sciences.* London: Wiley.

Collard R-C (2014) Putting animals back together, taking commodities apart. *Annals of the Association of American Geographers* 104(1): 151–165.

Collard RC (2020) *Animal traffic: Lively capital in the global exotic pet trade.* Durham: Duke University Press.

Collard RC and Dempsey J (2013) Life for sale? The politics of lively commodities. *Environment and Planning A* 45(11): 2682–2699.

Conrad S (2012) Enlightenment in global history: A historiographical critique. *The American Historical Review* 117(4): 999–1027.

Cooper MH (2017) Open up and say "baa": Examining the stomachs of ruminant livestock and the real subsumption of nature. *Society & Natural Resources* 30(7): 812–828.

Coulter K (2016) *Animals, work, and the promise of interspecies solidarity.* New York: Palgrave Macmillan US.

Davis J, Moulton AA, Van Sant L and Williams B (2019) Anthropocene, Capitalocene, … Plantationocene? A manifesto for ecological justice in an age of global crises. *Geography Compass* 13(5): e12438.

de Leeuw S and Hunt S (2018) Unsettling decolonizing geographies. *Geography Compass* 12(7): e12376.

Ernwein M, Ginn F and Palmer J (2021) *The work that plants do: Life, labour and the future of vegetal economies.* London: Transcript Verlag.

Esson J, Noxolo P, Baxter R, Daley P and Byron M (2017) The 2017 RGS-IBG Chair's theme: Decolonising geographical knowledges, or reproducing coloniality? *Area* 49(3): 384–388.

Falcon J (2023) Toward a critical posthuman geography. *Cultural Geographies* 30(1): 19–34.

Fitzsimmons M (1989) The matter of nature. *Antipode* 21: 106–120.

Folkers A and Opitz S (2022) Low-carbon cows: From microbial metabolism to the symbiotic planet. *Social Studies of Science* 52(3): 330–352.

Gillespie K and Collard RC (2015) *Critical animal geographies: Politics, intersections and hierarchies in a multispecies world.* Abingdon: Taylor & Francis.

Giraud EH (2019) *What comes after entanglement? Activism, anthropocentrism, and an ethics of exclusion.* Durham: Duke University Press.

Goldstein J and Johnson E (2015) Biomimicry: New natures, new enclosures. *Theory, Culture and Society* 32(1): 61–81.

Greenhough B and Roe E (2011) Ethics, space, and somatic sensibilities: Comparing relationships between scientific researchers and their human and animal experimental subjects. *Environment and Planning D: Society and Space* 29(1): 47–66.

Greenhough B and Roe E (2019) Attuning to laboratory animals and telling stories: Learning animal geography research skills from animal technologists. *Environment and Planning D: Society and Space* 37(2): 367–384.

Guthman J (2019) *Wilted: Pathogens, chemicals, and the fragile future of the strawberry industry*. Oakland: University of California Press.

Hamilton C (2017) *Defiant earth: The fate of humans in the Anthropocene*. London: Wiley.

Haraway DJ (2008) *When species meet*. Minneapolis: University of Minnesota Press.

Haraway DJ (2016) *Staying with the trouble: Making kin in the Chthulucene*. Durham: Duke University Press.

Hawthorne C (2019) Black matters are spatial matters: Black geographies for the twenty-first century. *Geography Compass* 13(11): e12468.

Hinchliffe S (2022) Postcolonial global health, post-colony microbes and antimicrobial resistance. *Theory, Culture & Society* 39(3): 145–168.

Hinchliffe S, Bingham N, Allen J and Carter S (2016) *Pathological lives: Disease, space and biopolitics*. London: Blackwell.

Hinchliffe S and Ward KJ (2014) Geographies of folded life: How immunity reframes biosecurity. *Geoforum* 53: 136–144.

Hörl E and Burton JE (2017) *General ecology: The new ecological paradigm*. New York: Bloomsbury Publishing.

Hornborg A (2014) Technology as fetish: Marx, Latour, and the cultural foundations of capitalism. *Theory, Culture & Society* 31(4): 119–140.

Hornborg A (2017) Dithering while the planet burns: Anthropologists' approaches to the Anthropocene. *Reviews in Anthropology* 46(2–3): 61–77.

Hovorka AJ (2016) Animal geographies I: Globalizing and decolonizing. *Progress in Human Geography* 41(3): 382–394.

Hunt S (2014) Ontologies of indigeneity: The politics of embodying a concept. *Cultural Geographies* 21(1): 27–32.

Jazeel T (2019) *Postcolonialism*. Abingdon: Taylor & Francis.

Keulartz J (2012) The emergence of enlightened anthropocentrism in ecological restoration. *Nature and Culture* 7(1): 48–71.

Klaver I, Keulartz J, Van den Belt H and Gremmen B (2002) Born to be wild: A pluralistic ethics concerning introduced large herbivores in the Netherlands. *Environmental Ethics* 24(1): 3–21.

Loftus A (2019) Political ecology I: Where is political ecology? *Progress in Human Geography* 43(1): 172–182.

Lorimer J (2016) Gut buddies: Multispecies studies and the microbiome. *Environmental Humanities* 8(1): 57–76.

Lorimer J (2020) *The probiotic planet: Using life to manage life*. Minneapolis: University of Minnesota Press.

Lorimer J and Driessen C (2013) Bovine biopolitics and the promise of monsters in the rewilding of Heck cattle. *Geoforum* 48: 249–259.

Malm A (2018) *The progress of this storm: Nature and society in a warming world.* New York: Verso UK.

Margulies JD (2019) On coming into animal presence with photovoice. *Environment and Planning E: Nature and Space* 2(4): 850–873.

Margulies JD and Bersaglio B (2018) Furthering post-human political ecologies. *Geoforum* 94: 103–106.

Moore J (2016) Name the system! Anthropocenes & the Capitalocene alternative. In: Jason W Moore. Available at: https://jasonwmoore.wordpress.com/2016/10/09/name-the-system-anthropocenes-the-capitalocene-alternative/ [accessed April 2023].

Moore JW (2015) *Capitalism in the web of life: Ecology and the accumulation of capital.* New York: Verso.

Moulton AA (2023) Towards the arboreal side-effects of marronage: Black geographies and ecologies of the Jamaican forest. *Environment and Planning E: Nature and Space* 6(1): 3–23.

Narayanan Y (2017) Street dogs at the intersection of colonialism and informality: 'Subaltern animism' as a posthuman critique of Indian cities. *Environment and Planning D: Society and Space* 35(3): 475–494.

Nelson SH (2014) Resilience and the neoliberal counter-revolution: From ecologies of control to production of the common. *Resilience* 2(1): 1–17.

Noxolo P (2022) Geographies of race and ethnicity 1: Black geographies. *Progress in Human Geography* 46(5): 1232–1240.

O'Connor JR (1998) *Natural causes: Essays in ecological Marxism.* Guildford: Guilford Publications.

Palmer J (2021) Putting forests to work? Enrolling vegetal labor in the socioecological fix of bioenergy resource making. *Annals of the American Association of Geographers* 111(1): 141–156.

Patel R and Moore JW (2017) *A history of the world in seven cheap things: A guide to capitalism, nature, and the future of the planet.* Oakland: University of California Press.

Perreault T, Bridge G and McCarthy J (2015) *The Routledge handbook of political ecology.* Abingdon: Taylor & Francis.

Porcher J (2017) *The ethics of animal labor: A collaborative utopia.* Amsterdam: Springer International Publishing.

Radcliffe SA (2017) Decolonising geographical knowledges. *Transactions of the Institute of British Geographers* 42(3): 329–333.

Robbins P (2019) *Political ecology: A critical introduction.* London: Wiley.

Shukin N (2009) *Animal capital: Rendering life in biopolitical times.* Minneapolis: University of Minnesota Press.

Smith LT (2021) *Decolonizing methodologies: Research and indigenous peoples.* New York: Bloomsbury Academic.

Smith N (2010) *Uneven development: Nature, capital, and the production of space.* Athens, Georgia: University of Georgia Press.

Srinivasan K (2016) Towards a political animal geography? *Political Geography* 50: 76–78.

Srinivasan K (2019) Remaking more-than-human society: Thought experiments on street dogs as "nature". *Transactions of the Institute of British Geographers* 44(2): 376–391.

Srinivasan K and Kasturirangan R (2016) Political ecology, development, and human exceptionalism. *Geoforum* 75: 125–128.

Srinivasan K, Kurz T, Kuttuva P and Pearson C (2019) Reorienting rabies research and practice: Lessons from India. *Palgrave Communications* 5(1): 152.

Star SL (1991) Power, technologies and the phenomenology of conventions: On being allergic to onions. In: Law J (ed) *A sociology of monsters?* London: Routledge, pp. 26–56.

Sundberg J (2014) Decolonizing posthumanist geographies. *Cultural Geographies* 21(1): 33–47.

Swyngedouw E (1996) The city as a hybrid: On nature, society and cyborg urbanization. *Capitalism Nature Socialism* 7(2): 65–80.

Swyngedouw E (2004) *Social power and the urbanization of water: Flows of power.* Oxford: Oxford University Press.

Swyngedouw E and Ernstson H (2018) Interrupting the anthropo-obscene: Immuno-biopolitics and depoliticizing ontologies in the Anthropocene. *Theory, Culture & Society* 35(6): 3–30.

Thrift N (2000) Afterwords. *Environment and Planning D-Society & Space* 18(2): 213–255.

Todd Z (2016) An indigenous feminist's take on the ontological turn: 'Ontology' is just another word for colonialism. *Journal of Historical Sociology* 29(1): 4–22.

Tsing AL (2015) *The mushroom at the end of the world: On the possibility of life in capitalist ruins.* Princeton, NJ: Princeton University Press.

Tuck E and Yang KW (2012) Decolonization is not a metaphor. *Decolonization: Indigeneity, Education & Society* 1(1): 1–40.

Wadiwel D (2018) Chicken harvesting machine: Animal labor, resistance, and the time of production. *South Atlantic Quarterly* 117(3): 527–549.

Wainwright J (2005) Politics of nature: A review of three recent works by Bruno Latour. *Capitalism Nature Socialism* 16(1): 115–127.

Wakefield S (2019) Making nature into infrastructure: The construction of oysters as a risk management solution in New York City. *Environment and Planning E: Nature and Space* 3(3): 761–785.

Wakefield S (2020) *Anthropocene back loop.* Oxford: Saint Philip Street Press.

Wakefield S, Chandler D and Grove K (2022) The asymmetrical Anthropocene: Resilience and the limits of posthumanism. *Cultural Geographies* 29(3): 389–404.

Whatmore S (2002) *Hybrid geographies: Natures, cultures, spaces.* London: Sage.

Whyte KP (2018) Indigenous science (fiction) for the Anthropocene: Ancestral dystopias and fantasies of climate change crises. *Environment and Planning E: Nature and Space* 1(1–2): 224–242.

Wolfe C (2012) *Before the law: Humans and other animals in a biopolitical frame.* Chicago: University of Chicago Press.

Epilogue

Cooling down

We have been on a heady tour through the literatures of more-than-humanism. We have moved far from the humanist world of rational minds floating in bodies that are bounded from their environments. We have encountered animals with agency, technologies that shape society, and geological forces with the power to reconfigure civilisations. We have learnt to place science in its social context, tracing the materials and embodied practices through which knowledge is made. We are better equipped to recognise multiple forms of environmental expertise. In developing this multi-natural model of the world and how it might be known, we have disturbed the modern settlement between Science and Politics, shattering a one-world world, to present a political pluriverse of contested environmental futures. By way of conclusion, we would like to circle back to the key terms we asked you to reflect on in the opening prologue:

Nature. Animal. Human. Science.

What do these words mean to you now? What images come to mind?

Again, there remains no right answer, and we would still hope to find some variation. But after reading this book, we might expect our readers to be transitioning towards some of the following:

Nature: the great green world out there, separated from Society. A valued place or thing that is often under threat, as well as an external force with the power to harm. You might imagine a park, a garden, the countryside, or the wilderness?

Becomes

Natures: dynamic assemblages of organisms and elements, including humans. Animated by nonlinear processes and constantly changing at different speeds. Still valued as a set of places and experiences, as well as an external force with the power to harm. But now also found in cities, laboratories, on screens, and in the body. Coming in hybrid, cyborg, feral, and other monstrous and impure forms.

***

Animal: a mobile, living organism visible to the naked eye. Generally, not a human. Perhaps a dog or cat? Or maybe a tiger, panda, or polar bear? These might be seen as beasts of lesser moral status?

Becomes

Animal: still a mobile, living organism, but now expanded to include a range of more obscure, uncharismatic beings. A being with its own lifeworld, geographical experience, and health and welfare needs. An ecological actor. Sometimes a person. Worthy of ethical consideration and moral status. Includes humans.

***

Human: a person. A special lifeform, blessed with language and a thinking (perhaps even rational) mind, superior to animals. Living in a body that is separate from the environment. Perhaps you saw yourself, a friend, a statue, or a famous person?

Becomes

Human: a special animal. Commonly sharing specific competencies like language or the ability to use tools. Blessed with large, powerful, and embodied minds. Composed of microbes, entangled with the environment, and responsible (albeit unequally) for changing planetary dynamics. Sociable and political. Capable of reason but shaped by affect and emotion.

***

Science: the truth about the natural world. An objective way of producing knowledge that is not shaped by personal and social interests. Perhaps you see a person in a white coat in a laboratory, or in a suit reassuring the public? Maybe an explorer in some natural environment?

Becomes

Science: one valuable method for producing knowledge about the world. One of several legitimate forms of expertise. Involves hard work, skill, and lots of technology. Shaped by location and social context. Confers power to govern people and environments and should be subservient to democratic processes.

***

Were your new definitions similar to ours? Do you support the shifts we are proposing here? These are provocative and contested assertations and you are perfectly entitled to disagree.

Appendix
Interview with Professor Dame Sarah Whatmore

Sarah Whatmore is Professor of Environment and Public Policy at the University of Oxford. She is one of the key figures behind the emergence of more-than-human geography, and the term is commonly linked to her book *Hybrid Geographies*, which was published in 2002. Sarah developed her approach through a range of research projects exploring topics spanning wildlife conservation, flood risk mapping, and alternative food networks. She has collaborated with a wide range of human and physical geographers, developing new approaches to interdisciplinary research and public engagement with science. In recent years, she helped to establish the Social Science Expert Group within the Science Advisory Council at the UK Government's Department of Environment Food and Rural Affairs (Defra). This interview was conducted in March 2023. We start with the origins of hybrid geographies, move back to discuss Sarah's earlier research, before skipping forward to her recent work on the relationships between science and politics.

———

Jamie: Let's start with *Hybrid Geographies*. Can you tell us the story of how the book came together?

Sarah: I'd been on fellowship, and I went to Santa Cruz, Madison, and Australia. For the first time in a long time at that point in my career, I could actually do some systematic reading. Santa Cruz in particular was really important. Donna [Haraway] was there, and Margaret Fitzsimmons, a bunch of folk just thinking very differently.[1] It felt like a liberation. This was in the second half of the '90s. I came back with a whole load of reading and case studies. Some of the chapters in *Hybrid Geographies*, I had written previously as papers with Lorraine Thorne (Whatmore and Thorne, 1998, 2000). And then the final chapter was the ethics piece, which was a rewrite of a paper that I'd written out of the stuff that I'd been reading and doing on that fellowship – I think it first came out in *Society & Space* in the late '90s (Whatmore, 1997).

Everybody seems to identify that last chapter in the book as the point at which the more-than-human comes into being. I'm not sure that it does. I mean, all the arguments are there, but it is very much more focused on arguing against the notion of *post*-humanism that was predominant in that period through the work of Katherine Hayles (1999) and Cary Wolfe (2010) and others mostly coming out of the humanities. But one of the issues that we had with that tradition was its resistance to the type of empirical engagement that is common in the social sciences. We found the whole post-thing was like other 'posts', just not very productive. The arguments I was trying to make in *Hybrid Geographies* were against the post-version of humanism. Ultimately, the notion of hybridities is unsatisfactory, however much I try to resolve it in the last chapter by saying, "It's not this kind of hybridity and it's not that kind of hybridity. It's another kind of hybridity". There never was a 'nature'/'culture' divide. There wasn't an historical 'before' when it made sense. It has always been and always will be mixed up.

Jamie: So, there is the risk that hybridity looks like a mixture of two types of thing, isn't there?

Sarah: Yes, absolutely, and I spent a lot of time in the concluding chapter saying why that's a bad thing. I would never trash Donna's work, but I think there is an element of that in the *cyborg manifesto*. Katherine Hayles is a more digital AI variant of the same thing. Cary's work doesn't carry that take quite so much, but at that stage – like me – he hasn't got the language to put it any other way than post-humanism. And he'd be quite upfront about that.

Jamie: And were you taking hybrid from Latour and *We Have Never Been Modern*?

Sarah: So, I was taking hybrid in part from Latour, but in part actually from geography. This is the other thing, the way that geographers' writing is often overlooked, shall we say, by our humanities friends and colleagues. There is a whole tradition in geography, and it's part of the argument I'm trying to make in the book, that never did accept that the world is either social over here or physical and material over there. It might be a thin thread at times, but you can trace through geographical thinking, individuals or currents that are trying to hold onto a different way of framing the world. For me, that's the most important thing geography has to offer. I know I'm in a minority in thinking that. There are, you know, many people on either side of the discipline who would very much like to forget the other half.

Jamie: So, this would be work on landscapes by Carl Sauer, for example?

Sarah: Yes, Margaret [Fitzsimmons] was his granddaughter. She had his entire book collection, and she was a really interesting interlocutor when I was at Santa Cruz. There was the Sauer legacy, the thinking by people who were trying to write about landscape not just as a physical entity you go into, but as a whole way of being in the world that is not first and foremost about either sight or talk. That we're already there, and in order to develop theories and ideas that privilege sight or talk, you have somehow to extract yourself from the way that we inhabit the world in an everyday sense. I'm sure all this is picked up in John's (Wylie, 2007) landscape book. You learn those things as a student, through particular approaches and systematic ways of thinking. You unlearn or you distance yourself from your everyday experience. And of course, everybody's everyday experience is different, but arguably that's one of the features that the more-than-human is trying to hold onto.

Jamie: And Tim Ingold (2000) is making a similar argument about the same time. Were you reading that work or was that happening in parallel?

Sarah: It was sort of happening in parallel. I read Ingold's work for an earlier project. He was particularly obsessed at the time with the idea of dwelling and building, which, you know, goes right back to his discipline and our discipline's founding days in the nineteenth century. I would say that's a good example of a noninteraction. I think we were at some of the same conferences, and I was certainly doing a lot of anthropology stuff at the time, maybe because of the folk in Santa Cruz.

Jamie: So, there's the landscape tradition, but Margaret was also coming out of a Marxist tradition. She has that piece, *The Matter of Nature* (Fitzsimmons, 1989), where she says that Marxists have forgotten about materiality...

Sarah: Correct, and I would say she's channelling Carl Sauer and Marxism in a really fruitful and generative sort of way. Also, as a person she was not unlike Donna Haraway in her passion for life's diversity. They were neighbours and both massively committed to their dogs. Margaret had a special van because she had such a huge dog, and this dog would emerge from the back, and those of us who were a bit scared of big dogs...

Jamie: So even back then dogs were very much on the scene?

Sarah: Oh yes, absolutely. They were big dog walkers. And, you know, like most of the States, they go in much more for breeds than we do. It's got to be a thoroughbred, and hers was one of those waterdogs that rescue people – I can't remember what the proper name is. Anyway, it was very hairy and very large, but, you know, very sweet and cuddly.

Jamie: And were they thinking with dogs already at that point, or were dogs not yet on the radar as subjects of geographical inquiry?

Sarah: Companion animals were definitely on the radar. I can remember going in a van with this dog to a farmer's market somewhere in that part of California, Half Moon Bay, I think. These markets were interesting in those days, different to our equivalents in terms of their political significance as well as what they sold. There were stalls there that weren't just about human food. They were about alternative companion animal feedstuffs, and so on. It seemed to be much more a continuum there than it was here at the time.

Jamie: And at that time, Donna was writing about primatology and then about cyborgs...

Sarah: She was, but very committed to feminist thinking. I would say that, and dogs, were her primary passions. And the anthropology department at that time had a lot of very serious, interesting, diverse feminist thinkers. They had a wonderfully named – it wasn't called the anthropology department, now what was it called?

Jamie: Was this the *History of Consciousness* programme?

Sarah: Yeah, it was a really interesting and different kind of enterprise.

Jamie: And that feminist thinking also comes into *Hybrid Geographies* as another strand of thought?

Sarah: Yes, yes, absolutely. Possibly not one terribly recognisable to any particular brand of feminism. But, you know, I grew up in the later years of second wave feminism, trying to broaden the idea of what counts as work and how do you count it, right through to why do we always adopt analytical styles in the academy that require you first to distance yourself from everyday life. I think feminism has got lots of different strands that were trying to tackle that, including ecofeminism. I found ecofeminism quite difficult to digest in some versions. I thought people like Val Plumwood were onto some interesting things, but it was a real discovery for me to find and get into Donna Haraway's work.

Jamie: So, after Santa Cruz you went to Australia, and we have the Australian strand of feminism and the work of Val Plumwood. But were you also beginning to think about indigenous ontologies, and some of the histories of Australia in different ways?

Sarah: Yes.

Jamie: Could you claim that as an influence on your thinking?

Sarah: Yes. I would say that the chapter in *Hybrid Geographies* about Unsettling Country – well, it's a section, and it's the section that comes most directly from this fellowship, which was about property. The two chapters in this section are trying to reimagine, rethink concepts and practices of property ownership, not only from the critical legal studies point of view, which was rife at that time, but to try and rethink it in more-than-human terms. Even critical legal studies maintained the primacy of the subject of property, the owner, and the institutions that validated ownership. The object of property got almost no mention whatsoever. It just was an object of property, end of, you needn't think about that anymore. The first trip I made to Australia was quite explicitly to look at the Mabo ruling.[2] In other words, it was one of the case studies through which I wanted to look at the colonial encounter and the imposition of Western property practices in other parts of the world. Then by the time I got to Australia, the Mabo ruling was out and the parliamentary response to the ruling was actively underway. And I was very fortunate to have several contacts with critical legal scholars as well as geographers, who were following this closely and drew my attention to key academic sources. And that chapter is mostly an attempt to think about the matter in question, but also to try and demonstrate that a central feature of the Mabo ruling, which chimes with the more-than-human as against the post-human, is the legal argument that there never was an absence of native title. That is a falsehood, an historical falsehood and that what their ruling was doing, unlike the conservative opposition to it, was reinstating something that was already there.

Jamie: And were you in conversation with indigenous scholars?

Sarah: Not really in person as the analytical material for that particular chapter was predominantly based on a close reading of legal and parliamentary documents and public and scholarly commentaries rather than on interviews, including a lot from the *Aboriginal Law Bulletin,* the principal outlet for indigenous legal scholarship at the time. I was based in Melbourne and I would say I was interacting most with geographers – people like Jane Jacobs and various of her colleagues, who had done work mainly on the conjuring of aboriginal communities for legal purposes by anthropologists. In order to substantiate aboriginal land claims, anthropologists were one of the key intermediaries in legal processes that required an articulation, in Western terms, of indigenous communities' connection to a piece of land, river, water, etc.

Jamie: One of the more current criticisms, particularly against Latour, is the argument that he doesn't acknowledge the indigenous ontologies that precede the claims of hybridity. This criticism particularly comes up around the concept of multinaturalism that he takes from de Castro. And the argument that there are indigenous scholars who have been writing about South America for a while.

Sarah: I think it's wonderful that the academy has changed sufficiently that these voices are now heard directly as academic voices. But you're born when you're born, and I don't think there was enough of that then. In the 'empirical' phase of Latour's body of work, which to my mind is the highpoint, I don't remember him venturing much beyond European case studies (Latour 2013). I'm less familiar with his later, more 'gaia' orientated writings with which I think these critiques are most associated, but I'm not here to defend Latour. We all have frailties. He certainly did. But you can only do so much and his is such a rich legacy. I'm sure that the critiques have valid points to make.

Jamie: So, we have started in the middle of the story. We started with *Hybrid Geographies,* and I want to go onto science and politics later, but perhaps you could give us the back story, how did you come to be interested in geography?

Sarah: How did I begin? Well, it would be jolly neat, wouldn't it, if I could say hand on heart that I always had a discomfort with the idea that we could separate out our own experience from the world that makes up those experiences. Maybe there was some unarticulated version of that going on. I can remember that if at school there had been an A-level in anthropology, I would probably have done that. There is something about that trio of subjects [geography, anthropology and archaeology] and their histories which include many very difficult aspects of their histories, not least their colonial associations, as well as some very positive aspects such as this refusal to let go of the importance of the more-than-human, and all the heterogenous components of that which attracted me. I nearly read archaeology at university, and actually quite often these days I find that I'm drawn more strongly to archaeological than to geographical practices. I think geography has got a bit stuck somehow in its urge to be 'relevant' and 'problem-solving'. Where there is something about *what* archaeologists' study that seems to keep alive a kind of intellectual passion, something about its – you know, with caveats – its integrity as a subject and the objects it studies, that less readily shift according to the fashions and demands of the day.

I still think there are people keeping a vein of this 'more-than-human' distinctiveness alive in geography. But at my worst moments I think we have been overtaken as a discipline by a number of things that have distracted our attention. One is the whole environmental, climate change imperative, whereby you become oriented towards the future. It's all about forecasting and it's so imperative that any deviation from having the biggest impact possible is somehow letting the planet down. Two is tendencies in both the physical and the human sides of geography, to turn away from the middle ground, so to speak. They want to be 'proper' social scientists or natural scientists and they are a bit embarrassed frankly, to inhabit this discipline called geography, because it's neither of those things and may, consequently, compromise the status of their work.

Jamie: So you've always been interested in that interface…

Sarah: Oh always, for as long as I can remember.

Jamie: And so taking you back to the beginning, your PhD research…

Sarah: Let's go back as far as the Masters (MPhil.) So, I did a Masters in planning and built environments, and my thesis was on Marxist rent theory and the ownership of agricultural land by financial institutions. At that time, I could have told you chapter and verse about the minutiae of arguments about Marxist rent theory. I was interested in the concept of property and how it shapes the socio-material world. I've always been interested in property. I should have done law really, looking back. After that, I wanted to do something 'useful' in the world so I went to work for the GLC [Greater London Council] in policy research, at the interface between housing and planning. And it was in the days building up to the Thatcher [Conservative Prime Minister] government's abolition of the GLC, so it was fascinating time to work there. I led a report against council house sales and some other really interesting things, but mostly I spent my time speech writing, which was a fascinating digression, but I missed the research.

Jamie: Is that when Ken Livingstone [Labour politician] was leader of the Council?

Sarah: Correct, so he was facing off Thatcher across the river.

Jamie: At the high point of '80s politics in London. In the heart of an almost Marxist establishment, or at least a Left establishment?

Sarah: Indeed. So, I was in the housing department, which was in the middle of a roundabout, and it was a hexagonal, mostly concrete building, with very few windows, not in the fancy-looking building on the river immediately opposite the Houses of Parliament. It was exactly like being in a university, except more applied. But in the fancy building, where Ken and co hung out, there was the equivalent of the 'cabinet' in the Westminster government, and that was full amazing people, including academics, doing fantastic work. There was a series of really good analyses of various aspects of the London economy that came out of that time. There was one on food that was way ahead of its time. Just wonderful, amazing, amazing people.

But I wanted to get back to doing primary research with the prospect of an academic career in mind. So, I took a job as a research assistant on the first of what became a series of ESRC grant funded research projects [Economic and Social Research Council, one of the UK government's bodies responsible for funding academic research] secured by Richard Munton at UCL [University College London], and Terry Marsden at Southbank [then, Polytechnic], to investigate the changing ownership and management of agricultural land. I think initially that we were looking at the land in the London greenbelt before expanding to work in Dorset too. About a year in, I agreed with them that I would do my PhD part-time, alongside doing this job. It was on women in farming, which in those days meant women married to farmers for the most part. I worked with a group of women in Dorset and in various bits of the greenbelt and wrote a feminist analysis. It was trying to argue for something that I called – you can hear the echoes of my Marxist training – the family exploitation thesis. Marxists had long been predicting the demise of the family farm, on the grounds that they could not compete with corporate agriculture in optimising the exploitation of the hired workers, etc., etc. And my argument was forget the hired workers, there were hardly any left on family farms by this stage, and look instead to the exploitation of women within the family who, at that time (1980s) often contributed to the farm work but rarely had a stake in the property or gained recognition as farmers in their own right.

Jamie: Could you claim that at that point there was already an interest in how the materiality of farming configured the economy or the nature of the labour practices, that prefaced this interest in the more than-human?

Sarah: I would say the continuity for me became an interest in property, particularly landed property, and the way it shapes various aspects of the materiality of social arrangements and social life. And I've come back to that at various points along the way. That's what I was doing right from Masters level. And much later on, when I started to read Latour and co on science studies, my immediate thoughts were can one do something similar with the legal sides of this, with the property sides of this. And the fellowship that I applied to do was about that, and became part two of *Hybrid Geographies*.

Jamie: And you went to Bristol University in '89, '90 and Bristol was coming to the fore as this incredibly innovative…

Sarah: Bristol was an absolutely amazing department at that time. When I started as a so-called 'new blood' lecturer, it was a small department and it's important to underscore that. It was in a transition phase, with a strong reputation then in an important intellectual phase in the discipline – the so-called 'quantitative revolution' with Peter Haggett et al (including the early David Harvey). Harvey had come and gone by the time I joined and several retirements were in the offing. So, I was the first of a series of new recruits, including Nigel Thrift who I think was next to arrive as the senior human geography professor. I remember being made aware that the department had been very successful in the first national research assessment exercise and that, as the only department in the University to come top in those early exercises, they got a lot of resource and investment. One of the first things we did was to set up the MSc in Society and Space and which became the flagship of the department's reputation at the core of another important intellectual phase in the discipline centred on an intense engagement with continental philosophy and social theory. For a while, in the late '90s and early 2000s the human geography research culture became known as the 'Bristol Sound' and attracted a generation of outstanding postgraduate students who now populate the senior echelons of several British geography departments. There was a buzz, there was a real buzz, and it was a great, mind-expanding place to be.

Jamie: One thing that came from that period is nonrepresentational theory and that developed alongside the emergence of more-than-human geographies. How would you characterise the influence of Nigel and people working with Nigel on that?

Sarah: I arrived in Bristol having just got a biggish grant to do a project on environmental planning gain, and I would say that's probably the last project or bunch of publications that was not influenced by reading either the types of philosophical or the STS materials we all got into reading then. It's the last point in the trajectory of my interest in property not influenced by those literatures. And then when Nigel arrived – this is how I remember it, he may remember it differently – I'd just got money to run a project on commoditising wildlife in various guises, working with Lorraine [Thorne]. And Nigel and I overlapped in certain things that we were reading at the time. I would say loosely, some continental philosophy, Deleuze, acolytes of Deleuze, Bergson and so forth, and we also overlapped in reading and being interested in some of that early STS stuff. but we were empirically interested in very different kinds of things – nature, animals and land in my case, creative arts and industries and urban change in Nigel's case. I have been rather deliberate in not situating my work under the 'non-rep' label because, whilst it made space for doing the bodily and the material in that broader theoretical sense, it didn't quite know what to do with, or wasn't very interested in, I think would be a better way of putting it in nature, ecology and the living world.

Jamie: And the environment was less in the ether as an everyday concern?

Sarah: Oh, absolutely, absolutely. Also, where it was what people were doing, it was not being done in an analytically very interesting way, at least from my point of view. Environmental work in those days tended to fall into one of three camps - instrumentalist or problem-solving; environmental discourse analysis; or political ecology. We were having conversations through all of this and were early readers of each other's work, for example, but I've not contributed to a non-rep book per se and I was keen to avoid the more-than-human project being wrapped up as a sort of subset of 'non-rep'.

Jamie: That's interesting, because in this book we have them very much as part and parcel of the same thing, but perhaps emerging or joining later...

Sarah: So, I would say they were parallel impulses. I wouldn't overplay the fact that we both at the time happened to be at Bristol. Yes, there were lots of conversations ongoing. I'm sure those conversations were intertwined in no end of imaginative and novel ways through the MSc [in Society and Space], through all the people studying doctorates and so on. And if you think about some of the grad students who came out at the time, either on Nigel's side or on mine, you can see how those different but overlapping impulses have been amplified.

Jamie: If you trace a concept like affect, which is owned by both parties, and has roots in von Uexkull, and then in Deleuze and other ways of thinking. More-than-human work gets interested in learning to be affected, and bodily practices and knowing, which seem to offer a methodological overlap, and even an epistemological overlap about the nature of knowledge with non-rep...

Sarah: So, there are definite overlaps. Training bodily senses, for example, one goes in the direction of creative arts, the other goes in the direction of animal geographies. But in close quarters, where I quite explicitly engage with a term from Nigel which is slightly pre his non-rep and pre my more-than-human, is spatial formations.

His *Spatial Formations* book (Thrift, 1996), was the name of our project on wildlife and you can see all kinds of threads that go into those other projects later on.

Jamie: And for that, you're both borrowing on actor-network theory (ANT)?

Sarah: I don't think either of us were ever very content with actor-network theory, but we found it quite a good jumping off point. I won't speak for Nigel, but certainly one of our dissatisfactions with actor-network theory was that it comes from a set of intellectual critiques and challenges at the very core of the mainstream social sciences which had long been conceived of a radically human-ist project. It is uninformed by and uninterested in the questions that geography, archaeology, anthropology have posed for such a long period of time, hence it's so late to questions of 'nature'. There are all kinds of interesting things about ANT, such as the way it forces you to do social science differently, which we were both interested in. But in my case, the novelty it assumed in re-introducing other dimensions of the material world into the business of studying social life suffered from a failure to learn from all those traditions in geographical/anthropological/archaeological work that had found ways to hold onto the importance of this heterogeneity.

Jamie: And both of you are uneasy with the flat ontology?

Sarah: Yes.

Jamie: Nigel doesn't like that actor-network theory doesn't deal with specific human competencies, and you're not happy with the ecology of actor-network, which is very flat.

Sarah: Absolutely. But at the time, ANT was doing the most to disturb some of the central tenets of the social sciences, and both of us were sure there was something about the particularity of the discipline of geography that could deal with these shortcomings more productively. Certainly, in my case, there's a good reason why this discipline is not just another social science, and I think we've got something to say back to this discussion.

Jamie: And at this point, your empirical materials are quite varied. I mean, your spatial formations paper goes to Ancient Rome, doesn't it? And then you've got GM [Genetic Modification], which was a hot topic at the time. But you were moving between different cases to test out some of these ideas?

Sarah: Yes, and in a rather crude way it goes back to the "it's not 'post', it's 'more-than'" by deliberately trying to engage with earlier spatial formations. Just trying to ram the point home with,

Here's another example that didn't require the Enlightenment or any of the other central tenets of humanism to exist for similar kinds of practical makings of the divisions and distinctions by which we characterise our worlds. Here's one from Rome.

So we intersected the treatment of wild animals, specifically *leopardus*, in the context of the combats staged in the Roman amphitheatre with the contemporary treatment of wild animals, specifically *caiman latirostris*, under CITES [the Convention on International Trade in Endangered Species of Wild Flora and Fauna]. And the whole project was an effort to emphasise of the various mobilities of animal life against the then dominant notion in conservation biology that creatures inhabit particular places and what we need to do is put big fences up to make them stay put.

Jamie: So, that critique of wilderness, the wildness versus wilderness, which is also in the book.

Sarah: Yes.

Jamie: And there is an Australian take on that as well, isn't there, around *terra nullis*. And you've got William Cronon and others making similar arguments in environmental history around the same time, haven't you?

Sarah: Yes, it was fairly consciously an argument against the dominant – by which I mean not only academic, but popular versions of the 'end of the world' narrative. The Bill McKibben *End of Nature* type line. Partly for practical, or what some people would call political reasons, that his remedy didn't seem to me to be a terribly viable one. And partly for intellectual reasons, that his analysis didn't seem to me to be very tenable either. It was to try and articulate those things differently.

Jamie: Particularly because McKibben suggests that there was once a nature that has now come to an end?

Sarah: Correct. You know, you would never know from his account, despite the fact that he's from North America, that there were peopled ecologies prior to European colonialism...

Jamie: So, that brings us nicely to where we began, with the fellowship and the writing of *Hybrid Geographies*. So, let's move onto *Urban Natures*, which is the next big project that emerges shortly after you leave Bristol, what are the origins of that? You are going back to the city, thinking about wildlife out of place…

Sarah: Yes, exactly. So, if we've done the temporal challenge, let's do a spatial challenge it doesn't all appear to be in a game park in South Africa, as it were! But also – and I think crucially – to pick up the efforts at the time to radically disrupt humanist versions of mainstream social science. This project wants to pick up that more corporeal thread that before talk, before the visual, we're already inhabiting a world in which our experiences and understandings are made of encounters with all kinds of others.

Jamie: I remember there are stories about urban water voles…

Sarah: About allotments, about cultivating. So, Steve [Hinchliffe] and I came up with this tripartite research proposal to investigate different types of ecological spaces: cultivated, wild and feral, inhabited by animal life in the city, and we took case studies in Birmingham and Bristol and explored those, so that we could map which ones were where.

Jamie: At a time where the policy landscape was quite amenable to urban ecology?

Sarah: So, we were still in the era of DoE, Department of Environment, long since abandoned, sadly. And they produced quite an interesting policy initiative on making cities liveable, I think it was in the days when John Prescott had been made deputy prime minister and drove this agenda called Liveable Cities. That was the policy context into which this project entered. And there were all kinds of good things about that, not least that making cities more liveable for people meant making them more liveable for more-than people. Of course, there are downsides too, but that was the policy context. Part of it was to empirically investigate this proposition, and part of it was to argue, when we got to the more policy side of it, that rather than the DoE telling everybody how to do it, that actually there were lots of communities already perfectly appreciative of this co-habitability, and practicing it in novel and interesting ways.

Jamie: So, is that where this interest in public engagement, participatory approaches, that leads into the flood risk mapping project begins?

Sarah: Yes, that's a fair genealogy. One of the things that struck us in the urban wildlife project – *Habitable Cities* – must have been at least in part about the policy configuration at the time in which we were operating. So, this *Liveable Cities* thing came out of DoE and makes almost no space for British – to use the Whitehall vernacular for the four nations – British communities to know or do anything about this that might usefully inform government policy design or implementation. This approach was in immense contrast to colleagues working in the Global South, where the whole of the rhetoric and to some extent practice of the Department for International Development, the ODI, was to work with communities in the Global South to inform the agencies bringing money and so forth, what their local expertise was. It was like chalk and cheese. And so, in a very small way, in the urban wildlife project, we wanted to try and get the voice of people already doing this for themselves into the conversation, that was at a fairly crucial point.

Of course, it all went off the boil when the [Conservative/Liberal Democrat] coalition government came in [after the 2010 general election]. And then the flood project that came a few years later with a different set of collaborators, centred on how to achieve more effective public engagement in environmental science and policy of environmental but in a much more intellectually worked through way. I'd done a lot of work between times on Isabelle Stengers' radical take on philosophy of science and practicing science differently. What was probably crucial in the development of my own thinking was the intellectual demands of working at the Open University, where you had to learn to articulate for a very non-specialist audience, some quite complex, philosophical ideas. Unusually for the OU at that time, we set about doing a new course for Masters level students, and the book element was called *Using Social Theory* (Pryke et al., 2003). And I had the task of writing up a version of what was, crudely put, 'what difference did a more-than-human approach make to doing geography?' using Stengers' work to inform the arguments. So, it was methodological in orientation and writing for that audience really focused the mind and made me do a lot of thinking through, that then fed into the next flood research project.

Jamie: And that distilled a research design for your work using these concepts?

Sarah: Correct. And it was quite radical epistemologically, because that OU chapter ends on the argument, that some of my colleagues never really accepted or warmed to, which challenges the old line in research methods that says, "Ah well, the social sciences differ from the natural sciences because our research subjects answer back, and therefore we have a whole series of methodologies that are all about hearing them answer back." And my chapter ended on the line that actually this doesn't really hold or, at least, its hold on the social sciences obscures the attention that you need pay in your research methodologies to what people do and with what other components in making that 'doing' take hold, as well as to what they say about what they're doing.

Jamie: But then you managed to find some amenable physical scientists and launched this pretty enormous project.

Sarah: Well, I have not been intending to lead another big collaborative project and had been lining myself up for the next solo book, which would have been a much longer exploration of Stengers' work in relation to the translation of environmental science into policy. When Philip Lowe, sadly no longer with us, announced that he had been appointed to direct a big new interdisciplinary, inter-research council programme called Rural Economy and Land Use (RELU). So, you can see we're getting back to where I started with financial institutions and agricultural land. Stuart Lane, who was a hydrological modeller in the geography department at Durham, ex-Cambridge, approached me and said,

> Look, I'm thinking we ought to do something here. I'm really interested in the stuff you've been doing on Stengers and experimenting with new ways of getting people to participate in constructing knowledge about problems that face them. I do flood risk management. Why don't we get together?

I knew nothing whatever about hydrology but started reading about it. I was interested in modelling as it just didn't seem to conform to that stylised account of the way that 'proper' science proceeds. So, a bunch of us got together to try to thrash something out with a set of methodological experiments (Competency Groups) derived from Stengers' writing on philosophy of science at its heart. I think it's fair to say that only Stuart and I, who had been regular participants in those worthy set-piece 'bridging the divide' sessions at geography conferences were really the only two people in the original group very interested in this philosophical stuff. Anyway, we put in a project proposal and somewhat to everyone's surprise, we got through the review process after a very long and rather painful process which I've written about this in Andrew Barry's book on interdisciplinarity (Whatmore, 2013).

Jamie: And this was a time when flooding was high on the agenda. You went to Pickering and there was a whole process by which it ended up solving the problem…

Sarah: It did.

Jamie: But not necessarily in a way that you anticipated when you embarked on the project?

Sarah: Indeed. So, the thing that was unusual about that project, which not a lot of people appreciate, was that the modelling was pretty standard technically, except for the fact that the modellers had to learn to work with people who lived with flood risk in particular places and who came to the Competency Group meetings with, in some cases, very strong views as to what the solution was. The thing that was really innovative was the methodology. It was experimental not least because we did not know whether it would work or not, whether it would generate anything of value if it did. And it happened that the first trial site for this methodology was in Pickering, a market town in north Yorkshire which we knew from a contact with somebody who worked for the regional Environment Agency had a controversy ongoing around the lack of flood defences. And of course, not only are you trying to find your way with a new group of people who live with this risk and are understandably exercised by it but you are also learning to work with the academic project team, which was a big interdisciplinary team across four different universities.

Jamie: One of the themes that comes up in our book is this idea of experiments and experimentation as a characteristic of a more-than-human epistemology. This was very much an experiment designed to generate surprises. It wasn't an experiment where you had a particular hypothesis that you were testing from the get-go?

Sarah: Yes.

Jamie: And serendipitous surprises in the Pickering case worked out such that eventually you secured a bund [flood defence measure]. But you hadn't conceived of that in advance?

Sarah: Correct. So, the reason that Pickering had never had any money spent on it in terms of flood defences was because the investment in flood risk management measures ends up, after a load of modelling, so on and so forth, to be a cost benefit calculation. Pickering, a very beautiful market town at the foot of the hills of the North York Moors had just never quite got over the line in term of the cost of the engineering interventions that dictated by the protocols of Environment Agency investment. We started our work in Pickering immediately after the town had experienced unseasonable flooding in the summer before we arrived to recruit local people to join the Competency Group. That event and the ongoing lack of flood defensive measures had led to a breakdown in relations between the community and the regional Environment Agency, so it was a very contested space when we went in. And the Competency Group methodology was designed for controversial situations, where your purpose was not to arrive at a consensus, but to keep alive and explore what the tensions were.

Anyway, Stuart and his RA [Research Assistant], Nick [Odoni], devised a user interface, almost like a video game, that enabled the people we recruited to the group to try out their ideas for managing flood risk. We developed a model specific to the Pickering catchment and the visual interface enabled anybody, even me, to use it and to see what the results were: what happened to the water, where did it go if you did x, y, and z? Anyway, after trying lots of ideas about nine, ten months in, we realised that a combination of suggestions for things which individually looked to have marginal effect, together seemed likely to have a potentially positive effect. We decided that we had enough confidence in our CG work to go public with it under the collective group name – the Ryedale Flood Research Group (RGSG). We staged an exhibition of our modelling work, visualisations, and suggested interventions. The exhibition helped to change the terms on which the Environment Agency and community could engage and, subsequently, they tested our modelling work for themselves, and the rest is history.

The local members of the RGSG group, one in particular, went on to engage directly with the regional Environment Agency in designing a series of woody debris dams up in the uplands, funded and installed by the Forestry Commission, and eventually a concrete culvert just outside the town, that enables the water that gets through the woody debris dams to be held back and dispersed before it hits the town. Not only have many other communities been inspired by the Pickering project but, just this year, it appeared on an ITV nature programme as an exemplar of 'natural flood management' with a reintroduced colony of beavers now constructing new woody debris dams in the catchment.

Jamie: And the hope was that you'd have a methodology that would be generalisable or used in other contexts?

Sarah: Catharina (Landstrom) is doing most these days to explore how lessons from this case and methodology can be adapted to other situations. I also tried to advance the idea of involving communities affected by flood risk in flood risk modelling and management at DEFRA with very mixed results. However, a couple of years after I stopped banging on about it at every possible opportunity, surprise, surprise, something called 'natural flood management' made its way into official policy in the Environment Agency nationally.

Jamie: So, we could claim that as a legacy in a roundabout way?

Sarah: In a very roundabout way, The Pickering case has undoubtedly helped to push that over the line.

Jamie: Have you been able to generalise the Competency Group methodology beyond this case and turn it into a set of methodological guidelines?

Sarah: So, it is doctoral students and postdocs on that project, who have gone on to run their own projects in different parts of the world, who have done most with it. I wouldn't want to say that I'm *au fait* with all the things that they have done. Certainly, Catharina's done a lot more with it, and has written up the methodology for other users (Landstrom, 2017, 2019). I still get regular enquiries from all kinds of people, including medics, who want to do public engagement that doesn't just rely on having a talking shop, that involves people affected by disease 'x' or environmental condition 'y' putting their hands-on knowledge, practical knowledge, know-how if you want, to work in better understanding that condition or that problem as they have experienced it.

Jamie: Finally, if we move to the latest chapter, where you've been working in a fairly senior government role. How much do you feel the more-than-human has been something you've been able to test out or bring to that work?

Sarah: Hmm, so government work is a curious thing. I've obviously always had a commitment to trying to link thinking differently to doing things differently in practice. From my brief stint at the GLC right through. I don't really know where that comes from and doesn't really have anything to do with the more-than-human. But during the period of my appointment to the Science Advisory Council at DEFRA [Department for the Environment Food and Rural Affairs], as one of a very small number of social scientists on the Council, I did manage to help set up and Chair a Social Science Expert Group which joined a number of more specialist advisory groups that feed into the Science Advisory Council. It is a legacy of which I'm proud as it has survived my departure from the Chair. It still exists, it is still valued, and there is now a cadre of social scientists employed inside DEFRA whom it supports.

Jamie: With an interest in engagement and participation?

Sarah: Yes. In fact, the most recent product of that Social Science Expert Group was on public engagement. I would say that the philosophical dimensions of competency groups are slightly lost in translation. But the notion that got the most traction is that communities affected by environmental hazards and risks, like flooding, have useful knowledge and perspectives which can inform their management in many useful ways.

Notes

1 Sadly, not long after this conversation was recorded, we received the announcement of Margaret Fitzsimmons' death on 6 April 2023, and some weeks later that of Henry Buller – another more-than-human geographer who engaged in policy work too.

2 The Australian Institute for Aboriginal and Torres Strait Islanders Studies explains that: 'The Mabo Case was a significant legal case in Australia that recognised the land rights of the Meriam people, traditional owners of the Murray Islands in the Torres Strait. The Mabo Case was successful in overturning the myth that at the time of colonisation Australia was 'terra nullius' or land belonging to no one. The

High Court recognised the fact that Indigenous peoples had lived in Australia for thousands of years and enjoyed rights to their land according to their own laws and customs' AIATSIS (2023) *The Mabo case*. Available at: https://aiatsis.gov.au/explore/mabo-case [accessed April 2023].

References

AIATSIS (2023) *The Mabo case*. Available at: https://aiatsis.gov.au/explore/mabo-case [accessed April 2023].

Fitzsimmons M (1989) The matter of nature. *Antipode* 21: 106–120.

Hayles NK (1999) *How we became posthuman: Virtual bodies in cybernetics, literature, and informatics*. Chicago, IL: University of Chicago Press.

Ingold T (2000) *The perception of the environment: Essays on livelihood, dwelling and skill*. London: Routledge.

Landström C (2017) *Transdisciplinary environmental research: A practical approach*. New York: Springer International Publishing.

Landström C (2019) *Environmental participation: Practices engaging the public with science and governance*. New York: Springer International Publishing.

Latour B (2013) *The making of law: An ethnography of the Conseil d'État*. Oxford: Polity Press.

Pryke M, Rose G and Whatmore S (2003) *Using social theory: Thinking through research*. London; Thousand Oaks, CA: SAGE Publications in association with the Open University.

Thrift N (1996) *Spatial formations*. London: Sage.

Whatmore S (1997) Dissecting the autonomous self: Hybrid cartographies for a relational ethics. *Environment and Planning D-Society & Space* 15(1): 37–53.

Whatmore S (1999) Hybrid geographies: Rethinking the 'human' in human geography. In: al. MDe (ed) *Human geography today*. London: Polity, pp. 22–39.

Whatmore S and Thorne L (1998) Wild(er)ness: Reconfiguring the geographies of wildlife. *Transactions of the Institute of British Geographers* 23(4): 435–454.

Whatmore S and Thorne L (2000) Elephants on the move: Spatial formations of wildlife exchange. *Environment and Planning D-Society & Space* 18(2): 185–203.

Whatmore SJ (2013) Reflections on an experiment in geographical practice. In: Barry A and Born G (eds) *Interdisciplinarity: Reconfigurations of the social and natural sciences*. London: Routledge, pp. 161.

Wolfe C (2010) *What is posthumanism?* Minneapolis: University of Minnesota Press.

Wylie J (2007) *Landscape*. London: Routledge.

Index

Note: **Bold** page numbers refer to tables; *italic* page numbers refer to figures and page numbers followed by "n" denote endnotes.